Starting With Stories

Pam Schiller, Ph.D and Pat Phipps, Ed.D

Starting With Stories

Engaging Multiple Intelligences Through Children's Books

Pam Schiller and Pat Phipps

Illustrations: Kathy Ferrell and Debi Johnson

gryphon house

Beltsville, MD

Dedication

To the teachers who use multiple intelligences as a framework for curriculum and to the children who flourish in your care.

Pat Phipps and Pam Schiller

© 2006 Pam Schiller and Pat Phipps

Printed in the United States of America

Published by Gryphon House, Inc.
10726 Tucker Street, Beltsville, MD 20705
301.595.9500; 301.595.0051 (fax);
800.638.0928 (toll-free)

Visit us on the web at www.ghbooks.com

Illustrations: Kathy Farrell and Debi Johnson

Cover Photograph: Straight Shots.

Library of Congress Cataloging-in-Publication Data

Schiller, Pamela Byrne.
  Starting with stories : engaging multiple intelligences through children's
books / Pam Schiller, Pat Phipps ; Illustrations, Kathy Ferrell and Debbie Wright.
      p. cm.
  Includes bibliographical references and index.
  ISBN-13: 978-0-87659-297-7 (alk. paper)
  ISBN-10: 0-87659-297-3 (alk. paper)
  1. Early childhood education--Activity programs. 2. Multiple
intelligences. 3. Children's books. I. Phipps, Pat. II. Ferrell, Kathy.
  III. Wright, Debbie. IV. Title.
  LB1139.35.A37S364 2006
  372.21--dc22
                            2006015192

Bulk purchase

Gryphon House books are available for special premiums and sales promotions as well as for fund-raising use. Special editions or book excerpts also can be created to specification. For details, contact the Director of Marketing at Gryphon House.

Disclaimer

Gryphon House, Inc. and the authors cannot be held responsible for damage, mishap, or injury incurred during the use of or because of activities in this book. Appropriate and reasonable caution and adult supervision of children involved in activities and corresponding to the age and capability of each child involved, is recommended at all times. Do not leave children unattended at any time. Observe safety and caution at all times.

Every effort has been made to locate copyright and permission information.

 Gryphon House is a member of the Green Press Initiative, a nonprofit program dedicated to supporting publishers in their efforts to reduce their use of fiber sourced forests. For further information visit www.greenpressinitiative.org.

Table of Contents

Introduction

Starting With Stories is a comprehensive, literature-based curriculum for children ages three to five. There are more than 1200 activities based on 100 children's books. Activities for each title support not only literacy skills and concepts but also support all eight multiple intelligences using multi-curricular activities. In other words, this book provides everything you need to teach both critical skills and concepts while addressing individual learning styles and preferences.

In today's climate of accountability, early childhood teachers must be more intentional and purposeful in their instruction. It is important to use every opportunity to prepare children for school readiness. However, it is important to remember that school readiness is more than a collection of facts. School readiness encompasses children's levels of self-confidence, their curiosity, the ability to relate to others and be cooperative, the ability to demonstrate self-control and intentionality, and the ability to communicate effectively. Each of these important characteristics grows and develops in a classroom that provides experiences that nurture the individual child. A teacher who knows the many ways children can express their abilities (multiple intelligences) and who teaches in an environment where best practices are guided by the research, ensures that all children enter school ready to learn.

Starting With Stories Literacy Support

In preschool, children need exposure to activities that support four basic literacy skills:

- ❍ oral language development (vocabulary and sentence structure)
- ❍ phonological awareness (rhyme, alliteration, and onomatopoeia)
- ❍ letter knowledge (visual recognition of upper- and lowercase letters)
- ❍ print awareness (understanding the many ways in which print communicates)

The 100 children's books in *Starting With Stories* are springboards that provide opportunities for children to practice each literacy skill. For example, after reading *Right Outside My Window*, talk with the children about what they see outside their own bedroom windows. On a second reading of *To Market, To Market*, ask the children to fill in the rhyming words. Children have a great time finding the *onomatopoeic* words (words that imitate the sounds they describe) while reading *Dinosaurumpus* and *Listen to the Rain*. Finding and matching letters is put into perfect context when children recite *Chicka Chicka Boom Boom*. Quality, child-centered literature is the best "teacher" of literacy skills.

Inter-Curriculum Daily and Special Activities

Daily lesson plans based on the children's books in *Starting With Stories* offer six ideas for learning centers or small group interaction—covering all eight multiple intelligences. The match of learning centers and multiple intelligences results in activities that are not only fun-filled and creative but have a natural appeal to children. Special activities include music and movement, field trips, games, home-school connections, and classroom visits, all connected to the literature and aligned with the eight multiple intelligences.

Multiple Intelligences

The best curriculum plans offer young children numerous opportunities to make meaningful connections, not only to academic content, but also to their daily lives. One of the best ways to provide appropriate, meaningful learning experiences for children is to integrate the curriculum by applying a multiple intelligences approach.

The theory of multiple intelligences, eight ways of demonstrating one's abilities, as first introduced by Dr. Howard Gardner in 1983 in his book, *Frames of Mind: The Theory of Multiple Intelligences*, places an emphasis on learning through meaningful experiences. An ideal way to provide meaningful learning experiences for children is through a rich curriculum that integrates subject content with the multiple intelligences, and there's probably no better medium for this integration than through children's literature.

For young children, meaningful learning experiences are active, hands-on, concrete activities and ongoing interactions with appropriate materials, equipment, and persons in the learning environment. Classroom environments that use learning centers with thematic instruction engage the full range of intelligences.

Schiller and Phipps in *The Complete Daily Curriculum for Early Childhood* provide a more detailed discussion of Gardner's theory of multiple intelligences. However, the chart below outlines the various types of learning experiences in which children with strengths in that particular intelligence like to engage, as well as strategies that teachers can use to develop each intelligence.

Intelligence	What Learners Like to Do	Teaching Strategies
Linguistic	Read, write, and listen; tell stories, rhymes, riddles, and tongue twisters; play verbal memory and word games; create jingles, raps, and creative drama scenes	Circle time, sharing time, reading to class, talking books and cassettes, dictated stories, storytelling, journal keeping, writing activities, word games, brainstorming, books, group discussions, guest speakers, peer tutoring, creative drama, giving reports, individualized reading, cooperative learning
Logical-Mathematical	Ask questions; explore patterns and relationships; do experiments, figure things out, and solve problems; play checkers, board games, and other strategy games; engage in classification activities, counting and number games	Problem-solving activities, logic puzzles and games, creating story problems, thinking skill activities, creating codes, divergent questioning, using technology, patterning activities, scientific demonstrations, diagrams, graphs, charts, categorizing activities

Intelligence	What Learners Like to Do	Teaching Strategies
Spatial	Put things together, take things apart, and do woodwork activities; make collages, sculptures, and constructions; draw, paint, and do other art projects; design and build things with Legos and other types of blocks; look at pictures; daydream and visualize	Variety of art materials, graphic-rich environment, mapping activities, visual aids, puzzles and mazes, color cues, mental imaging activities, illustrations and drawings, junk boxes, posters and pictures, collages, wordless picture books, paintings, manipulatives, construction kits, museum trips, charts and graphs
Bodily-Kinesthetic	Participate in hands-on active learning activities; engage in gross and fine motor activities; move around the classroom, touch and explore objects; dance, do creative dramatics and role playing; use body language, gesture, and touch people while talking to them; hear or read action-packed stories; participate in sports and games; move, twitch, tap, or fidget while sitting; fix things and build models	Creative movement, puppet theater, art and craft activities, aerobic and fitness activities, field trips, manipulatives, construction activities, sports, outdoor activities, projects, tactile activities, gardening, scavenger hunts, making collections, body maps, cooking activities
Musical	Sing, hum, and/or whistle tunes; play musical instruments; listen to and respond to music; make up lyrics; listen to music while engaged in classroom activities; use movement, tapping, humming, or singing to convey information	Singing, humming, listening to mood music, giving musical presentations, listening to a variety of music, rhythm instruments, whistling, raps and chants, music software, books with sing-along cassettes, creating songs, melody instruments
Naturalist	Experience nature or the natural surroundings; take walks and collect samples of rocks, soil; classifying insects, birds, rock; care for plants and animals; spend time outdoors; go on field trips, do science projects; work on projects that protect the environment	Nature walks, class gardens, outdoor activities, recycling activities, data gathering activities, science and nature books, nature centers, nature collages, nature collections, field trips, bird watches, outdoor scavenger hunts, class pets, ant farms, science and discovery centers, museums
Interpersonal	Socialize with peers; talk to people; have lots of friends; to be selected by others to help; mediate conflicts and organize activities; organize, communicate, and sometimes manipulate others; work on cooperative projects	Cooperative groups, peer sharing, classroom visitors, conflict resolution activities, social interactions, learning centers, peer tutoring, class meetings, role plays, board games, brainstorming, circle times
Intrapersonal	Work alone and pursue personal interests—projects and hobbies; follow own instincts; be original; engage in self-paced, self-selected, and individualized projects and activities; express self in own unique style of dress, behavior, and general attitude; reflect on activities	Problem-solving activities, relaxation activities, individual projects, journal writing, self-directed learning, self-help activities, quiet time, reflection time, individual games, learning centers

By utilizing teaching strategies that focus on individual children, such as a multiple intelligences approach, teachers can help children internalize a deep understanding of what is to be learned.

Using This Book

Starting With Stories can be used to enhance your existing curriculum or as a literature-based curriculum. The thematic guide in the appendix allows you to integrate the children's books into your existing curriculum. However, there are sufficient books under each theme to develop curriculum around the selections. The lesson plans offer a variety of choices and are interesting and extensive enough to last for days. This allows a hundred books to go a long way—easily covering a full year of instruction. The majority of the books work with several multiple themes. This is a perfect application of one of the fundamental findings of early brain development research—the more connections children make to what they learn, the more fluid and complex their comprehension.

The appendix also has other useful tools: letters to families that explain the use of multiple intelligence theory, letters to accompany some of the literature titles with home-school connections, open house suggestions, and strategies for implementing interactive story times with children.

It's all here—all you have to do is select a children's book!

References

Armstrong, Thomas. 1994. *Multiple intelligences in the classroom.* Alexandria, VA: ASTD.

Gardner, H. 1983. *Frames of mind: The theory of multiple intelligences.* New York: Basic Books.

Phipps, P. 2003. Integrating multiple intelligences throughout the curriculum (a chapter in the *DLM Early Childhood Express Research Booklet*). Columbus, OH: SRA/McGraw-Hill.

Phipps, P. 1997. *Multiple intelligences in the early childhood classroom.* Columbus, OH: SRA/McGraw-Hill.

Schiller, P. & Phipps, P. 2002. *The complete daily curriculum for early childhood* Beltsville, MD: Gryphon House.

Schiller, P. 1999. *Start smart: building brain power in the early years.* Beltsville, MD: Gryphon House.

Schiller, P. 2001. *Creating readers.* Beltsville, MD: Gryphon House.

Books & Activities

Abiyoyo

Author: Pete Seeger. Illustrator: Michael Hayes

About the Book
A South African folktale about a boy and his father who, after being banished from town for making mischief, are welcomed back when they find a way to make the scary giant, Abiyoyo, disappear.

Learning Literacy

Segmentation
❍ Encourage the children to clap the syllables in Abiyoyo's name. *How many syllables do you hear?*

Phonological Awareness
❍ Discuss the sound words used to describe the little boy's ukulele, the father's wand, and the saw. Explain that these words are *onomatopoeic* words. They sound like the sound they are describing. *What onomatopoeic word might be used to describe the giant's dance steps?*

Comprehension
❍ Ask the children why they think the townspeople were afraid of Abiyoyo.
❍ Reread the story, stopping at the point where the boy and his father awaken and see the giant. Ask the children what they think the boy and his father might do to stop the giant.

Print Awareness/Letter Knowledge
❍ Show the children the cover of the book. Point out the book title. Ask the children to identify the letters in the title. *Which letters appear in the title more than one time?*

Special Activities

❍ Visit a music store. Examine the ukuleles and other string instruments. Point out percussion and wind instruments. Ask the children how these groups of instruments are different from string instruments. (Musical, Naturalist)
❍ Attend a magic show or invite a magician to put on a show at school. (Linguistic, Interpersonal)
❍ Provide items such as cardboard tubes from coat hangers, streamers, sequins, jewels, and feathers, and invite the children to make magic wands out of them. (Spatial, Bodily-Kinesthetic)
❍ Dance the "Giant Stomp." Play ukulele music and invite the children to dance like Abiyoyo. (Bodily-Kinesthetic, Musical, Interpersonal, Intrapersonal)
❍ Play *Abiyoyo and Other Songs and Stories* CD by Peter Seeger, Smithsonian Folkways.
❍ Recite the poem, "Our Mother Plays the Ukulele" with the children. (Linguistic)

Our Mother Plays the Ukulele
by Pam Schiller
Our mother plays the ukulele,
She strums and hums and sings so gaily.
We clap our hands and tap our toes,
As merrily from song to song she goes.

When our birthdays come each year,
The very first sound we expect to hear
Is "Happy Birthday" sung so gaily,
To the strings of our mother's ukulele.

Learning Activities

Art *(Linguistic, Spatial)*
Read from the section of the book that describes the giant. Invite the children to use paper, markers, and crayons to draw a picture of Abiyoyo.

Dramatic Play *(Linguistic, Interpersonal)*
Provide a couple of stiff cardboard tubes from coat hangers for the children to use as magic wands, and a "ukulele" made from rubber bands wrapped around a shallow box. Invite the children to re-enact the story.

Blocks *(Spatial, Bodily-Kinesthetic, Interpersonal)*
Provide boxes, paper towel tubes, paper sacks, and other materials, and challenge the children to build the town in the story. Invite the children to re-enact the part of the story where Abiyoyo is coming to town.

Music *(Linguistic, Musical)*
Provide a ukulele. Encourage the children to sing the "Abiyoyo" song to the strum of the ukulele.

Discovery *(Logical-Mathematical, Spatial)*
Encourage the children to use boxes, bags, empty paper towel tubes, and other materials to construct Abiyoyo. Help the children to place their Abiyoyo between a light source and a wall, and ask, *Does the shadow of this Abiyoyo look like the shadow in the book, when Abiyoyo is standing in front of the sun?*

Writing *(Linguistic, Naturalist)*
Set out magnetic letters. Encourage the children to spell *Abiyoyo.* Ask questions: *Can you spell Abiyoyo backwards? What is the giant's name when it is spelled backwards? Which name suits him better?*

Let's Keep Reading

Abiyoyo Returns by Pete Seeger
The Judge by Margot Zemach
The Little Old Lady Who Was Not Afraid of Anything by Linda Williams

Thinking About What We Learned

1. Which parts of the story might really happen? Which parts are only make-believe?

Alicia's Happy Day

Author: Meg Starr

Illustrators: Ying-Hwa Hu and Cornelius Van Wright

About the Book

Alicia celebrates her birthday in style. She is greeted by neighbors, shopkeepers, animals, and more. She enjoys a party with her family and friends.

Learning Literacy

Oral Language

❍ Discuss words that may be new to the children, such as *salsa, pigeons, ribbon,* and *peel.*

❍ Talk with the children about the names that Alicia uses for her mother and father (*mammi* and *poppi*).

❍ Invite the children to talk about the many different names they call their mothers and fathers. List the names on chart paper as the children say them.

❍ Talk with the children about the expression *helado de coco (coconut ice cream).* Explain that it is made with sugar, milk, eggs, and vanilla. Look at the picture in the book of the Icey man. Ask the children, *What is an Icey man?*

Comprehension

❍ Ask the children the following questions: *Which happy birthday wish did you like best? Why? How do you celebrate your birthday? What do you think a "twirly-swirly" day is like?*

Print Awareness

❍ Make a list of the many ways people wish Alicia a happy birthday. Encourage the children to pick the birthday wishes they like best.

Special Activities

❍ Have an "Everybody's Birthday" celebration. Let the children help choose the theme, help make the invitations and cake, select the music and games, and decorate the room. (Linguistic, Logical-Mathematical, Spatial, Bodily-Kinesthetic, Musical, Naturalist, Interpersonal, Intrapersonal)

❍ Play salsa music and encourage the children to dance. (Bodily-Kinesthetic, Musical, Intrapersonal)

❍ Encourage the children to draw and write on the sidewalk with chalk. Print *Happy Birthday* and challenge the children to copy the letters. Draw a cake and invite the children to add the candles. (Linguistic, Logical-Mathematical, Spatial, Bodily-Kinesthetic)

❍ Play Simon Says using a sign that says "Walk" and one that says "Don't Walk." For example, say, *Simon says* and hold up the "Walk" sign, inviting the children to walk. Then say *Simon says* and hold up the "Don't Walk" sign, so the children will stop. As children become more proficient, add more signs. (Linguistic, Logical-Mathematical, Bodily-Kinesthetic, Interpersonal)

Learning Activities

Dramatic Play *(Musical, Interpersonal, Intrapersonal)*

Provide props for a birthday party, such as hats, streamers, pretend cake, and wrapped boxes for presents. Invite the children to have a pretend birthday party. Encourage them to take turns being the birthday girl or boy and to sing "Happy Birthday" to each honoree.

Math *(Logical-Mathematical, Naturalist)*

Cut ice cream cone shapes from construction paper. Cut scoops (circles) of ice cream from white, brown, and pink construction paper. Arrange four or five scoops of "ice cream" in a pattern on two "cones." Encourage the children to copy the patterns.

Fine Motor *(Linguistic, Bodily-Kinesthetic, Interpersonal)*

Demonstrate how you can peel an orange to create a "ribbon of peel." From construction paper, cut orange circles about 6" in diameter. Draw a dotted line around in continuous circles starting in the center and working out to the edge of the paper. Challenge the children to cut the line to make paper versions of the ribbon peels.

Snack *(Linguistic, Logical-Mathematical, Bodily-Kinesthetic, Interpersonal)*

Help each child make coconut ice cream by placing ½ cup of milk, 1 tablespoon of sugar, ¼ teaspoon of vanilla, and ½ teaspoon of coconut extract in a quart-size resealable plastic bag. Place it inside a gallon-size resealable plastic bag and add ice cubes and 3 tablespoons of rock salt. Shake until the ice cream freezes—about 10–12 minutes.

Games *(Spatial)*

Make birthday puzzles by cutting up the fronts of cake boxes to create puzzles. Vary the difficulty of the puzzles by cutting some of the boxes into more pieces than others. Encourage the children to put the puzzles together, beginning with simple puzzles and progressing to puzzles that are more difficult.

Writing *(Linguistic, Bodily-Kinesthetic)*

Print *Happy Birthday* on a piece of chart paper. Encourage the children to copy the greeting using magnetic letters. Place blue fingerpaint on top of a white plastic tablecloth. Encourage the children to write *Happy Birthday* in the fingerpaint with their finger. Ask, *Does it look like the sky writing in the story?*

Let's Keep Reading

Moira's Birthday by Robert Munsch
Not Yet, Yvette by Helen Ketteman

Thinking About What We Learned

1. How did the helado de coco taste?
2. Why do you think Alicia had a good birthday?

Alphabet Soup: A Feast of Letters

Author and Illustrator: Scott Gustafson

About the Book

Otter finds a large old soup pot in his new home. He invites 26 friends to a potluck house-warming party. Each guest is asked to bring a soup-worthy ingredient, and the animals bring foods that start with the same letter as their names (armadillo brings asparagus, zebra brings zucchini).

Learning Literacy

Phonological Awareness

❍ As you read about each individual animal and that animal's contributions to the potluck, encourage the children to find objects on the page that begin with the same sound as the first letter in the animal's name.

Comprehension

❍ Ask the children the following questions: *What gave Otter the idea to make a soup? How does he let everyone know that he is having a potluck dinner? What is a potluck dinner?*

Print Awareness/Letter Knowledge/ Phonological Awareness

❍ Copy a section of text from the book, such as the section about Bear the baker. Underline the words that begin with the letter "b". Ask, *How many words begin with the letter b?* Print other sentences from the book·and point out the alliteration.

Letter Knowledge

❍ Place magnetic letters on a board. Challenge the children to help you sort the letters into those with straight lines, those with curved lines, and those with both straight lines and curved lines.

Special Activities

❍ Take a trip to the zoo. Ask the children, *Can you find one animal for each letter of the alphabet?* (Linguistic, Logical-Mathematical, Naturalist, Interpersonal)

❍ Make an alphabet soup. Make a list of things that you can put into the soup that represent as many of the alphabet letters as possible. Send a list of the items home with the children and ask each family to contribute one of the items for the soup. Match the items to the alphabet before they go into the soup. Be sure to toss in some alphabet-shaped noodles. (Linguistic, Logical-Mathematical, Naturalist, Interpersonal)

❍ Invite the children to try Hula Hoops, like the hedgehog does in the book. Getting a Hula Hoop to spin is not as easy as it looks. (Bodily-Kinesthetic, Intrapersonal)

❍ Have the children select a partner. Instruct each pair of children to think of a way they can combine their bodies to form a letter of the alphabet. (Spatial, Bodily-Kinesthetic, Interpersonal)

❍ Sing the "Alphabet Song." Sing it forward and sing it backward. Singing the letters in both directions keeps children from simply memorizing the letters in alphabetical order. (Linguistic, Musical, Naturalist)

Learning Activities

Art

(Linguistic, Spatial)
Provide lime-colored tempera paint and paper and encourage the children to paint "lime letters."

Listening

(Linguistic, Intrapersonal)
Record the story, emphasizing the repetitive consonant sounds in the description of each animal and the item it brought to add to the soup. Place the book and the tape in the listening center.

Blocks

(Spatial, Bodily-Kinesthetic, Interpersonal)
Challenge the children to make alphabet letters with blocks. Talk with them as they work. Ask questions: *Can you make curved letters or only straight letters? Can you spell your name with the blocks?*

Music

(Linguistic, Musical, Intrapersonal)
Provide rhythm band instruments. Encourage the children to sing "The Alphabet Song" to the beat of a drum or the jingle of a tambourine. Challenge them to use one of the instruments to create beats to accompany the spelling of their names.

Language

(Linguistic, Naturalist)
Help the children to sort magnetic letters into those with straight lines, those with curved lines, and those with both straight lines and curved lines.

Writing

(Linguistic, Intrapersonal)
Give each child a handful of alphabet cereal. Invite the children to find all the letters of their names. After they spell their names with the cereal, invite them to eat the cereal.

Let's Keep Reading

Chicka Chicka Boom Boom by Bill Martin, Jr. and John Archambault
Stone Soup by Marcia Brown

Thinking About What We Learned

1. What do you think about Otter's potluck house-warming party? Which animal was your favorite?
2. Name some letters with straight lines. Is the first letter of your name a straight letter, a curved letter, or a letter that is both straight and curved?

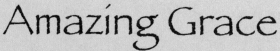

Amazing Grace

Author: Mary Hoffman. Illustrator: Caroline Binch

About the Book

Grace loves stories. She loves acting out the role of the lead characters in books. When her teacher announces that the class is going to put on the play, "Peter Pan," Grace wants to try out for the role of Peter Pan. Her classmates make her doubt her ability to play the part because she is an African American girl whereas Peter Pan is a Caucasian boy. Grace's mother and grandmother remind Grace that she can be anything she wants if she puts her mind to it. With renewed confidence, Grace tries out for the part and is unanimously voted into the role of Peter.

Learning Literacy

Oral Language

❍ Grace calls her grandmother *nana*. Ask the children, *What do you call your grandmother?* List the children's answers on chart paper.

❍ Ask the children the following questions: *Why do you think the title of the book is* Amazing Grace? *What does* amazing *mean? What other descriptive words describe Grace?*

❍ Discuss words that may be new to the children, such as *audition, ballet, fortune, companion, genie,* and *kingdom.*

Comprehension

❍ Ask the children the following questions: *Have you ever pretended to be a character you have read about in a book or seen in a movie? How would the story be different if Grace had been a boy?*

Special Activities

❍ Take the children to see a live play. (Linguistic, Musical, Interpersonal)

❍ Put on a simple play. Both "Little Red Hen" and "The Giant Turnip" provide simple story lines that can easily be converted into a play . Have the children make tickets, programs, and posters, and help them make costumes and props. Add music where appropriate. Invite another class to come see the performance. (Linguistic, Spatial, Logical-Mathematical, Bodily-Kinesthetic, Musical, Interpersonal)

❍ Play music and encourage the children to pretend to fly. (Bodily-Kinesthetic, Musical, Interpersonal, Intrapersonal)

Learning Activities

Construction *(Linguistic, Spatial)*
Provide a box that the children can use as a puppet stage. Encourage the children to think about how they would want to alter the box to create a stage. Follow the children's instructions as they suggest how to cut the box. Encourage the children to decorate the stage. Provide puppets and challenge the children to put on a play.

Listening *(Musical)*
Play the music from the CD *Peter Pan* by James Newton Howard. Encourage the children to pick their favorite songs.

Dramatic Play *(Spatial/Bodily Kinesthetic, Interpersonal)*
Fill the center with costumes for the children to use to pretend that they are characters from books. If you have the materials to make a Peter Pan costume, add them to the center.

Math *(Logical-Mathematical, Naturalist)*
Make a graph of characters you have read about during the past week. Encourage the children to vote for the characters they would most like to be. Help the children tally the votes to determine which character was picked most frequently.

Library *(Linguistic)*
Fill the library with the books mentioned in the first part of the story as the base for Grace's role play. For example, books about Anansi, Hiawatha, Mowgli, and Aladdin, as well as books about pirates. Talk about the characters with the children. Keep a copy of *Amazing Grace* in the center so that children can refer to the pages that show her in character.

Writing *(Spatial, Intrapersonal)*
Encourage the children to talk about times when someone hurt their feelings. Write down their stories as they tell them. Encourage them to draw pictures to go with their stories.

Let's Keep Reading

The Itsy Bitsy Spider by Iza Trapani
The Little Engine That Could by Watty Piper

Thinking About What We Learned

1. Which character did you pretend to be in the dramatic play center? What did you wear?
2. What would somebody say you can do amazingly well?

Anansi and the Talking Melon

Retold by Eric A. Kimmel. Illustrator: Janet Stevens

About the Book
Anansi, the trickster spider, is at it again—at Elephant's expense. Anansi drops into Elephant's garden and eats so much melon he is too full to move. Bored, Anansi decides to play a trick on Elephant. From inside the melon, Anansi starts talking, convincing poor Elephant that he has a talking melon. Elephant picks up his treasure and takes off on a journey to show the talking melon to King Monkey. Chaos ensues.

Learning Literacy

Oral Language
- Discuss words that may be new to the children, such as *melon, bored, thorn tree, hoeing, bore, ridiculous,* and *warthog.*
- Bring a melon into the classroom. Ask the children to describe its texture, its weight, and its smell. Cut the melon and serve slices to the children. *How does it taste?*

Comprehension
- Ask the children the following questions: *Have you ever been bored? What did you do to entertain yourself? What things did the animals in the book do that we know animals in real life can't do? What do you think will happen now that Anansi has moved to the bananas?*

Special Activities

- Visit a produce store. Find the melons. Ask questions: *How many different types of melons can you find? Can you find a melon that looks like the one in Elephant's garden? Are all the melons the same weight?* Weigh several melons. *How much do the melons cost?* (Logical-Mathematical, Naturalist)
- Play Spider Melon Roll. Take a couple of balls outdoors. Show the children how to walk on all fours like a spider. Define a start and a finish line. Pair the children and have each pair race from the start to finish line, moving like spiders and finding a way to move the ball without their hands. (Spatial, Bodily-Kinesthetic, Interpersonal, Intrapersonal)
- Sing "Anansi the Spider" to the tune of "The Itsy Bitsy Spider." Encourage the children to make up hand motions to go with the song. (Linguistic, Bodily-Kinesthetic, Musical)

Anansi the Spider
by Pam Schiller
Anansi the spider ate too much honeydew.
Tricked Mr. Elephant by calling out, "Yoo-hoo!"
Filled with delight, Elephant cried, "Yippee!"
And he took the talking melon
To see the King Monkey.

Learning Activities

Art *(Spatial)*
Provide cantaloupe skin, paper, and tempera paint in a shallow pan or in a Styrofoam meat tray. Have the children dip the outer skin of the melon in the paint and then press it onto the drawing paper to make interesting and original prints. Ask, *How does the texture of the melon skin affect the print on the paper?*

Dramatic Play *(Linguistic, Interpersonal, Intrapersonal)*
Create a large "melon" by draping a piece of orange fabric, blanket, sheet, or pieces of bulletin board paper over a small table. Make the melon large enough for a child to get inside. Provide additional props for the animals (perhaps stuffed animals) and encourage the children to re-enact the story.

Language *(Logical-Mathematical, Interpersonal, Intrapersonal)*
Away from the children, spray paint several tennis balls orange. Cut a small hole or slit in each ball (adult-only step) and insert a small plastic spider. Encourage the children to talk as if they were the spiders in the "melons."

Math *(Logical-Mathematical, Bodily-Kinesthetic)*
Paint five 6" paper plates orange to look like melons, and put out several pairs of tweezers and beads. Print the numerals 1–5 in the center of each plate (one number per plate). Challenge the children to use tweezers to move the correct number of beads onto the plates.
Safety Note: Use child-safe tweezers.

Music *(Musical, Intrapersonal)*
Away from the children, spray paint several tennis balls orange. Cut a small hole or slit in each ball (adult-only step) and insert jingle bells in them. Place one bell in the first ball, two in the next, and so on, up to five. Encourage the children to make music with the bell balls. Challenge them to arrange the balls in order from the softest sound to the loudest sound.

Science *(Naturalist)*
Provide several pictures of spiders. Challenge the children to find a spider that looks like Anansi. Invite the children to sort the spiders by size, color, whether they are scary or not, and so on.

Let's Keep Reading

Anansi and the Moss-Covered Rock by Eric A. Kimmel
Flossie and the Fox by Patricia Missack
Rosie's Walk by Pat Hutchins

Thinking About What We Learned

1. Do you think it was okay that Anansi played a trick on Elephant? Why? Why not?
2. What was the funniest thing that happened in the story?

Animal Orchestra: A Counting Book

Author and Illustrator: Scott Gustafson

About the Book

One "Maestro Toucan" introduces the musicians in his animal orchestra, from the "two double basses" to the "ten flutes." The final spread shows the entire ensemble on stage.

Learning Literacy

Oral Language

❍ Talk with the children about each instrument and how it is played. Explain to the children that instruments are classified as *percussion, string, brass,* or *wind* based on how the instrument makes its sound. Common string instruments include the guitar, violin, and piano. Wind instruments include the flute, oboe, clarinet, and saxophone. Brass instruments include the trumpet, French horn, trombone, and tuba. Drums and cymbals are percussion instruments.

Comprehension

❍ Ask the children the following questions: *Do you think animals can really play instruments? What is the role of the conductor? Which instrument would you like to play?*

Print Awareness

❍ Ask the children to brainstorm a list of percussion sounds they can make with their bodies (clapping, slapping knees, tapping feet, and clucking tongues). List their ideas on chart paper.

Letter Knowledge

❍ Discuss the orchestra as a family of instruments. Compare it to the letters of the alphabet. Explain to the children that a family is made up of family members, just as an orchestra is made up of many different instruments, and the alphabet is made up of different letters.

Special Activities

❍ Visit a high school orchestra. Obtain permission for the children to sit beside musicians within the orchestra. Talk with the children about the difference in the way the music sounds depending on where you are sitting. (Logical-Mathematical, Musical, Naturalist, Intrapersonal).

❍ Make a large floor puzzle with enough pieces for every child to have one piece to add to the puzzle. Describe the puzzle as pieces that go together to make a whole, in the same way that instruments combine to make an orchestra and letters combine to make the alphabet. (Linguistic, Logical-Mathematical, Spatial, Interpersonal)

❍ Give one or two children rhythm instruments (homemade or purchased). Put on classical music and encourage the children to play along. Start by having only one child play, and gradually give other children more instruments until everyone is playing. Discuss how the sound of the music changes with each additional instrument. (Linguistic, Logical-Mathematical, Bodily-Kinesthetic, Musical, Naturalist, Interpersonal)

Learning Activities

Art *(Spatial, Musical)*
Provide crayons and paper. Play classical music and invite the children to color to the tempo of the music.

Listening *(Linguistic, Musical)*
Make a recording of *Animal Orchestra*. Place the book and the tape in the listening center.

Blocks *(Bodily-Kinesthetic, Spatial, Interpersonal)*
Have the children work together to build a structure. Give each builder four blocks and let them take turns adding one block at a time to the community structure.

Music *(Musical, Naturalist, Intrapersonal)*
Provide homemade musical instruments for the children to explore. Set out tin cans of various sizes and drumsticks or dowels to use to tap the cans. For wind instruments, take four or five clean, empty plastic bottles and tape them together from smallest to largest. Show the children how blowing over the tops of the bottles creates a harmonic sound. Ask questions: *Which instruments do you like the best? Why?*

Discovery *(Logical-Mathematical, Bodily-Kinesthetic, Musical, Interpersonal, Intrapersonal)*
Put bells inside margarine containers; cover and shake. Encourage the children to rub sandpaper together. Provide various boxes and drumsticks or dowels for the children to use to tap the boxes. Talk with the children about the various sounds they are making. Ask questions: *Are all the sounds percussive? Which sounds do you like the best?*

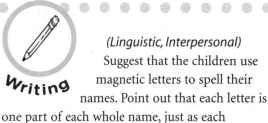

Writing *(Linguistic, Interpersonal)*
Suggest that the children use magnetic letters to spell their names. Point out that each letter is one part of each whole name, just as each instrument is one part of a whole orchestra.

Let's Keep Reading

Ben's Trumpet by Rachel Isadora
Max Found Two Sticks by Brian Pinkney
Zin! Zin! Zin! A Violin by Lloyd Moss

Thinking About What We Learned

1. What did you learn about orchestras today?
2. Which type of instrument do you like best? Why?

Apples Here!

Author and Illustrator: Will Hubbell

About the Book

Beautiful illustrations and simple text tell the story of apples from bloom to fruit to market and into homes. Some of the traditions and holiday customs associated with apples are mentioned.

Learning Literacy

Oral Language

❍ Pass an apple around for the children to feel. Talk about the texture of the skin and the weight of the apple. Serve apples slices. Cut the apple as the children watch. Introduce the children to the names for each part of the apple: *stem, skin, core, meat,* and *seeds.*

Phonological Awareness

❍ Sing "Apples and Bananas" (see appendix page 232) with the children. Print *apples* at the top of a sheet of chart paper, then *aypuls* beneath it, followed by *eeples, ipples,* and *upples.* Help the children pronounce each word, and ask the children whether the sounds of the words sound the same as the names of the first letters of each word. Explain to the children that the letters are vowels and that in these words they sound the same as the name of the letter because they are long vowels, and that all long vowels say their letter name.

Comprehension

❍ Ask the children the following questions: *Have you ever picked apples from a tree? Where? How did you reach them? Have you ever seen apples growing on a tree? How do you think the pickers reach the apples at the top of the tree? How are apples like oranges? How are they different? Does the color of an apple affect the taste of the apple?*

Print Awareness

❍ Show the children the cover of the book. Point out *apple.* Ask the children to identify the letters in the word, and ask them which letter shows up in apple more than once.

Special Activities

❍ Take a trip to an apple farm, or visit a produce stand. Examine the apples. Ask, *How many different kinds of apples are there?* Upon returning to the classroom, write a group story about the visit. Include a list of the apples that were at the farm or stand. Encourage the children to draw pictures that illustrate their favorite parts of the trip. (Linguistic, Logical-Mathematical, Spatial, Interpersonal, Interpersonal)

❍ Challenge the children to balance apples on their heads. Encourage them to take a few steps. Can they keep the apples balanced on their head? (Bodily-Kinesthetic)

❍ Tell the children the story of Johnny Appleseed (many versions available). Sing "Johnny Appleseed." (Linguistic, Musical, Naturalist)

Johnny Appleseed

Oh, the earth is good to me,
And so I thank the earth,
For giving me the things I need—
The sun, the rain, and the apple seed.
The earth is good to me.

Chicago Public Library
Oriole Park
9/22/2015   4:58:20 PM
-Patron Receipt-

ITEMS BORROWED:

1:
Title: All around town! : exploring your com
Item #: R0178613577
Due Date: 10/13/2015

2:
Title: How to prepare your child for kinderg
Item #: R0103731198
Due Date: 10/13/2015

3:
Title: A grand old tree /
Item #: R0405646203
Due Date: 10/13/2015

4:
Title: Tell me, tree : all about trees for kids
Item #: R0202746751
Due Date: 10/13/2015

5:
Title: Are trees alive? /
Item #: R0178613666
Due Date: 10/13/2015

6:
Title: Starting with stories: engaging multi
Item #: R0164033105
Due Date: 10/13/2015

-Please retain for your records-

MFRANK

Learning Activities

Art

(Spatial, Bodily-Kinesthetic)
Give the children a bowl of apple seeds, paper, glue and several pairs of tweezers. Encourage the children to pick up the apple seeds with the tweezers, dip them into the glue, and place them onto their collage. **Safety Note:** Be sure children use child-safe tweezers. If child-safe tweezers are not available, encourage the children to use their fingers instead.

Math

(Logical-Mathematical)
Show the children how to cut an apple in half and then into fourths. Provide construction paper apples and encourage the children to cut them into halves and then into fourths. Provide squares of paper and encourage the children to cut the squares into halves and fourths.

Cooking

(Linguistic, Logical Mathematical)
With the children, make apple cider. Mix 32 ounces of apple juice, 1 teaspoon of cinnamon, ¼ cup of lemon juice, and 2 tablespoons of honey. Heat in an old-style coffee pot. **Safety Note:** The coffee pot will get hot. Keep it out of reach of the children. Cool to room temperature and serve. Ask questions: *Which is sweeter, apple juice or the cider? What ingredient makes the cider sweet?*

Science

(Naturalist)
Dip cotton balls into extracts or massage oils with an apple blossom scent and them place them into film canisters or a similar type of canister to create Aroma Canisters. Hide one of the canisters. Then encourage the children to smell the othe canister and then use their noses to sniff out the matching scent. Ask questions: *Have you ever smelled real apple blossoms? Do you think apple blossoms smell the same as an apple?*

Listening

(Musical, Naturalist)
Provide a bowl of apple seeds. Encourage the children to place the seeds inside plastic containers of various sizes and then shake the containers to hear the sound the seeds make. Encourage the children to explore the sound of the seeds in each container. Ask questions: *Which sounds do you like the best? Why?*

Snack

(Linguistic, Musical, Naturalist, Interpersonal, Intrapersonal)
Provide a variety of apples for children to sample. Try to obtain the apples mentioned in the book: McIntosh, Gala, and Golden Delicious. Encourage the children to discuss which apple they like best. Ask questions: *Which apple is the sweetest? Which one is the most tart? How do apples sound when you chew them?*

Let's Keep Reading

Apples and Pumpkins by Anne Rockwell
How Do Apples Grow? by Betsy Maestro
Johnny Appleseed by Patricia Demuth

Thinking About What We Learned

1. Which apple did you like best? Which one was the sweetest?
2. What foods can be made with apples?

Barnyard Banter

Author and Illustrator: Denise Fleming

About the Book

A goose chasing a butterfly through the barnyard creates a rhyming and rhythmic ruckus among the animals that live there.

Learning Literacy

Oral Language

❍ Discuss words that may be new to the children, such as *banter, muck, wallow, rafters, padlock,* and so on.

❍ Take time with the children to look closely at the illustrations. Denise Fleming used textured paints to create the illustrations in *Barnyard Banter*. She poured cotton pulp through stencils to create the textured effect of the settings for the animals. Talk with the children about the illustrations. Have them describe the look of the grass and scenery, as well as the fur and feathers that cover the animals. Compare Denise Fleming's illustrations to those in other books.

Phonological Awareness

❍ Encourage the children to help you identify the onomatopoeic words in the story, such as *meow, cluck, moo,* and *cock-a-doodle-doo*. Remind the children that onomatopoeic words are words that imitate the sounds they are trying to describe.

Comprehension

❍ Ask the children the following questions: *Why was the goose chasing the butterfly? Which animal in the book is your favorite? Why? Are there animals that could be added to the story?*

Special Activities

❍ Play Duck, Duck, Goose. Invite the children to sit in a circle. Select one child to be IT. Encourage IT to walk around the circle behind the children tapping each child on the head lightly saying, "Duck, duck, duck, duck" and eventually, "Goose." When IT taps a child on the head and says, "Goose," that child stands and chases IT around the circle trying to tag her. If IT gets back to the chaser's place in the circle and sits down before being tagged, the chaser becomes IT. If the chaser tags IT, IT must try again. (Bodily-Kinesthetic, Interpersonal)

❍ Take a field trip to a local farm, if possible. Make a list of all the animals in *Barnyard Banter* before leaving on the trip. See if you can find all the animals in the book at the farm. Check them off the list as you find them. (Linguistic, Naturalist)

❍ Go on a nature walk to look for butterflies. (Naturalist)

❍ Create an animal choir. Ask children which animal in the story they would like to represent. Place the children in groups according to their choices. Sing "Old MacDonald" changing the word *farm* to *choir* and E-I-E-I-O to *do-re-mi-fa-so*. When you point to a group of "animals," have them make the sounds that animal group made in the story. Point to one group for the *cows here* and another group for the *ducks there,* and then go back and forth between the two groups. Sing a second verse using two different groups. (Musical, Intrapersonal)

Learning Activities

Art

(Spatial)
Create textured paints by adding sand and sawdust to regular tempera paint. Provide drawing paper, tempera paint, and sponges shaped like animals. Invite the children to make sponge print animals with the paint. Explain to the children that Denise Fleming used textured paints to create her illustrations in *Barnyard Banter*.

Gross Motor

(Bodily-Kinesthetic, Interpersonal)
Show the children how to waddle like a goose. Blow bubbles and have the children waddle to catch the bubbles. *Is waddling easier or more difficult than walking?*

Blocks

(Logical-Mathematical, Spatial, Naturalist)
Provide farm animals and props and encourage the children to create their own barnyard. Ask questions: *Which animals can be penned together? Which animals need to be by the water? Which animals need the barn?*

Listening

(Musical, Naturalist)
Provide pictures of farm animals and a tape of sounds that the animals make. Have the children listen to the tape and match the correct animal to the sounds on the tape.

Games

(Interpersonal, Intrapersonal)
Cut goose footprints from orange construction paper or from orange plastic sheeting or vinyl. Arrange the prints on the floor in a path as if they were actual goose footprints. Hide a butterfly somewhere at the end of the footprint path. Challenge children to follow the goose footprints and find the butterfly. Then hide the butterfly again and arrange the goose footprints in a new path.

Writing

(Linguistic)
Print *goose* and *butterfly* on a sheet of paper. Encourage the children to use magnetic letters to copy the words.

Let's Keep Reading

In the Small, Small Pond by Denise Fleming
Olmo and the Blue Butterfly by Alma Flor Ada

Thinking About What We Learned

1. Have you ever chased a butterfly? Did you catch it? Why is it difficult to catch a butterfly?
2. Can you name some of the onomatopoeic sounds in the story?

Beatrice's Goat

Author: Page McBrier. Illustrator: Lori Lohstoeter

About the Book
Beatrice dreams of attending school with other village children of Kisinga (western Uganda), but instead she must take care of her five younger siblings and help her mother in the fields. Everything starts to change, however, when Beatrice and her family receive a goat, "a lucky gift," says her mother, from a charitable organization.

Learning Literacy

Oral Language
❍ Tell the children that this story is a true story, and that such stories are called non-fiction. Invite the children to recall times they wanted something they could not have.
❍ Show the children the picture in the book where Beatrice is watching the children in school. Ask the children about the school in the picture. *How is school in the village of Kisinga different from our school?*

Comprehension
❍ Ask the children the following questions: *Why did Beatrice name the goat Mugisa? What does Mugisa mean? Would Beatrice have been able to go to school without the goat?*

Print Awareness/Letter Knowledge
❍ Print *Beatrice* on chart paper. Ask the children the following questions: *What is the first letter in her name? Does anyone in the class have a name that begins with the same letter as Beatrice's name?*

Special Activities
❍ Visit a zoo or farm or some other location where children can observe goats. Ask questions: *What do they eat? What color are they?* Explain to the children what a goatee is. (Linguistic, Logical-Mathematical, Naturalist)

❍ A popular game for children in Uganda is similar to our Hula Hoops™. Encourage the children to play with Hula Hoops™. (Spatial, Bodily-Kinesthetic, Musical Interpersonal)
❍ Beatrice lives in a village called Kisinga, in western Uganda. Find her town on a map. Discuss some interesting facts about Uganda. (Linguistic, Logical-Mathematical, Spatial, Naturalist, Interpersonal, Intrapersonal)

● Uganda has substantial natural resources, including fertile soil, regular rainfall, and sizable mineral deposits of copper and cobalt.
● Agriculture employs over 80% of the work force.
● Coffee is Uganda's primary export.
● Uganda's flag is red, yellow, and black.

❍ Challenge the children to raise $100 (art sales, bake sales, and so on) so that they can sponsor a goat. Send the contribution to the address below. The organization will provide you with information about the recipient of your donation. Encourage the children to stay in contact with their recipient. (Linguistic, Logical-Mathematical, Interpersonal, Intrapersonal)

Heifer Project International
P.O. Box 8058
Little Rock, AR 72203
Telephone: (800) 422-0474

Learning Activities

Cooking

(Linguistic, Logical-Mathematical, Spatial, Bodily-Kinesthetic, Interpersonal)

Make "Kashata Na Nazi" (Ugandan Coconut Candy). Melt 2 cups of sugar in a medium-sized iron skillet, stirring constantly until it melts (adult-only step). While the sugar is still white, add 2 cups of moist coconut, 1 teaspoon of cinnamon, and ½ teaspoon of salt. Stir hard for 30 seconds. Pour into a pan lined with wax paper. Cut into 1½" squares while still hot. Cool until set.

Music

(Linguistic, Musical)

Play music from Uganda. Examples include *Music From Uganda* from the Caprice Series, *Dance My Children, Dance* by Samile, and *African Lullaby* from Ellipsis Arts. Encourage the children to discuss how music from Uganda is different from music in the United States.

Dramatic Play

(Linguistic, Interpersonal)

Provide materials the children can use to play school, such as chalkboard slates, books, paper, pencils, and so on.

Outside

(Spatial, Bodily-Kinesthetic, Interpersonal)

Provide water, straw, and a dirt area (or tub of dirt). Invite the children to wet the dirt and attempt to create mud houses like the one that Beatrice and her family live in. Demonstrate how the straw helps give form to the mud.

Math

(Logical-Mathematical, Interpersonal, Intrapersonal)

Beatrice has five brothers and sisters, which makes six children in her family. Provide paper plates, cups, and silverware. Invite the children to set the table for Beatrice's family. Remind the children to set a place for Beatrice's mama.

Writing

(Linguistic)

Set out several sets of magnetic letters. Print *Mugisa*, *Mulindwa*, and *Kihembo* on chart paper, and encourage the children to copy the names of the goats.

Let's Keep Reading

Faith the Cow by Susan Bame Hoover
Uncle Willie and the Soup Kitchen by Dyanne Disalvo-Ryan

Thinking About What We Learned

1. Think of something you have wanted as badly as Beatrice wanted to go to school. What was/is it? Did you get it? What are some things we can do to make waiting less difficult?
2. Do you think that Beatrice's brothers and sisters will get to go to school? Why?

Be Brown!

Author: Barbara Bottner. Illustrator: Barry Gott

About the Book
A bossy little boy meets a rambunctious puppy that simply will not obey the boy's commands. Can he teach the dog to obey?

Learning Literacy

Oral Language
○ Read the book again. Stop on each page and ask the children if the command the little boy gives the dog sounds like something someone might say to them.

Comprehension
○ Ask the children the following questions: *Do you have a dog? Does your dog obey commands? Why do you think the dog in* Be Brown! *won't obey the boy's commands? What is the dog's name? Why do you think the dog's name is Brown? How would the story be different if the dog's name were Black?*

Print Awareness/Phonological Awareness
○ Print *Be Brown!* on chart paper. Talk with the children about the beginning letter of each word. Point out that when consecutive words (words that are next to each other) begin with the same sound it is called *alliteration*. Say *Be Brown!* several times. Can the children hear that the /b/ sound is repeated? Talk about the exclamation point.

Special Activities

○ Visit a veterinarian's office or a pet store. Ask the veterinarian or pet store employee to talk to the children about dogs. (Linguistic, Naturalist, Interpersonal)

○ Play music and encourage the children to howl at the moon just as Brown howls at the moon. (Musical, Intrapersonal)
○ Play Pin the Nose on the Dog, as you would play Pin the Tail on the Donkey. (Spatial, Bodily-Kinesthetic, Interpersonal)
○ Sing and move to "My Dog Rags," sung to the tune of "Five Little Ducks." Discuss the second verse. *Why do you think Rags won't obey?* (Bodily-Kinesthetic, Musical, Interpersonal)

My Dog Rags
(additional verse by Pam Schiller)
I have a dog and his name is Rags. (point to self)
He eats so much that his tummy sags. (rub tummy)
His ears flip flop and his tail wigwags, (hold hands by ears and flop them—hold hand behind back and wag it)
And when he walks he zig, zig, zags! (zigzag)
Flip flop, wigwag, zig zag. (combine actions from last three lines)

My dog Rags he loves to play.
He rolls around in the mud all day. (roll arm over arm)
I whistle for him but he won't obey! (point to mouth)
He always runs the other way. (point over shoulder)
Flip flop, wigwag, hey, hey. (flop hands by ears, wag hand behind back, and then place hands beside mouth)

Learning Activities

Art *(Spatial)*
Suggest that the children use brown paint and paper to paint a brown dog. Ask, *Does he look like the dog in the story?*

Language *(Linguistic, Intrapersonal)*
Encourage the children to dictate a couple of sentences about how the little boy feels when the dog is not paying any attention to him. Provide smiling faces, frowning faces, frustrated faces, and crying faces. Encourage the children to pick the faces that represent the way they think the little boy feels.

Dramatic Play *(Linguistic, Interpersonal)*
Provide stuffed dogs and pretend bones or other types of doggy treats. Encourage the children to pretend they are running an obedience school. Explain what an obedience school is. Ask questions: *What makes the puppies behave? Would obedience school help Brown?*

Listening *(Linguistic, Musical)*
Record the story on a cassette tape. Encourage the children to make up a tune to sing the words to, instead of reading them. Use a ringing bell to signal that it is time to turn the page. Place the book and the tape in the listening center and encourage the children to listen to the story.

Gross Motor *(Linguistic, Bodily-Kinesthetic, Interpersonal)*
Suggest that the children pretend to be dogs doing tricks, such as sitting, rolling over, shaking paws, and so on.

Math *(Logical-Mathematical)*
Provide brown fingerpaint and paper. Show the children how to make a fist, press it into the paint, and then onto paper to make a paw print. Print the numeral 5 on their papers, and encourage the children to put five paw prints on the paper.

Let's Keep Reading

Good Dog, Carl by Alexandra Day
Harry the Dirty Dog by Gene Zion
The Pokey Puppy by Jeanette Sebring Lowrey

Thinking About What We Learned

1. What is the puppy doing in the book instead of listening to the little boy?
2. How does the little boy feel at the end of the story?

Blueberries for Sal

Author and Illustrator: Robert McCloskey

About the Book
A human child and a bear cub get mixed up while picking blueberries on a mountain. Children love this story.

Learning Literacy

Oral Language
○ Introduce words that may be new to the children, such as *tin, pail, blueberries, clump, struggle, hustle, tramped/tramping, stump, partridge,* and so on.

Phonological Awareness
○ The story is filled with *onomatopoeic* words (words that imitate the sounds they are describing). Help the children find the *onomatopoeic* sounds in the story, such as *kerplunk, munch, gulp,* and *garumpf.*

Comprehension
○ Show the children the pictures of Sal and her mother. Encourage the children to point out things in Sal's kitchen that they remember seeing in their own kitchens. Ask the children how their kitchens are different from Sal's.
○ Remind the children how, in the story, Mother Bear told Baby Bear to eat plenty of berries so his tummy would be full before he went into hibernation for the winter. Talk with the children about hibernation. Define *hibernation* and discuss other animals that hibernate in the winter. *Where do bears hibernate?*

Special Activities

○ Encourage the children to make a list of all the ways Sal and Baby Bear are alike, and then a list of the ways in which Sal and Baby Bear are different. (Linguistic, Naturalist, Interpersonal, Intrapersonal)
○ Invite the children to participate in the action story, "Going on a Bear Hunt." (Bodily-Kinesthetic, Musical)
○ Create an imaginary mountain in the classroom by draping a sheet over a table. Invite the children to recreate what Sal and Baby Bear experienced when they were on opposite sides of the mountain. Ask, *How can you let someone know you are on the other side of the mountain when that person can't see you?* (Logical-Mathematical, Intrapersonal)
○ Encourage the children to draw a picture of Sal and Baby Bear on opposite sides of the mountain. You may want to draw hills in the middle of pieces of drawing paper to get the children started. Talk with children as they draw: *Can Baby Bear see Sal? Can Sal see Baby Bear? Why? Why not?* (Spatial)

Learning Activities

Art *(Linguistic, Spatial)*

Mix 1 teaspoon glycerin, ½ half cup of liquid soap, and ½ cup water in a pail. Add blue tempera paint until the bubbles leave blue circles on the paper. Invite the children to blow circles to represent blueberries. Write *blueberries* on a card and invite the children to copy the word onto their papers beside their blueberry bubbles.

Listening *(Bodily-Kinesthetic, Musical)*

Encourage the children to drop a variety of items, such as small balls, buttons, and cotton balls into a bucket or pail. Ask the children to pay special attention to the sound each item makes when it hits the bottom of the bucket or pail. Encourage the children to describe the sound each item makes.

Discovery *(Logical-Mathematical, Spatial)*

Make dye by boiling blueberries or, for a less dramatic shade of blue, simply let blueberries sit in a small amount of water until the water is blue. Provide paper and brushes and encourage the children to use the dye as paint.

Math *(Logical-Mathematical, Intrapersonal)*

Provide pictures of foods that include blueberries; for example, blueberry muffins, blueberry yogurt, blueberry pancakes, blueberries in fruit salad, and blueberries by themselves. Encourage the children to place large cutout blueberries on a graph that represents their favorite way of eating blueberries.

Gross Motor *(Interpersonal, Intrapersonal)*

Create a bear cave by draping a sheet over a table. Encourage the children to pretend they are bears who will be spending the winter sleeping in the cave. Ask, *What do you want to put in the cave to make it comfortable all winter long?* Encourage the children to furnish the cave.

Science *(Linguistic, Naturalist)*

Suggest that the children examine photographs of or books about bears, looking for the differences in different types of bears. Ask questions: *Which bears are larger? Which are smaller? Is a polar bear a bear? Why? Why not?*

Let's Keep Reading

Are You My Mother? by Philip D. Eastman
Henrietta's First Winter by Lewis Rob

Thinking About What We Learned

1. Have you ever been lost from your mother? If so, how did you feel?
2. If blueberries are blue and blackberries are black, what other name could we use for strawberries?

Bob

Author and Illustrator: Tracey Campbell Pearson

About the Book
A rooster leaves the coop to find his voice. He learns to meow, bark, ribbit, and much more before he finally learns to cock-a-doodle-do. His ability to imitate other animals comes in handy when he has to outwit a fox.

Learning Literacy

Oral Language
○ Invite the children to demonstrate the movements related to each animal in the story; for example, wagging like a dog, hopping like a frog, and chewing like a cow.

Phonological Awareness
○ Point out that the animal sounds in the book are *onomatopoeic* sounds. These are words that imitate the sounds they are describing. Make a list of onomatopoeic sounds used in the story.

Comprehension
○ Ask the children the following questions: *Who tells Bob he is a rooster? How does Bob learn to cluck? How does he learn to meow? Who taught Bob to crow like a rooster? How did Bob fool the fox?*

Special Activities

○ Visit a farm. Make a list of the animals from the book and then see if the children can find them during your trip. Ask, *Do any of the roosters look like Bob?* (Linguistic, Naturalist)
○ Sing "Old MacDonald Had a Farm." Sing about each animal in the story. (Linguistic, Musical, Interpersonal)
○ Fill the library with non-fiction books about roosters. Ask questions: *Do any of the roosters look like Bob? How many roosters like Bob can you find?* (Logical-Mathematical, Spatial, Intrapersonal)
○ Teach the children "Bob's Song," to the tune of "Five Little Ducks." (Linguistic, Musical)

Bob's Song
by Pam Schiller
Twenty-two hens were sitting in a coop.
A hungry brown fox came around to snoop.
A hen for dinner sounded so good to him,
So he snuck right up through moonlight dim.

One brave rooster couldn't go to sleep,
So he saw the fox was about to leap,
"Cock-a-doodle do" he shouted out,
But the fox didn't even turn about.

The brave little rooster tried again,
Using the language of his friends.
"Meow," "woof," "ribbit," "moo, moo, moo,"
And the terrified fox: back home he flew.

Learning Activities

Art *(Spatial)*
Encourage the children to use white and red paint, black paper, and paintbrushes to speckle their black paper with white paint and then add red paint anywhere they choose. Ask, *Does your artwork remind you of Bob?*

Listening *(Musical, Naturalist, Interpersonal)*
Provide plastic farm animals or photos of farm animals. Record animal sounds on a cassette tape. Challenge the children to listen to the sounds and match those sounds to the plastic animals.

Blocks *(Linguistic, Spatial, Bodily-Kinesthetic, Naturalist)*
Suggest that the children use plastic farm animals and props to build a farm and re-enact the story.

Math *(Linguistic, Logical-Mathematical, Intrapersonal)*
Give the children feathers in a variety of colors. Provide a feather pattern and ask the children to copy it. Challenge the children to use the feathers to create patterns of their own. Encourage the children to describe their patterns to you.

Gross Motor *(Linguistic, Bodily-Kinesthetic)*
Use masking tape to create a line on the floor. Invite the children to walk the line like the animals in the story, hopping like a frog, strutting like a rooster, wagging like a dog, and chewing like a cow.

Writing *(Linguistic, Bodily-Kinesthetic)*
Print the farm animal names—*Bob, Fred,* and *Henrietta*—on index cards. Provide fingerpaint, and encourage the children to dab their fingerprints along the shapes of the letters.

Let's Keep Reading

Barnyard Banter by Denise Fleming
Myrtle by Tracey Campbell Pearson

Thinking About What We Learned

1. What did the fox want in the hen coop?
2. Which was your favorite activity today? Why?

Brown Bear, Brown Bear, What Do You See?

Author: Bill Martin, Jr. Illustrator: Eric Carle

About the Book

Brown Bear, Brown Bear, What Do You See? is a simple repetitive story that uses interlocking predictability to introduce children to animals, colors, and, most importantly, to the joys of rhythm and rhyme in language. This is a great book for children to use as a first "reader." The predictable text and clear illustrations provide enough clues to help even very young children read.

Learning Literacy

Oral Language

❍ Teach the children the American Sign Language signs (see appendix pages 235-236) for some of the animals in the story.

Segmentation

❍ Invite the children to clap the words in the story as you read it to them.

Phonological Awareness

❍ Print *Brown Bear, Brown Bear* on a piece of chart paper. Point out the *alliteration*. Explain to the children that alliteration happens when words start with the same sound. Print *red bird* on chart paper. Ask the children to help you make these words alliterative. Demonstrate changing the word *red* to *blue*. Explain how the words are now alliterative. Underline the letter "b" at the beginning of each word. Repeat the activity, using *yellow duck* (change to *daffy duck*) and *purple cat* (change to *cute cat*). Encourage the children to come up with other descriptive words that are alliterative.

Comprehension

❍ Ask the children the following questions: *How do you know which animal will be on the next page of the book?*

Special Activities

❍ Arrange for the children to "read" the book to a classroom of younger children. (Linguistic, Interpersonal, Intrapersonal)

❍ Make a class baggie book. To make a baggie book, gather enough resealable plastic bags to hold 9" x 12" sheets of paper. Give the children sheets of 9" x 12" drawing paper, and invite them to draw all animals in the story. Print the appropriate text next to each drawing and place the drawings back to back in the plastic bags. Staple the bags together along their edges, and cover the staples with vinyl tape. (Linguistic, Spatial, Interpersonal)

❍ Sing the words in *Brown Bear, Brown Bear, What Do You See?* to the tune of "Twinkle, Twinkle, Little Star." (Linguistic, Musical)

❍ Encourage the children to act out the story, making the appropriate animal movements with the introduction of each new animal. Ask the children to shade their eyes as though they are looking when they "see" a new animal. (Linguistic, Bodily-Kinesthetic, Interpersonal)

Learning Activities

Art

(Spatial, Interpersonal)
Suggest that the children use paper, animal-shaped sponges, and tempera paint to create pictures using different colors for the animals than the ones used in the story (make a white duck instead of a yellow duck, for example).

Music

(Musical, Intrapersonal)
Invite the children to use different musical instruments, their voices, and various classroom objects to create sound effects for each animal in the story. Provide a tape recorder and invite the children to record their sound effects as they "read" the story.

Blocks

(Spatial, Naturalist, Interpersonal)
Provide blocks, boxes, small sticks, construction paper, and other props for building animal homes. Encourage the children to build homes for the animals in the book—a nest for the bird, a barn for the sheep, a pond for the duck, a cave for the bear, and so on.

Science

(Logical-Mathematical, Naturalist)
Provide a book about birds. Ask the children to see how many different colors of birds they can find. Provide colored squares of construction paper for the children to use to denote the colors of the birds they find. Ask, *How many colors of birds did we find?*

Gross Motor

(Bodily-Kinesthetic, Interpersonal)
Ask the children to jump like frogs, waddle like ducks, and lumber like bears. Make a start line and a finish line with masking tape. Encourage the children to get in pairs and race each other, one as a duck and one as a frog, and so on. Ask the other children to guess who will arrive at the finish line first.

Writing

(Linguistic)
Place *Brown Bear, Brown Bear, What Do You See?* in the writing center. Encourage the children to use magnetic letters to copy the title of the book.

Let's Keep Reading

From Head to Toe by Eric Carle
Panda Bear, Panda Bear, What Do You See? by Bill Martin, Jr.
Polar Bear, Polar Bear, What Do You Hear? by Bill Martin, Jr.

Thinking About What We Learned

1. How would the story be different if you read it backwards?
2. What animal would you add to the story? What color would your animal be?

The Bug Cemetery

Author: Frances Hill. Illustrator: Vera Rosenberry

About the Book

A little boy finds a dead ladybug and decides to start a bug cemetery. The cemetery soon grows with more insects and eventually becomes the final resting place for a neighbor's cat. The sadness of losing things the children really care about changes the way they feel about their cemetery. This is a great book about life, love, loss, and death.

Learning Literacy

Oral Language

○ Define words in the story that may be new to the children, such as *tombstone, mound, funeral, cemetery, initiative,* and *mourners.*

Comprehension

○ Ask the children the following questions: *Why do the boys decide to let their cemetery become a garden? Have you ever lost a pet? How did you feel?*

Print Awareness

○ Make a list of the insects that the children might have buried in their cemetery. Look at the tombstones the children created for their cemetery. Ask, *Can you name the insects buried in the cemetery by looking at the names on the tombstones?*

Special Activities

○ Provide lemons, water, sugar, and a pitcher. Help the children make lemonade and set up a lemonade stand. Make signs. Help the children sell the lemonade to their parents when they stop by to pick up their children. (Linguistic, Logical-Mathematical, Interpersonal)

○ Plant a garden on the playground. Label each plant and flower. Allow the children to select the seeds and plants for their garden. Select a helper to take care of the garden each day. Teach them to weed, water, and trim plants as necessary. (Linguistic, Spatial, Naturalist, Interpersonal, Intrapersonal)

○ Invite the children to sing and move to "The Insect Song" to the tune of "Head, Shoulders, Knees, and Toes." (Logical-Mathematical, Bodily-Kinesthetic, Musical, Interpersonal)

The Insect Song

Head, thorax, abdomen,
Abdomen.
Head, thorax, abdomen,
Abdomen.
Six legs, four wings, antennae two.
Head, thorax, abdomen,
Abdomen.

Learning Activities

Art *(Spatial)*
Make blotto prints. Give each child a folded piece of construction paper. Open the folded paper. Place a blob of tempera paint on one side of the paper and then fold and press. When opening the paper, the design will look like a butterfly. Invite the children to add antennae and bodies to their butterfly designs.

Music *(Musical, Intrapersonal)*
Provide a cassette tape of different types of music. Encourage the children to select music they might use at a funeral for bugs.

Discovery *(Logical-Mathematical, Naturalist)*
Provide photos of insects and animals. Encourage the children to sort the photos into two categories: animals and insects. Mention the difference between the two categories. Explain that insects have six legs, two antennae, three body parts, and an exoskeleton.

Sand Table *(Linguistic, Spatial, Bodily-Kinesthetic, Intrapersonal)*
Give the children plastic insects. Encourage them to bury the insects in the sand. Provide stones and invite the children to decorate a stone for each insect. Label each grave with the name of the insect.

Language *(Linguistic, Spatial)*
Encourage the children to use paint and rocks to make tombstones. It might be easier for them to draw on the tombstone with markers instead of paint. With the children's permission, print on the tombstones the names of the insects for which the children are making the stones.

Science *(Naturalist)*
Provide seeds, topsoil, and cups. Invite the children to plant the seeds. When the seeds sprout, transplant them into the ground.

Let's Keep Reading

The Tenth Good Thing About Barney by Judith Viorst

Thinking About What We Learned

1. What do you think is good about a bug cemetery?
2. Why did the children cry at Buster's funeral?

Busy Fingers

Author: C.W. Bowie. Illustrator: Fred Willingham

About the Book

Rhyming text and beautiful illustrations describe all the wonderful things our fingers can do.

Learning Literacy

Oral Language

❍ Teach the children several fingerplays (see appendix page 233). Talk about how children can use their fingers to complement the rhymes.

Comprehension

❍ Ask the children the following questions: *What have you used your fingers for today? Is it easier to pick something up with your fingers or your toes?*

Print Awareness

❍ Make a list of things you use your hands to say; for example, *hello, goodbye, I love you, I am four years old, come here, there it is*, and so on. Teach the children how to say *I love you* using American Sign Language (see appendix page 236).

Special Activities

❍ Sing "The Itsy Bitsy Spider" with the children. Talk with them about how they use their fingers to make spiders. Sing the song again. Encourage the children to make their own finger spiders. Explain that there is not just one way to make the spider crawl up the spout. (Bodily-Kinesthetic, Musical, Intrapersonal)

❍ Provide special nice-smelling soap and hand lotion. Make a special event of hand washing. Talk about the importance of the children's washing their hands several times a day. (Linguistic, Bodily-Kinesthetic, Interpersonal)

❍ Do exercises. Talk with the children about the ways we use our fingers when we exercise. For example, *When doing toe touches, do you use your fingers?* Have the children think of exercises that require them to use their fingers. Have the children think of exercises that they do not need their fingers to do. Ask a volunteer to place tally marks on a chart that provides a column for "Exercises That Require Fingers" and a column for "Exercises That Require No Fingers." (Logical-Mathematical, Spatial, Naturalist)

Learning Activities

Art

(Spatial, Bodily-Kinesthetic)
Give the children red and green fingerpaint and paper to paint a picture. Ask questions: *What designs can you make with your fingers? What designs can you make using your whole hand?*

Math

(Logical-Mathematical, Bodily-Kinesthetic)
Provide numeral cards 1–5 (or 1–10,). Invite the children to draw a card and then use their fingers to show the number represented on the card. Talk about how the children might answer the question using their fingers.
Ask the children to use their fingers to show how old they are.

Blocks

(Spatial, Interpersonal)
Provide cars and trucks to push. Talk with the children about how they use their fingers to handle the vehicles.

Sand Table

(Bodily-Kinesthetic, Interpersonal)
Encourage the children to play with the toys in the sand table. Talk with them about how they use their hands to handle the sand.

Dramatic Play

(Spatial, Bodily-Kinesthetic, Musical, Interpersonal, Intrapersonal)
Show the children how to make shadow puppets. Place a light source near a wall. Demonstrate different types of shadow puppets the children can make with their fingers and hands. Invite the children to dance their shadow puppets to the beat of music.

Writing

(Linguistic, Naturalist, Intrapersonal)
Challenge the children to make a list of things they use their fingers to do. Provide crayons and encourage them to illustrate some of the items on their list, or if they prefer to, invite them to decorate the list. Ask the children which things on the list relate to eating, playing, and dressing.

Let's Keep Reading

Busy Toes by C. W. Bowie
Here Are My Hands by Bill Martin, Jr. and John Archambault

Thinking About What We Learned

1. Show me three things you can use your fingers to say.
2. Do you think dogs wish they had fingers?

Can I Keep Him?

Author and Illustrator: Steven Kellogg

About the Book

A young boy asks to bring home outrageous pets—a tiger, a bear cub, and even another little boy. Despite his pleas, his mom doesn't allow him to keep any of the prospective pets, but he still manages to find a friend.

Learning Literacy

Comprehension

❍ Ask the children the following questions: *Do you have a pet at home? What does your pet eat? Who cares for your pet? Would you like to have any of the unusual pets mentioned in the story? Which one? Why? How would you care for the pet?*

Print Awareness

❍ Make a list of each of the unusual pets mentioned in the book. Beside each animal, list the type of food it would require for feeding and the type of place it would require for sleeping.

Print Awareness/Oral Language

❍ Encourage the children to write or dictate a class letter to the mother in the story, asking to keep one of the unusual pets. Help the children explain to the mother why they would like to keep the pet and how they would take care of the pet. Transcribe their letter onto chart paper as they create it.

Special Activities

❍ Visit a pet store. Before leaving, make a list of pets the children expect to see. Take the list to the pet store and check off the animals that the children actually see. Upon returning to the classroom, revisit the list. Ask the children, *Did we find all the animals that we listed? Did we find animals that weren't on our list?* (Linguistic, Naturalist)

❍ Sing "Evan's Silly Pets" to the tune of "Johnny Works With One Hammer." Encourage the children to make up actions to go with each verse. Challenge them to make up additional verses to the song. Sing the song, substituting numbers for the adjectives describing each pet. For example, *two snakes, seven bears*, and so on. (Linguistic, Logical-Mathematical, Bodily-Kinesthetic, Musical)

Evan's Silly Pets
by Pam Schiller

Evan has some silly pets, silly pets, silly pets.
Evan has some silly pets he's taking to the vets.

Evan has hungry snakes, hungry snakes, hungry snakes.
Evan has hungry snakes eating chocolate cakes.

Evan has rowdy bears, rowdy bears, rowdy bears.
Evan has rowdy bears rolling down the stairs

Additional verses:
Dancing pigs…dancing jiggy jigs.
Talking birds…saying funny words.

Learning Activities

Art *(Spatial, Intrapersonal)*
Invite the children to draw pictures of pets they would like to own. Provide photographs of pets for those children who do not feel they can draw a pet. Encourage all the children to add things to their pictures that describe where their pets would sleep and what their pets would eat.

Math *(Logical-Mathematical, Musical)*
Sew jingle bells to five animal collars. Place one bell on the first collar, two on the next, three on the next, and so on. Encourage the children to order the collars from the one that makes the loudest noise when shaken to the one that makes the softest sound.

Dramatic Play *(Interpersonal, Intrapersonal)*
Suggest that the children use props, such as pretend bones, dog bowls, stethoscopes, boxes for cages, and stuffed animals, to set up an imaginary veterinary clinic.

Science *(Naturalist)*
Provide a live pet for the center, if possible. Give the children photographs of animals, some of which are pets and some of which are not pets. Invite the children to sort the pictures.

Gross Motor *(Bodily-Kinesthetic, Interpersonal)*
Provide a dog bowl, bones, a fishbowl, and a beanbag. Encourage the children to toss the bones into the dog bowl, or the beanbag into the fishbowl.

Writing *(Linguistic)*
Print *tiger*, *bear*, and *dog* on large index cards. Provide tracing paper and crayons or markers. Encourage the children to trace the animal names.

Let's Keep Reading
A Bicycle for Rosaura by Daniel Barbott
Pet Show by Ezra Jack Keats
Whistle for Willie by Ezra Jack Keats

Thinking About What We Learned
1. Who should be responsible for taking care of a pet? Why?
2. How do you call a dog to come to you? What about a cat? What about a bird? What about a fish?

Caps for Sale

Author and Illustrator: Esphyr Slobodkina

About the Book

This is the tale of a peddler, his caps, and some mischievous monkeys. The peddler walks the street with his caps stacked on his head. When he gets tired, he stops for a nap under a tree. While he naps, a group of monkeys takes his caps. When he wakes up, he has to figure out how to get his caps back from the thieves.

Learning Literacy

Oral Language

❍ Discuss the words in the book that may be new to the children, such as *peddler, thieves, ordinary, wares,* and *checked.*

Book Knowledge and Appreciation

❍ Ask the children to identify the line in the story that is always the same. Explain to the children that when a story uses the same line several times, that line is a *predictable line.* Predictable lines allow the children to read along with the reader.

Comprehension

❍ Ask the children the following questions: *How does the phrase* monkey see, monkey do *fit this story? Does the peddler always wear his hats in the same order on his head? Why do you think he always wears his hats the same way?*

Special Activities

❍ Organize a hat day. Encourage the children to wear a hat of their choice. When everyone has arrived, have a hat parade or a hat show-and-tell. (Bodily-Kinesthetic, Intrapersonal)

❍ Play Monkey See, Monkey Do. Have one child be IT. Invite IT to create an action and encourage all the "little monkeys" to copy IT's action. (Bodily-Kinesthetic, Interpersonal)

❍ Read the action story, "Monkey See, Monkey Do" (see appendix page 232). Encourage the children to follow the actions suggested in the story. (Linguistic, Bodily-Kinesthetic)

❍ Sew jingle bells to baseball caps or another similar type of cap. Play upbeat music and invite the children to put on the hats and dance a jingle dance. (Bodily-Kinesthetic, Musical, Interpersonal)

Learning Activities

Art *(Spatial, Intrapersonal)*
Cut cap shapes from construction paper. Give the children markers, sequins, buttons, ribbon, rickrack, lace, beads, and bangles to decorate their cap shapes in their own unique ways.

Listening *(Musical, Interpersonal)*
Provide a tape recorder. Encourage the children to tape themselves singing *caps for sale, caps for sale*, or saying *tsk, tsk, tsk.*

Dramatic Play *(Linguistic, Interpersonal)*
Provide caps (baseball caps work well) for the children. Encourage the children to re-enact the story. If the colors of the caps match the colors of the caps in the story, suggest that the children make up a new order and use that order to create their own chant.

Math *(Logical-Mathematical, Naturalist)*
Cut out small felt cap shapes in each of the colors mentioned in the book. Challenge children to arrange the caps in the same order as the caps the peddler wears.

Games *(Bodily-Kinesthetic, Interpersonal)*
Provide a cap and a beanbag. Turn the cap underside up and challenge children to toss the beanbag into the cap.

Science *(Naturalist)*
Provide pictures of animals and ask the children to sort the pictures according to which animals live in trees and which live on the ground.

Let's Keep Reading

Who Took the Farmer's Hat? by Joan Nodset
Whose Hat Is That? by Ron Roy

Thinking About What We Learned

1. Which part of the story do you like best? Why?
2. If you were a peddler, what would you sell and how would you sell it? If you were a cap peddler, how would you carry your hats?

Catch That Goat

Author and Illustrator: Polly Alakija

About the Book

Ayoka is supposed to watch the goat, but the goat gets away. Ayoka searches the streets for the goat, but she always seems to be just minutes behind the missing goat. When Ayoka finally finds the goat, she finds more than she bargained for.

Learning Literacy

Oral Language

❍ Look through the book without reading the story. Have a volunteer find the goat on each page. Ask the children, *What is the goat doing?*

❍ Define words in the story that may be unfamiliar to the children, such as *boli* and *paint pot*. Ask the children why they think the paint pots are called paint pots. Ask, *How are they different from the easel paint cups?*

❍ The illustrations in the book do a wonderful job showing the Nigerian marketplace. Ask the children to compare the marketplace to our malls.

Comprehension

❍ Ask the children the following questions: *Why did the goat run away? Where do you think he was going? How did Ayoka feel near the end of the story when her mother asked her, "Ayoka! Have you seen my goat?" How can you tell how she felt?* Show the children the page in the book where Ayoka's mother asks her about the goat.

Special Activities

❍ Visit a zoo, farm, or some other location where the children can observe goats. Ask questions: *What do the goats eat? What color are they? Can you see a goatee on the goats?* (Linguistic, Logical-Mathematical, Naturalist, Interpersonal)

❍ Explain to the children that *Catch That Goat* is a Nigerian story, and that Ayoka lives in Nigeria. Show the children where Nigeria is on a map. Discuss some interesting facts about Nigeria. (Linguistic, Logical-Mathematical, Spatial, Naturalist, Interpersonal)

● Nigeria is in west-central Africa.
● The Nigerian flag is green and white.
● Nigerian children play many games with seeds.

❍ Play Catch the Tail, a popular Nigerian game. Divide the children into teams of four. Ask each team to form a chain. Give the first child and last child in each team a scarf, and instruct the scarf holders to place their scarves in their pockets or tie them to their belts. The first person in each line leads that team in the chase, and tries to catch a "tail" from one of the other teams. A team wins when that team catches a "tail" from another team. (Bodily-Kinesthetic, Interpersonal)

❍ Hide examples of the marketplace items described in the story and a stuffed toy goat, and invite the children to search for them. Leave clues to help the children find the hidden items and the goat. (Logical-Mathematical, Interpersonal)

Learning Activities

Art *(Linguistic, Spatial)*
Provide easel paper, brushes, and paint pots (instead of normal paint cups). Use small coffee cans to represent paint pots. Explain to the children that *paint pots* is another way of saying *paint cups*.

Fine Motor *(Bodily-Kinesthetic, Interpersonal)*
Play the Seed Game, a popular Nigerian game. Give each child six seeds, such as acorns or walnuts, in their shells. Use masking tape to create two 12" start lines on the table or the floor about 12" apart. Each child lines up his or her seeds on one start line. The children take turns trying to hit each other's seeds by flicking their seeds with their index fingers.

Discovery *(Logical-Mathematical, Naturalist)*
Give the children several different pairs of sunglasses. Encourage the children to look through each pair. Ask questions: *Which pair is darkest? Is there a pair with blue lenses? How does the color of the lens change the color of things you see through the lenses?*

Math *(Logical-Mathematical)*
Provide numerals to match pictures of each of the missing items. Have the children match the correct numeral to each set of items.

Dramatic Play *(Linguistic, Interpersonal)*
Provide a toy stuffed goat and examples of the various items that the goat takes in the book. Encourage the children to re-enact the story using the props.

Music *(Musical, Intrapersonal)*
Play Nigerian music (one example is *The Rough Guide to the Music of Nigeria and Ghana*) Invite the children to select a piece of music to accompany the story. Ask the children why they selected the piece. *Does it sound like a busy marketplace? Does it sound like a running goat?*

Let's Keep Reading

Gingerbread Baby by Jan Brett

Thinking About What We Learned

1. Do you think that the goat was glad to be found? Why?
2. Which item in the marketplace did you find most interesting? Why?

Chicka Chicka Boom Boom

Authors: Bill Martin, Jr. and John Archambault
Illustrator: Lois Ehlert

About the Book
This is a rhythmic, rhyming chant in which lowercase letters climb up a coconut tree, but will there be enough room for all of them?

Learning Literacy

Oral Language

❍ Invite the children to recite the chant from the book, substituting a different kind of tree. For example, *maple tree, willow tree, tall palm tree,* or *chinaberry tree.* Ask, *How many syllables does the replacement tree need to have?* Clap the syllables in *coconut tree* and then in the possible replacement trees. Ask, *Which tree sounds right?*

Phonological Awareness

❍ Point out the rhyming words in the story; for example, *b* and *c*, *g* and *tree*, and so on. Read the story a second time, stopping at the end of sentences that rhyme with previous lines and let the children fill in the correct words.

Comprehension

❍ Ask the children the following questions: *Why did the letters fall from the tree? Do you think the letters will fall sooner when the mama and papa letters climb the tree? Why do you think the uppercase letters are the parents and the lowercase letters are the children?*

Special Activities

❍ Take *Chicka Chicka Boom Boom* outdoors. Give two children a rope and invite them to swing it low to the ground. Read the book while the other children jump over the rope. (Bodily-Kinesthetic, Musical, Interpersonal)

❍ Invite the children to act out the story. Place a label around each child's neck depicting the letter each child represents. Encourage the children to help create the labels and props (to their level of capability). (Linguistic, Spatial, Bodily-Kinesthetic, Interpersonal, Intrapersonal)

❍ Invite the children to sing the "Alphabet Forward and Backwards Song" to the traditional tune. (Linguistic, Musical, Naturalist)

The Alphabet Forward and Backwards Song
A, B, C, D, E, F, G,
H, I, J, K, L, M, N, O, P,
Q, R, S, T, U, V,
W, X, Y, and Z.
Now, I've said my ABC's.
Won't you sing them backwards with me?
Z, Y, X, W, V, U, T,
S, R, Q, P, O, N, M, L, K,
J, I, H, G, F, E,
D, C, B, and A.
Now, I've sung from Z to A.
I like letters either way.

Learning Activities

Art

(Spatial)
Provide drawing paper, crayons, and upper- and lowercase letters cut from sandpaper. Show the children how to make rubbings by placing the letters under drawing paper and rubbing the surface of the paper with crayons.

Listening

(Musical)
Ask a parent to tape record the story. Place the book and the tape in the listening center for the children to enjoy. Ask, *Can anyone guess who the reader might be?*

Fine Motor

(Linguistic, Bodily-Kinesthetic)
Set out playdough and help the children shape it into letters.

Science

(Logical-Mathematical, Naturalist)
Stick a fat pipe cleaner into a ball of playdough to create a mock tree trunk. Bend the top of the pipe cleaner slightly. Give the children lightweight washers and have them place the washers on the pipe cleaner one at a time until the trunk bends so much that it dumps the washers.

Gross Motor

(Bodily-Kinesthetic, Interpersonal, Intrapersonal)
Encourage the children to work in pairs to make letter shapes with their bodies.

Writing

(Linguistic, Naturalist)
Give the children upper- and lowercase magnetic or felt letters and have them match the lowercase letters to the uppercase letters.

Let's Keep Reading

Eating the Alphabet by Lois Ehlert

Thinking About What We Learned

1. Have you ever climbed a tree? What was it like? Did someone help you up? Did someone help you get back down?
2. Which letter in the story do you like best? Why?

Cloudy With a Chance of Meatballs

Author: Judi Barrett. Illustrator: Ron Barrett

About the Book

Grandpa tells a bedtime story about a town, Chewandswallow, with no food stores. All the food comes from the sky. It rains soup and juice. It snows mashed potatoes and a storm blows in hamburgers. However, when the weather takes a turn for the worse, the town inhabitants have to move away.

Learning Literacy

Comprehension

❍ Ask the children the following questions: *If the sky could provide any food you wanted, which food would you ask for? How would the story be different if the town had no toy stores?*

Print Awareness

❍ Write *Chewandswallow* on a piece of chart paper. Demonstrate how the town name is a combination of three words. Draw a line between the words and rewrite the town name as three words. Ask the children why they think the author named the town *Chewandswallow.*

Print Awareness/Oral Language

❍ Make a list of the bad-weather words used in the story. See if the children can remember which food fell with each type of weather. Introduce the word *inclement.*

Special Activities

❍ Sing "The Raindrop Song." Invite the children to change the lyrics to include items they would like to have fall from the sky, instead of the lemondrops and gumdrops already mentioned in the lyrics. (Linguistic, Musical, Intrapersonal)

❍ Talk about how the weather varies across the country. Show the children a weather map from the newspaper. Describe the symbols used to represent each weather type. Set up a weather station in the dramatic play center. Provide props, such as maps, weather symbols, and so on. (Linguistic, Logical-Mathematical, Naturalist, Interpersonal)

❍ Sing "On Top of Spaghetti." Ask the children if they can think of another type of food that could roll along the same course the meatball in the book rolled. Sing the song with the new item substituted for the meatball. (Linguistic, Musical, Naturalist)

❍ During outdoor play, show the children how to roll like meatballs (do forward rolls). Make sure you are rolling on a soft surface. (Spatial, Bodily-Kinesthetic)

❍ Sing the "Weather Song" to the tune of "Clementine." (Linguistic, Musical, Naturalist Interpersonal)

Weather Song

Sunny, sunny,
Sunny, sunny,
It is sunny in the sky.
S-U-N-N-Y, sunny,
It is sunny in the sky.

Additional verses:
Windy…
Rainy…

Learning Activities

Art

(Spatial, Intrapersonal)
Suggest that the children use crayons, markers, and paper to draw pictures of their favorite foods falling from the sky.

Gross Motor

(Bodily-Kinesthetic)
Roll brown construction paper or bulletin board paper into balls to represent meatballs. Provide a laundry basket and encourage the children to toss the "meatballs" into the basket.

Blocks

(Spatial, Interpersonal)
Encourage the children to use props, such as different blocks, plastic foods, and other props, to build a replica of Chewandswallow.

Science

(Logical-Mathematical, Naturalist)
Provide a basket containing lightweight and slightly heavier play food items. Encourage the children to drop the items from over their heads and see which items fall quickly and which items fall slowly. Invite the children to sort the items into those two categories.

Fine Motor

(Bodily-Kinesthetic, Naturalist)
Provide brown playdough for the children to roll it into "meatballs." Encourage them to sort the "meatballs" in groups from largest to smallest, and to try to roll the meatballs. Show the children what a meatball press looks like, and let the children experiment with pressing their playdough into meatballs.

Snack

(Linguistic, Musical, Naturalist)
Serve the children several different textures of foods, such as yogurt, crackers, pretzels, Jell-O®, carrots, and bananas. Encourage the children to describe the sounds each type of food makes as they chew.

Let's Keep Reading

Chicken Soup With Rice by Maurice Sendak
Strega Nona by Tomie dePaola
Today Is Monday by Eric Carle

Thinking About What We Learned

1. What is your favorite part of the story? Why?
2. Would you like to live in a town where food fell from the sky? Why? Why not?

A Cool Drink of Water

Author and Photographer: Barbara Kerley

About the Book
Everyone enjoys a cool drink of water. This book is a photographic celebration of that cool drink of water.

Learning Literacy

Oral Language
❍ Teach children the American Sign Language sign for *water* (see appendix page 236).

Comprehension
❍ Ask the children the following questions: *When do you most want a cool drink of water? What other beverages do people drink?*
❍ Talk with the children about how much fun it is to play in the water.

Print Awareness
❍ With the children, make a list of all the places water might come from.

Special Activities

❍ Take a field trip to a water bottling plant. Find out where the water comes from. Ask, *Where will the bottles of water go when they leave the plant?* (Linguistic, Naturalist)
❍ Take a field trip to a lake, river, or ocean. Talk with the children about the fun water provides when the children play in it. (Linguistic, Interpersonal, Intrapersonal)
❍ Play classical music. Encourage the children to move creatively, as though they were floating on water. Show them how to roll like a wave, float like a boat, swim like a fish, and splash like children playing, inviting them to do variations of the same movements. When you pretend to float, maneuver through the classroom as you would a maze. With the children, count the different ways you can move in water. (Linguistic, Logical-Mathematical, Bodily-Kinesthetic, Musical, Interpersonal, Intrapersonal)

Learning Activities

Art

(Spatial)

Invite the children to paint with watercolor paints, paintbrushes, and paper. Talk with them as they work. Discuss the use of water to help spread the paint: *Do the colors get lighter or darker when you add more water?*

Music

(Musical, Naturalist)

Make tone bottles. Fill six glass bottles with different amounts of water. Give the children rhythm sticks or short lengths of dowel rods and encourage them to tap the bottles gently to hear the different sounds they make, and then to arrange the bottles in order from the highest sound to the lowest sound. **Safety Note:** Supervise closely.

Discovery

(Logical-Mathematical, Intrapersonal)

Provide water in several different containers, such as a clay pot, plastic pitcher, plastic bottle, thermos, cooler, brass pot, and so on. Invite the children to sample the water from each container. Ask, *Does the water taste different when served from a different container?*

Water Table

(Logical-Mathematical, Bodily-Kinesthetic, Musical, Interpersonal, Intrapersonal)

Provide sponges, bars of soap, basters, cups and funnels. Talk with the children as they play in the water. *How does the water feel on your hands? What sounds can you make with water? Do things on the bottom of the tub look larger than they are?*

Listening

(Musical, Naturalist)

Play a nature tape that uses the different sounds of water, such as rain, waterfalls, and ocean waves, as means of relaxation. Talk with the children about the sounds. Ask the children to name the sources of water they hear on the tape.

Writing

(Linguistic, Spatial, Bodily-Kinesthetic, Intrapersonal)

Give the children several markers and paper cups with their names on the bottoms and encourage them to decorate their cups.

Let's Keep Reading

Water Dance by Thomas Locker
Water, Water, Everywhere by Mark Rauzon

Thinking About What We Learned

1. What is your favorite way to drink water?
2. Do you like to play in the water? Why?

Dance

Author: Bill T. Jones. Photographer: Susan Kuklin

About the Book
This book is a photo tribute to the power of dance and to the beauty of the human body in all its forms.

Learning Literacy

Oral Language
- Look at the photos in the book. Ask, *How many parts of his body does Bill use when he dances?* Make a list.
- Show the children the pages where Bill makes lines and curves with his body, and ask a few volunteers to demonstrate the same lines and curves.

Comprehension
- Ask the children the following questions: *Do you like to dance? Why? When do you dance? Where?*

Special Activities
- Visit a dance studio. Encourage the dancers to make the same moves that Bill does. Ask questions: *How many different kinds of dancing do you see? How many different kinds of dancing are there?* (Linguistic, Logical-Mathematical, Naturalist, Interpersonal, Intrapersonal)
- Teach the children to say the action chant, "Thelma Thumb" with you and to move their thumbs as the chant directs.

Thelma Thumb
Thelma Thumb is up and
*   Thelma Thumb is down.*
Thelma Thumb is dancing all
*   around the town.*
Dance her on your shoulders,
*   dance her on your head.*
Dance her on your knees and
*   tuck her into bed.*

Name other fingers: *Phillip Pointer, Terry Tall, Richie Ring,* and *Baby Finger.* Dance the Finger Family on other body parts. (Linguistic, Spatial, Bodily-Kinesthetic, Interpersonal, Intrapersonal)

- Teach the children the "It's a Simple Dance to Do" chant. (Linguistic, Spatial, Bodily-Kinesthetic, Interpersonal, Intrapersonal)

It's a Very Simple Dance to Do
It's a very simple dance to do.
Come on and do a dance with
*   me,*
It's just a little step or two.
I'll teach you how,
We'll start right now.

It's a very simple dance to do.

First you clap your hands, (clap
*   three times)*
Then stomp your feet. (stomp
*   three times)*
It's a very simple dance to do.

Wait, I forgot to tell you,
There's another little step or
*   two:*
Turn around (turn around)
And touch your toes. (touch
*   your toes)*
It's a very simple dance to do.

Clap your hands, (clap three
*   times)*
Stomp your feet, (stomp three
*   times)*
Turn around (turn around)
And touch your toes. (touch
*   your toes)*
It's a very simple dance to do.

Wait I forgot to tell you,
Clap your hands.
Stomp your feet.
Turn around
And touch your toes.
Pull your ears
And flap your arms,
Now stretch up high.
All fall down.
It's a very simple dance to do.

(Repeat last chorus)

Learning Activities

Art *(Spatial, Musical, Intrapersonal)*
Provide an easel, paint, and paper. Play classical music and encourage the children to let their paintbrushes "dance" across the paper in time with the music.

Gross Motor *(Logical-Mathematical, Bodily-Kinesthetic)*
Challenge the children to balance on one foot and hold their other foot beside their knees, and then encourage them to hold their foot out in front of them, behind them, and so on. Ask, *Which position is easiest to keep your balance?*

Dramatic Play *(Spatial, Interpersonal)*
Provide dance shoes and costumes for the children to explore.

Music *(Logical-Mathematical, Spatial, Bodily-Kinesthetic, Musical, Interpersonal, Intrapersonal)*
Invite children to play rhythm band instruments and to dance to the beat of the drums and the jingles of the tambourine and bells. Discuss *rhythm*, *meter*, and *beat*. Point out the one-to-one correspondence of beat and movement.

Language *(Bodily-Kinesthetic, Naturalist, Interpersonal, Intrapersonal)*
Challenge the children to use their bodies to demonstrate different states of being, such as *sad, happy, angry, joyful, sleepy,* and so on. Provide a mirror so the children can watch their actions.

Writing *(Linguistic, Spatial, Bodily-Kinesthetic)*
Challenge the children to work with a partner to contort their bodies into the shapes of different letters, such as *A, F, H, I, K, L, M, N, T, V, W, X,* and *Z.*

Let's Keep Reading

The Baby Dance by Kathy Henderson
Barnyard Dance by Sandra Boyton
Daddy Dances by Ann Taylor
Dance, Tanya by Patricia Lee Gouch

Thinking About What We Learned

1. What have you learned about dancing?
2. Can you show me a happy dance?

Dinosaurumpus!

Author: Tony Mitton. Illustrator: Guy Parker-Rees

About the Book
Wonderful, fun, and descriptive words tell the story of a group of dinosaurs on their way to a dinosaur romp.

Learning Literacy

Oral Language
❍ Discuss words in the story that may be new vocabulary for the children, such as *tread, swamp, shudder, sludgy, romp, shrieks,* and so on.

Phonological Awareness
❍ Read the story again to find all the *onomatopoeic* words.

Comprehension
❍ Ask the children the following questions: *How would the sounds of a dinosaur romp be different from a cat or dog romp? Which dinosaur is your favorite? Why? How can you tell meat-eating dinosaurs from plant-eating dinosaurs?* Look through the book and help the children figure out which dinosaurs eat plants and which ones eat meat.

Special Activities

❍ Cut an 80' piece of yarn or string to represent the length of a brontosaurus. Stretch the yarn across the floor or the playground. Encourage the children to walk, hop, skip, or crawl the length of the yarn. Talk about the size of the dinosaur. (Logical-Mathematical, Spatial, Bodily-Kinesthetic, Interpersonal, Intrapersonal)

❍ Talk about the noises dinosaurs make. Review those mentioned in the story. The pteranodon *eeeks* and the tyrannosaurus *roars*. Encourage the children to make dinosaur sounds. Ask, *Which dinosaur made the loudest sound?* (Musical, Naturalist)

❍ Ask the children to describe the ways dinosaurs move. Play some romping music and encourage the children to dance like dinosaurs. (Bodily-Kinesthetic, Musical, Naturalist, Intrapersonal)

Learning Activities

Dramatic Play *(Musical, Interpersonal, Intrapersonal)*
Provide a light source and music. Invite the children to dance like dinosaurs between the light source and the wall. Call attention to the size of their shadows. Challenge them to make their shadows larger.

Fine Motor *(Spatial, Bodily-Kinesthetic)*
Suggest that the children use clay or playdough to create dinosaurs. Talk with them about the body parts they are adding to the dinosaurs, such as tails, plates, wings, claws, and so on.

Games *(Linguistic, Interpersonal, Intrapersonal)*
Tie 24" lengths of yarn to individual magnetic letters. Place the letters inside a box and drape the ends of yarn over the outside of the box. Give each child an index card with *dinosaur* printed on it. Encourage the children take turns pulling a letter from the box and matching it the letters on their cards until all the letters in dinosaur are out of the box and in proper order.

Math *(Logical-Mathematical)*
Use masking tape to outline a dinosaur's footprint (4' long and 3' wide). Invite the children to see how many steps (heel to toe) it takes for them to walk across the footprint. Encourage the children to connect inch cubes—one per step—to represent the number of steps they take. Challenge children to estimate how many children might fit inside the footprint.

Science *(Naturalist)*
Provide several pictures of dinosaurs or plastic dinosaur counters. Encourage the children to name the dinosaurs. Challenge them to sort the dinosaurs based on whether they are herbivores or carnivores.

Writing *(Linguistic)*
Print *dinosaur* on chart paper. Provide magnetic letters and encourage children to use the letters to spell *dinosaur*. If the children are interested, print the names of different dinosaurs on the chart and let them copy the individual dinosaur names with the magnetic letters.

Let's Keep Reading

Dinosaur Time by Peggy Parish
Patrick's Dinosaur by Carol Carrick

Thinking About What We Learned

1. Do you think dinosaurs would need a big bed? How big?

Do Your Ears Hang Low? A Love Story

Author and Illustrator: Caroline Church

About the Book
Two bouncy floppy-eared puppies meet at the top of a hill and befriend each other to the tune of the much-loved children's song, "Do Your Ears Hang Low?"

Learning Literacy

Oral Language

❍ With the children, sing the words of *Do Your Ears Hang Low?* Explain to the children that this is a silly song. It doesn't really make sense, particularly when singing it about people, because people can't tie their ears in a knot or bow and can't throw them over their shoulders no matter how long their ears may be. Ask, *Why does the song make more sense when we sing it about floppy-eared puppies?*

Phonological Awareness

❍ Point out the rhyming words in the story, such as *low/fro/bow*, and *shoulder/soldier*.

Comprehension

❍ Ask the children the following questions: *Which of the puppies do you like the best? Why? What part of our ears could hang low? Could a person have ears that hang low enough to tie?*

Special Activities

❍ Visit a pet store. Ask questions: *Which puppies have long ears? Which puppies have short ears?* After returning to the classroom, invite the children to write stories about the trip. Encourage the children to illustrate their stories. (Linguistic, Spatial, Naturalist, Interpersonal, Intrapersonal)

❍ Sing "Where, Oh, Where Has My Little Dog Gone?" Have the children compare this song to "Do Your Ears Hang Low?" Ask, *Which things are mentioned in both songs?* (Linguistic, Logical-Mathematical, Musical)

❍ Play Dog and Bone. Ask the children to sit in a circle. Designate one child as IT. Invite IT to walk around the outside of the circle, carrying a paper or plastic bone and eventually dropping the bone behind a player. That player picks up the bone and chases IT around the circle. If she taps IT before he gets around the circle and sits in her place, IT goes to the "doghouse" (center of the circle). If the player doesn't tag IT before he takes her place in the circle, the player becomes the new IT and the game continues. (Bodily-Kinesthetic, Interpersonal)

Learning Activities

Art *(Spatial, Intrapersonal)*
Give the children recycled bows, glue, and paper. Encourage them to make a bow collage, bow sculpture, bow jewelry, or a string of bows. Provide fingerpaints and paper. Show the children how to make dog footprints by rolling their fists in the paint and then making prints on paper.

Fine Motor *(Bodily-Kinesthetic)*
Set out rope and ribbon for tying. Show children how to tie knots and how to tie bows. **Safety Note:** Supervise children carefully during this activity.

Discovery *(Naturalist, Interpersonal)*
Fill four different plastic eggs with the following items: 1" diameter ball of playdough, 2 tablespoons of water, 4 cotton balls, and 10 buttons. Note the color of egg holding each item. Glue the halves of the eggs together. Give the eggs to the children and ask them which eggs wobble the best.

Listening *(Linguistic, Musical)*
Record yourself and the children singing the words of *Do Your Ears Hang Low?* on a cassette tape. Give the book, tape, and a small drum to the children and encourage them to drum along with the rhythm of the song as they listen to the tape.

Dramatic Play *(Spatial, Interpersonal)*
Provide a variety of clip-on earrings (dangling, decorative stones, and so on) and a mirror for the children to explore. Ask questions as they try on the earrings. *Why do people wear earrings?*
Safety Note: Supervise children carefully during this activity.

Science *(Logical-Mathematical, Naturalist)*
Encourage the children to look at pictures of animals and then sort the animals in the by the lengths of their ears.

Let's Keep Reading

Eyes, Ears, Nose and Mouth by Beverly Friday
How Much Is That Doggie in the Window? by Iza Trapani

Thinking About What We Learned

1. Which part of the story is your favorite part?
2. Do you think the dogs will be friends from now on?

Don't Let the Pigeon Drive the Bus!

Author and Illustrator: Mo Willems

About the Book
Children find themselves participating in this hilarious story about a pigeon determined to drive a bus despite being told he cannot. The pigeon tries whining, cajoling, bargaining, and every other trick he knows just to get his way.

Learning Literacy

Oral Language
❍ Ask the children about the expressions on the pigeon's face on each page. *How can you tell how he is feeling? Which part of his face is most expressive?*
❍ Change the words to "Wheels on the Bus" to fit the story. Add to the lines below.
   The pigeon on the bus says, "Let me drive."…. All through the town.
   The pigeon on the bus says, "I'll just steer."… All through the town.
   The pigeon on the bus says, "Once around the block."… All through the town.

Comprehension
❍ Ask the children the following questions: *Do you think a pigeon could drive a bus? Why? Why not? Have you ever wanted to do something someone wouldn't let you do? Do you believe the pigeon's cousin, Herb, drives a bus? Why? Why not? What do you think would have happened if the pigeon got his way? What is the pigeon thinking of doing at the end of the book?*

Special Activities

❍ Take a field trip to a park or another spot where pigeons reside. Take food so the children can feed the pigeons. Discuss the pigeons. *What color are the pigeons? Do they prefer to walk around or fly around? How many feet do the pigeons have? Do they have arms? Without arms, how could a pigeon drive a bus?* (Logical-Mathematical, Spatial, Naturalist)
❍ Demonstrate walking like a pigeon. Encourage the children to walk like pigeons. (Bodily-Kinesthetic)
❍ Take a ride on a bus. Ask the driver to show you the parts of the bus mentioned in the book. Ask, *Where is the steering wheel? Where is the accelerator?* (Linguistic)
❍ Give the children two paper or plastic plates to hold and pretend they are wings. Play some music and encourage the children to fly like a pigeon to the music. When the children are finished flying, ask questions: *Why would a pigeon want to drive a bus when he could simply fly?* (Bodily-Kinesthetic, Musical, Interpersonal, Intrapersonal)
❍ Teach the children how to say *no* and *stop* using American Sign Language signs (see appendix page 236). (Spatial, Bodily-Kinesthetic)

Learning Activities

Art *(Spatial)*
Put out paper, crayons, and markers, and encourage the children to draw a pigeon.

Games *(Bodily-Kinesthetic, Interpersonal)*
Provide feathers (available at a hobby store or a teacher supply store) and a box. Create a throw line. Ask the children to stand behind the throw line and toss feathers into the box. Ask, *Is this difficult? Why?* Have the children try dropping the feathers. *Is it easier to get the feathers in the box by dropping them?*

Blocks *(Spatial, Bodily-Kinesthetic, Interpersonal)*
Encourage the children to build a road with blocks and then use toy cars, trucks, buses, and other vehicles on the road.

Math *(Logical-Mathematical, Naturalist, Interpersonal, Intrapersonal)*
Encourage the children to sort feathers by color and then arrange them from longest to shortest. Ask questions: *Which feather do you like best? Why did you choose that feather?*

Construction *(Linguistic, Spatial, Musical, Interpersonal)*
Help the children create a slogan they can use with the pigeon such as *No, Pigeon, No,* or *Pigeon, Fly.* Print their slogan on a banner for them and encourage them to illustrate the banner. Ask, *Will this convince the pigeon to quit begging?*

Writing *(Linguistic)*
Write *no* and *stop* on chart paper. Encourage the children to copy the words onto their own paper. Discuss how *Don't Let the Pigeon Drive the Bus!* uses *no* and *stop.*

Let's Keep Reading

A Bicycle for Rosaura by Daniel Bardott
The Pigeon Finds a Hot Dog! by Mo Willems

Thinking About What We Learned

1. What do you do when you want to do something and someone says you can't do it?
2. Do you think a pigeon would be a good bus driver? Why? Why not?

The Doorbell Rang

Author and Illustrator: Pat Hutchins

About the Book
Mother makes a batch of cookies. The children sit to eat their cookies while mother mops the floor. However, before they can eat their cookies, the doorbell rings and more children enter the story. This scenario repeats until there is only one cookie available for each child. This time, when the doorbell rings, it is not more children. It is grandma with another batch of cookies.

Learning Literacy

Book Knowledge and Appreciation
○ After reading the story several times, ask the children to find words or phrases that are repeated.

Comprehension
○ Ask the children the following questions: *What do you think would have happened if there had been more children at the door instead of grandma? What do you think the weather outside was like on the day the story took place?*

Print Awareness
○ Copy a recipe for chocolate chip cookies onto a chart tablet. Point out the ways a recipe is different from a paragraph of text. Point out the list of ingredients, the measurements, and the directions.

Letter Knowledge
○ Print *chocolate chip* on a piece of chart paper. Ask the children to identify the first two letters in each of the words. Say *chocolate chip* several times. Ask the children if they can hear the repetitive sounds or the /ch/. It is not important that the children identify the /ch/ blend, only that they hear the identical sounds in the words.

Special Activities

○ Visit a bakery. Watch the bakers as they bake cookies. Ask the children questions about the senses involved in this experience. *How does it smell inside the bakery? What items do you see in the bakery? What sounds are present? Is there a hum from the beaters? Is there a clinking sound from spoons hitting the sides of the mixing bowls? What is the temperature inside the bakery? Is it warm from the ovens?* If you are lucky enough to sample the bakery goods, discuss the taste of the goods. (Logical-Mathematical, Musical, Naturalist, Intrapersonal)

○ Place an 8' strip of bulletin board paper on the floor. Pour some tempera paint in a shallow pan and place it at one end of the strip. Fill a small tub with soapy water and place it with a towel at the opposite end of the paper. Invite the children to take off their shoes, step in the paint, and walk from one end of the paper to the other. At the other end, have the children step in the tub of water to wash their feet. After several children walk across the paper, call attention to how the footprints are increasing, just as they do in the book. (Spatial, Bodily-Kinesthetic)]

○ Recite "Who Took the Cookie From the Cookie Jar?" (Linguistic, Bodily-Kinesthetic, Musical, Interpersonal)

Learning Activities

Art *(Spatial)*

Encourage the children to use light brown and dark brown tempera paint, paper, and brushes to paint cookies, using the lighter paint for the cookies and then the darker paint to make dots (chocolate chips).

Gross Motor *(Bodily-Kinesthetic, Musical)*

Place a throw line on the floor with masking tape. Across from the line, place a service bell inside a box made to look like a cookie jar. Provide round beanbags to represent cookies, and challenge the children to toss the cookies into the cookie jar to make the bell ring.

Dramatic Play *(Linguistic, Logical-Mathematical, Interpersonal, Intrapersonal)*

Provide props such as rolling pins, playdough, cookie sheets, mixing bowls, spoons, and cookie cutters for cookie baking in the kitchen. Encourage the children to bake cookies. Ask them how they will know they have enough cookies for everyone to have at least one.

Math *(Logical-Mathematical)*

Cut cookie shapes from light brown felt. Provide large brown buttons for the children to use as chips to place on the cookies. Make a deck of numeral cards (1–8). Ask the children to draw numeral cards from the deck and then place the same number of chips on their cookies.

Games *(Logical-Mathematical, Interpersonal)*

Cut a giant cookie from construction paper to make a game board. Make circles on the cookie to represent chips. Arrange the chips in a trail between a start and stop spot on the board. Provide a spinner and a game piece for each player. The children spin the spinner and move the appropriate number of spaces.

Writing *(Linguistic)*

Print *cookie* on chart paper. Provide a cookie sheet and magnetic letters. Invite the children to copy the word using the magnetic letters. Challenge the children by writing *chocolate chip cookie* on the chart and inviting them to copy that, too.

Let's Keep Reading

If You Give a Mouse a Cookie by Laura Joffe Numeroff
One Hundred Hungry Ants by Elinor J. Princzes

Thinking About What We Learned

1. What is your favorite cookie? Have you ever helped bake your favorite cookie?
2. Have you ever had something that you really wanted to eat but there wasn't enough for everyone to have some? What did you do?

The Dot

Author and Illustrator: Peter H. Reynolds

About the Book
A teacher's encouragement helps a little girl find the artist within, and the lesson spreads.

Learning Literacy

Oral Language
○ Show the children a picture by the artist Georges Seurat. Explain that Seurat painted his pictures using dots. This type of art is call *pointillism.* Talk with the children about his paintings.

Comprehension
○ Ask the children the following questions: *Why did the teacher say the little girl had drawn a polar bear in a snowstorm? What color would the paper be if the picture were of a polar bear in a snowstorm? Why did the little girl decide to make more dot pictures? Would the story be different if the little girl had drawn a square instead of a dot?*

Print Awareness
○ Draw a dot on a piece of chart paper. Encourage the children to brainstorm a list of things the dot might represent, such as a snowflake, a flea, a grain of sand, a period, and so on.

Special Activities

○ Visit an art museum. Look for pictures with dots in them. Look for works of art that employ the pointillist technique. Discuss the various types of painting, asking the children to identify the pictures they like the most. Ask them about the feel and mood of the paintings and drawings: *Which paintings create a serious mood? Which paintings create a playful mood? Do colors make a difference?* (Linguistic, Logical-Mathematical, Spatial, Naturalist, Interpersonal, Intrapersonal)
○ Invite the children to play Drop the Dot as you would play Drop the Handkerchief. (Bodily-Kinesthetic, Interpersonal)
○ Play Step on the Dot. Cut large circles from butcher paper and place them on the floor. Play music. When the music stops, direct the children to place their toes on the dots. After a few rounds, be more specific. Request that the children put their toes on dots of a particular color. Play for as long as the children show interest. (Linguistic, Logical-Mathematical, Bodily-Kinesthetic, Musical, Naturalist, Interpersonal)
○ Reproduce or create Connect the Dot game sheets for the children to explore. (Logical-Mathematical, Spatial)

Learning Activities

Art *(Spatial, Naturalist)*
Invite the children to use paints and paper to paint dots of all sizes and colors.

Gross Motor *(Spatial, Bodily-Kinesthetic, Interpersonal)*
Place butcher paper on the wall. Provide long-handled brushes or short mops and invite the children to use the brushes or mops to make large dots on the paper.

Discovery *(Spatial, Interpersonal)*
Provide an overhead projector and several cutouts of dots, in sizes that range from pennies to oranges. Invite the children to use the dots to create a shadow picture.

Language *(Linguistic, Bodily-Kinesthetic)*
Encourage the children to use pencils and paper to write their names. Challenge the children to make their names using dots instead of lines.

Fine Motor *(Logical-Mathematical, Spatial)*
Cut several large dots from construction paper. Cut the circles into puzzles, and challenge the children to put the dot puzzles together.

Music *(Musical, Intrapersonal)*
Provide classical music, crayons, and paper, and invite the children to "feel" the music, and then create dots to the tempo and mood of the music.

Let's Keep Reading

Harold and the Purple Crayon by Crockett Johnson
Ten Black Dots by Donald Crews

Thinking About What We Learned

1. Describe the dots you made today.
2. What do you think the little boy in the story might make from his squiggle?

Dream Carver

Author: Diana Cohn. Illustrator: Amy Córdova

About the Book

Mateo carves small statues, called *juguetes*, like his father and his father before him, but Mateo dreams of larger and more colorful statues. His father tries to dissuade him from his dream, but to no avail. Mateo brings his dreams to life at the village fiesta and suddenly everyone understands.

Learning Literacy

Oral Language

❍ Discuss the differences between dreams, daydreams, and night dreams. Talk with the children about the meaning of *imagination*.

❍ Introduce words in the story that may be new vocabulary for the children, such as *nestled, ancient, rackety, molé, darted, machete,* and so on.

❍ Turn to the page in the book where Mateo is mixing his paints. Look at the labels on the jars. Teach the children the Spanish color words, *azul* (blue), *rojo* (red), *amarillo* (yellow), and *naranja* (orange).

❍ Show the children where Mexico is on a map. Point out the spot where Mateo lives by the Zapotec ruins (Central America). Share a few facts about Zapotec Indians.

  ● The ancient Zapotec Indians are well known for their weaving and their carving.
  ● The Zapotecs speak a combination of Spanish and their own Indian language.

Comprehension

❍ Ask the children the following questions: *What kind of statues did Mateo and his father carve? Why does Mateo like the fiesta so much?*

Special Activities

❍ Visit an art studio or an art class at the local high school or college. Encourage the children to observe the artists and ask questions about their choices of colors and techniques. (Spatial, Naturalist, Interpersonal)

❍ Visit an art museum. Ask questions: *Do you like the artwork in the museum? Why? Does any of the artwork look like the work of Mateo and his father?* (Spatial, Naturalist, Interpersonal)

❍ Provide a piñata and invite the children to break it. Hang the piñata over the branch of a tree or from a pulley, and let the children take turns trying to break it with a stiff cardboard tube from a coat hanger. Blindfold the children or ask them to close their eyes as they swing at the piñata. Explain that the piñata is a favorite fiesta game in Mexico, and it is often part of birthday parties. **Safety Note:** Limit swings to three in order to keep the children from swinging wildly. Make sure all children stand at least ten feet away from the piñata and the swinger. (Bodily-Kinesthetic, Interpersonal)

❍ Play Frozen Statues. Explain to the children that they can dance creatively while the music is playing but that when the music stops, they are to freeze in a statue position. (Spatial, Bodily-Kinesthetic, Musical, Interpersonal, Intrapersonal)

❍ Play music from Mexico. Encourage the children to dance. (Bodily-Kinesthetic, Musical, Interpersonal, Intrapersonal)

Learning Activities

Art

(Spatial)
Provide brushes, paper, and several vibrant and bold colors of paint. Encourage the children to paint colorful pictures similar to the statues Mateo paints.

Fine Motor

(Logical-Mathematical, Spatial, Bodily-Kinesthetic)
Help the children mix and shape Sawdust Dough. Mix 5 cups of sawdust (readily available at a lumberyard), 1 cup of wheat paste, and 4 cups of water. Shape the dough into small blocks and allow it to dry. Provide plastic knives. Challenge the children to use the knife to carve the blocks into animals.

Construction

(Spatial, Bodily-Kinesthetic)
Help the children mix Baker's Clay. Mix 1 cup of white flour, 1 cup of salt, and enough water to turn the mixture into soft clay. The children shape the dough into any design they wish. Cook the designs in a conventional oven at 225°, checking every 15 minutes for hardness. If you use a microwave, heat in 30-second intervals to desired hardness.

Music

(Musical, Naturalist, Interpersonal)
Provide Mexican musical instruments, such as maracas, a vihuela, guitarron, harp, and so on. Invite the children to try each instrument. Talk with them as they explore the instruments. If such instruments are unavailable, provide Mexican music for the children to listen to, and encourage them to describe the instruments they hear in the music.

Discovery

(Spatial)
Provide paint, brushes, and several scraps of wood. Invite the children to paint the wood. Talk with the children about the wooden sculptures that Mateo and his father paint. *What colors did they use? What colors did Mateo want to use? Which colors do you like best? How is painting on wood like painting on paper? How is it different?*

Writing

(Linguistic, Spatial, Intrapersonal)
Invite the children to tell you some of their dreams. Transcribe the dreams onto paper and let the children illustrate the pages on which you wrote their dreams.

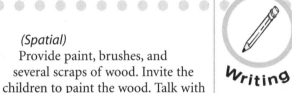

Let's Keep Reading
The Little Painter of Sabana Grande by Patricia Markun

Thinking About What We Learned
1. What did you learn about painting on wood today?
2. Which colors of paints did you use most often today?

Edward the Emu

Author: Sheena Knowles. Illustrator: Rod Clement

About the Book

This rhyming text tells the tale of Edward, an emu who grows bored with being an emu. He tries being a seal, a lion, and a snake. When he returns home, he finds another emu, and his boredom ends.

Learning Literacy

Oral Language

❍ Talk about emus with the children:

The emu is a large, feathered flightless bird from Australia. It is similar to ostriches, cassowaries, and kiwis. Emus are very fast and can run up to speeds of 30 miles per hour (50 kilometers per hour). Emus are also very good swimmers. Emus live in groups together called flocks. *Emus grow to be between 5' and 6' tall and weigh between 90 and 150 pounds. This makes the emu the size of most humans as adults. The female (mommy) emu, or hen, lays large green eggs but it is the male (daddy) emu that sits on the nest and cares for the baby emus when they hatch.*

Comprehension

❍ Ask the children the following questions: *Why was Edward unhappy? Have you ever pretended to be an animal? What does Edward do when he pretends to be a lion? Do you think Edward would have gone back home if he hadn't heard someone talking about the emus?*

Letter Knowledge

❍ Print *Edward* and *Edwina* on a piece of chart paper. Ask the children to identify the letters in each name and then to identify the letters that are the same in each name. Ask, *Do the names sound the same?*

Special Activities

❍ Take a trip to the zoo. Before leaving, make a list of all the animals that Edward pretended to be. Check the animals off the list as the children find them at the zoo. Examine the habits of each animal. Ask the children which animals they would most like to be. (Linguistic, Naturalist, Interpersonal)

❍ Encourage the children to imitate zoo animals. Invite them to sway like an elephant, leap like a lion, roll over like a bear, and clap like a seal. Encourage the children to think of other animal moves. Ask, *Which movements do you like best?* (Linguistic, Bodily-Kinesthetic, Intrapersonal)

❍ Place a sheet of butcher paper on the wall. Divide it into five sections and print the following words, one in each section: *fly, crawl, walk, swim,* and *hop*. Ask the children to draw pictures of animals in the proper sections. (Spatial, Naturalist)

Learning Activities

Blocks

(Spatial, Naturalist, Interpersonal, Intrapersonal)

Provide plastic zoo animals and additional zoo props for the children to build a zoo. Provide index cards and pencils so that the children can label the zoo cages. Discuss the arrangement of the animals: *How do you decide which animals go where?*

Dramatic Play

(Naturalist, Interpersonal)

Encourage the children to use animal costumes and masks to pretend to be the animals Edward visited in the zoo. Talk with the children about the characteristics of each animal. Encourage the children to do some of the animal activities mentioned in the story, such as slithering like a snake or lounging like a lion.

Games

(Logical-Mathematical, Spatial, Bodily-Kinesthetic)

Laminate and cut zoo animal photos into puzzle pieces. Encourage the children to complete the puzzles. Make sure to create puzzles that cover a range of ability levels.

Math

(Logical-Mathematical, Bodily-Kinesthetic)

Place different amounts of clay inside green plastic "emu" eggs to create eggs that vary in weight. Encourage the children to handle the eggs and arrange them from heaviest to lightest. Provide a scale so that children can check their tactile accuracy.

Sand Table

(Bodily-Kinesthetic, Interpersonal)

Away from the children, spray paint large plastic eggs with green paint. Bury the eggs in the sand table and add the children to find them. After they find the eggs, encourage the children to bury them again. Remind the children that emus lay their eggs in the sand and that they are green so that they are camouflaged.

Writing

(Linguistic, Bodily-Kinesthetic)

Print *zoo* on 5" x 7" index cards. Provide tracing paper and encourage the children to trace the over the letters of the word. Place the book in the center and encourage the children to copy Edward's name using magnetic letters.

Let's Keep Reading

At the Zoo by Paul Simon

Thinking About What We Learned

1. What did Edward learn?
2. Why do we have zoos? Do you think the animals wish they could be free from their cages?

Eight Animals Bake a Cake

Author: Susan Middleton Elya. Illustrator: Lee Chapman

About the Book

Eight animals whip up a cake. Everyone brings an important ingredient. All goes well until they take the cake from the oven and end up dropping it. The cow saves the day.

Learning Literacy

Oral Language/Comprehension

❍ Teach the children how to count to eight in Spanish: *uno, dos, tres, cuatro, cinco, seis, siete, ocho.*

❍ Review the Spanish names for the animals introduced in the story.

Comprehension

❍ Ask the children the following questions: *Why was the cake dropped? How would the story be different if there were only four animals?*

Special Activities

❍ Visit a bakery. Ask questions: *How many people bake a cake? What ingredients do they use? How would you describe the aromas in the bakery? Which pastry would you like to take home with you?* (Linguistic, Interpersonal, Intrapersonal)

❍ Find an upside-down cake recipe, either in a cookbook you own, or on a website, such as www.epicurious.com. Allow the children to help measure and mix the ingredients. To match the storyline, you may want to ask each child to bring one ingredient from home. (Linguistic, Logical-Mathematical, Interpersonal)

❍ Encourage the children to gallop the way the horse in the story does. Provide a unopened box of salt and encourage the children to gallop while holding the box. Ask, *What sound does the salt make?* (Bodily-Kinesthetic, Musical)

❍ Place small balls ("cherries") in a basket. Encourage the children to carry the basket on their heads, the way the cow carries the cherries in the book. Once they get the knack of balancing the basket, challenge them to walk in a zigzag pattern. (Spatial, Bodily-Kinesthetic, Interpersonal)

Learning Activities

Discovery

(Logical-Mathematical, Naturalist, Interpersonal)
Provide plastic animals or pictures of animals to represent each animal in the story. Provide labels or pictures of the ingredients needed for the cake. Challenge children to match the ingredients to the animals that brought them.

Listening

(Musical, Interpersonal, Intrapersonal)
Suggest that the children use a pretend microphone to sing the way the bird sang while waiting for the cake. Ask questions: *What kind of sounds might a bird make? What would a "cake waiting" song sound like?*

Dramatic Play

(Linguistic, Logical-Mathematical, Interpersonal)
Encourage the children to use props such as bowls, spoons, measuring cups and spoons, baking pans, and empty spice cans to pretend to bake a cake. Talk about which ingredients are needed and how much of each ingredient goes into the cake.

Math

(Logical-Mathematical, Interpersonal)
Encourage the children to use a set of eight plates, napkins, spoons, and cups to set a table for eight using one-to-one correspondence. Set out the props again, only this time provide uneven sets. With the children, discuss the concepts *greater than* and *less than* as they pertain to the unequal sets.

Gross Motor

(Bodily-Kinesthetic, Interpersonal)
Encourage the children to balance plastic eggs on their noses the way the dog does in the story. Ask questions: *Why is it so difficult? Is there an easier place to balance the egg? Can you balance it in your hand or on your elbow?*

Writing

(Linguistic, Spatial, Naturalist)
Print animal names in Spanish on chart paper, and encourage the children to place pictures of the animals beside their printed names. Invite the children to use the magnetic letters to copy the names. Encourage the children to illustrate the names that they copy.

Let's Keep Reading

Fox Tale Soup by Tony Bonning
Stone Soup by Marcia Brown

Thinking About What We Learned

1. Whose idea was it to bake the cake?
2. Do you like to help cook? What have you helped cook at home?

Epossumondas

Author: Coleen Salley. Illustrator: Janet Stevens

About the Book
A Louisiana possum, Epossumondas, interacts with a human mother and aunt. He travels between the two humans as a messenger of sorts, but is hampered by making one silly mistake after another.

Learning Literacy

Oral Language
- Discuss words and phrases that may be new to children, such as *sweet patootie, scrunched, churned, sense you were born with,* and *bedraggled.*
- If possible, show the children photos of real possums. Talk with the children about their habits, movements, and sounds.

Comprehension
- Ask the children the following questions: *What kind of animal was Epossumondas? Did you know that Epossumondas was going to step in the pies? How did you know? Whose hat does Epossumondas wear over the butter? What would have happened if Mama gave Epossumondas a basket, like the one she has on her arm at the end of the story, to carry things home from Auntie's house? Would that have solved the problem?*

Print Awareness/Letter Knowledge
- Write *Epossumondas* on a piece of chart paper. Ask the children if they think *Epossumondas* is a long or a short name. Write several children's names on the chart paper under *Epossumondas.* Ask the children questions such as, *Does anyone have a longer name? Which letter appears the most in* Epossumondas?

Special Activities

- Visit the zoo to see possums. Ask the children if the zoo possums look like Epossumondas. Upon returning, help the children write a story about the trip. (Linguistic, Naturalist, Interpersonal)
- Outdoors, tie a piece of string around clumps of dirt and encourage the children to drag the dirt around the playground. Ask, *What happens to the dirt after a few minutes of dragging?* (Logical-Mathematical, Bodily-Kinesthetic)
- Teach the children how to play Possum. Invite them to lie on the floor and pretend to be asleep. Tell them no matter what, they are not to move or "wake up." Tickle each child on the chin with a feather. Do they wake up? Ask, *Would a possum move?* (Bodily-Kinesthetic, Interpersonal)

Learning Activities

Discovery

(Logical-Mathematical, Naturalist, Interpersonal)
Give the children chunks of dried clay to crumble into the sand table. Show them how to squeeze and pinch the clay to make it crumble. Point out that the clay is similar to the cake that Epossumondas crumbles on the way to his mama's house.

Dramatic Play

(Spatial, Interpersonal, Intrapersonal)
Provide a variety of hats and dress-up clothes for the children to explore. Try to find props that look like the hats, shoes, and dresses worn by Auntie and Mama. Invite the children to select a favorite hat and a favorite outfit and to create voices for Auntie and Mama.

Fine Motor

(Logical-Mathematical, Bodily-Kinesthetic, Interpersonal)
Provide playdough, rolling pins, pie tins, measuring cups, plastic knives, and other utensils for the children to make pies. Show them how to cut the playdough to make crisscross lines on top of their pies to look like Mama's pies.

Gross Motor

(Linguistic, Bodily-Kinesthetic, Interpersonal)
Provide a hat, and a beanbag to represent butter. Challenge them each to place the "butter" beanbag on his head, then put on the hat and tiptoe the way Epossumondas does. Ask, *Is it difficult to balance the "butter?"*

Music

(Bodily-Kinesthetic, Musical)
Use masking tape to outline a pathway on the floor from Mama's house to Auntie's house. Encourage the children to pretend to tiptoe like Epossumondas, and to create a little song for Epossumondas to sing or to hum as he travels the path from Mama's to Auntie's and back again.

Science

(Naturalist, Interpersonal)
Encourage the children to look at photographs of possums, noting the unique characteristics of possums. Ask questions: *Do they look like Epossumondas? Why is there so little hair on their tails? What color are their ears and toes?*

Let's Keep Reading

Epaminondas and His Auntie by Sara Cone Bryant
The Princess and the Pizza by Mary Jane Auch
To Market, to Market by Anne Miranda
Why Epossumondas Has No Hair on His Tail by Coleen Salley

Thinking About What We Learned

1. Do you have an aunt like Epossumondas' Auntie?
2. Which activity did you enjoy most today? Why?

Exactly the Opposite

Author and Photographer: Tana Hoban

About the Book
Great photographs depict pairs of opposites.

Learning Literacy

Oral Language
❍ Gather items in a basket that you can use to illustrate opposites. For example, a jar or a bottle to demonstrate *open* and *shut* or *tall* and *short* blocks. Talk with the children about the examples of opposites in your basket, and then challenge the children to find things in the classroom that they can use to demonstrate opposites.

Comprehension
❍ Ask the children the following questions: *Which pairs of opposites did you see in the book? Can you use your hands to show me* open *and* shut, *and* front *and* back?

Special Activities
❍ Take a walk around the school. Invite the children to look for pairs of opposites or ways to show opposites. Make a list of the pairs of opposites the children find. (Linguistic, Logical-Mathematical, Spatial, Naturalist)
❍ Dance to music with a fast tempo, then to music with a slow tempo. Provide scarves or ribbons and encourage the children to move them to the beat of the music. (Bodily-Kinesthetic, Musical, Intrapersonal, Interpersonal)

❍ Sing songs and play games that relate or can be made to relate to opposites, such as "Go In and Out the Windows," "Red Light, Green Light," or "The Itsy Bitsy Spider." (Linguistic, Spatial, Bodily-Kinesthetic, Musical, Interpersonal)
❍ Sing "Sing a Song of Opposites" to the tune of "Mary Had a Little Lamb." Encourage the children to add to the verses. (Linguistic, Musical)

Sing a Song of Opposites
by Pam Schiller
This is big and this is small, (show with hands
    spread far apart and then close together)
This is big, this is small,
This is big and this is small,
Sing along with me.

Additional verses:
This is tall and this is short.
This is up and this is down.
This is in and this is out.
This is happy and this is sad.
This is fast and this is slow.
This is here and this is there.

Learning Activities

Art *(Logical-Mathematical, Spatial, Bodily-Kinesthetic, Intrapersonal)*

Mix the paints so that some are thick and some are thin. Put out the paint, paper, and wide and narrow brushes, and encourage the children to paint. Talk with the children as they work. *Is it easier to paint with thick paint or thin paint? Which brush is more fun to paint with?*

Blocks *(Spatial, Bodily-Kinesthetic, Interpersonal)*

Challenge the children to build tall and short towers. Talk with them as they build. *Which tower is more difficult to balance? What is the advantage of a tall tower over a short tower?*

Construction *(Linguistic, Spatial, Bodily-Kinesthetic)*

Make a weaving loom for children by cutting slits 1" apart in both sides of Styrofoam meat trays. Starting at the top of the tray and on the bottom side, run yarn back and forth across the tray through the slits on each side, and tie or tape them at the bottom and on the back of the tray. Provide ribbon, lace, pipe cleaners, and other interesting materials for weaving. Talk with the children about the *over* and *under* pattern.

Discovery *(Linguistic, Naturalist, Interpersonal)*

Set out a basket of items full of objects that illustrate the meaning of *opposite*. Encourage the children to explore the items in the basket, and then help them search the classroom for more items to add to the collection.

Gross Motor *(Linguistic, Bodily-Kinesthetic, Interpersonal)*

Invite the children to toss beanbags into a box. Provide a bottle and clothespins. Challenge the children to drop the clothespins into the bottle. Ask the children: *Where is the beanbag when it doesn't land in the box? Where is the clothespin when it doesn't make it into the bottle?*

Music *(Musical, Interpersonal, Intrapersonal)*

Suggest that the children try several rhythm instruments and determine if the sound the instrument makes is loud or soft. Ask, *Are there some instruments that are loud or soft depending on how you use them?* Encourage the children to make loud and soft sounds with the instruments.

Let's Keep Reading
Sing a Song of Opposites by Pam Schiller

Thinking About What We Learned

1. Which pair of opposites can you demonstrate with the light switch? Which pair of opposites can you demonstrate with the door?
2. What did you find out about the thick and thin paint?

A Family Like Yours

Author: Rebecca Kai Dotlich. Illustrator: Tammie Lyon

About the Book
This book provides a wonderfully inclusive description of families. Everyone will find their family represented somewhere within the book.

Learning Literacy

Oral Language
❍ Talk with the children about their families. Encourage the children to talk about how their families are alike and different.
❍ Discuss words that may be new to the children, such as *zillion, shore, galore, proper, aisles, operas, spare, pout, detail,* and *bellow.*

Phonological Awareness
❍ Reread *A Family Like Yours* a couple of times, stopping at the second words in rhyming word pairs, and encourage the children to complete the rhymes. Discuss rhyming words.

Comprehension
❍ Ask the children the following questions: *Was there a family like yours in the book? Which part of the book was like your family? How would you describe some of the families in the story?*
❍ Create a word web (see appendix page 230) about families. Print *family* in the center of a sheet of chart paper and draw a circle around the word. Encourage the children to tell you what they know about families and print their words and phrases on the paper, and draw lines connecting them to the *family* circle.

Special Activities

❍ Have a Family Night or Family Picnic at school. Invite the children's families to a potluck dinner. Ask each family to bring a dish to contribute to the meal. Help the children bake cookies for the dessert, make decorations, and draw family portraits to display. Consider teaching the children a few songs to sing as entertainment. (Linguistic, Logical-Mathematical, Spatial, Bodily-Kinesthetic, Musical, Interpersonal, Intrapersonal)
❍ Ask families to help their children make family trees. Send home a form for families to use, or let families come up with their own creative format for presentation. (Linguistic, Logical-Mathematical, Naturalist, Interpersonal)
❍ Sing "Where Is Thumbkin?" substituting family members for the names of the fingers; for example, *Where is mother,* or *Where is brother?* (Bodily-Kinesthetic, Musical, Interpersonal)
❍ Teach the children the family rhyme below. (Linguistic, Bodily-Kinesthetic)

I Help My Family
by Pam Schiller (suit actions to words)
I help my family when I can.
I fold the clothes.
I feed the dog.
I turn on the hose.
I crack the eggs.
I ice the cake.
Then I help eat
The good things we make.

Learning Activities

Art

(Spatial, Intrapersonal)
Encourage the children to draw family portraits. Help them label each family member. Display their portraits or use them to create a baggie book. (See the Language activity on this page for directions on making books.)

Language

(Linguistic, Spatial, Bodily-Kinesthetic, Interpersonal)
Help the children make individual Family Books. Staple five or six resealable plastic bags together across the bottom of the bags. Cover the staples with cloth tape to create a spine. Ask the children to bring photos of their families to place inside the plastic bags to create a Family Book.

Blocks

(Spatial, Bodily-Kinesthetic, Interpersonal)
Invite the children to use several boxes and pictures of different types of housing to build different kinds of homes. You may probably need to sit with the children and demonstrate how to build homes.

Math

(Logical-Mathematical, Naturalist)
Create a graph to show how many family members each child has. On a poster board, make a graph with 10 columns. At the top of the first column print a numeral 1 and draw a single stick figure. Continue across the columns printing the next numeral and drawing the correct number of stick figures. Encourage each child to place stick-on squares in the column that corresponds to the number of people in his or her family.

Dramatic Play

(Linguistic, Interpersonal)
Encourage the children to use a variety of props for serving dinner, such as a tablecloth, dishes, cups, microwave, dinner boxes, and fast food napkins to set the table for one of three different dinners—a formal table, a microwavable frozen dinner, and a fast food dinner.

Music

(Linguistic, Musical, Interpersonal, Intrapersonal)
Provide a variety of music for the children to sample, such as rock and roll, country, classical, blues, jazz, and so on. Include music from other cultures, such as mariachi or flamenco. Talk with the children about the music. Ask them what kind of music their families listen to. Point out that people have different tastes in music.

Let's Keep Reading

Amazing Grace by Mary Hoffman
Koala Lou by Mem Fox

Thinking About What We Learned

1. Do animals have families? Which part of *A Family Like Yours* shows animal families?
2. What did you learn about families today?

Fancy Nancy

Author: Jane O'Connor. Illustrator: Robin Preiss Glasser

About the Book
Nancy is a glamour queen who loves everything that is fancy. When she decides to teach her boring family to be "fancy" the fun begins. The story is filled with fancy vocabulary.

Learning Literacy

Oral Language
- Invite the children to discuss *fancy*. Brainstorm with them a list of fancy things.
- Talk with the children about the fancy words in the book, such as *fuchsia, frilly, tiara, stupendous, accessories, escort, chauffeur, darling, parfait, curtsy,* and *dressing gown*.

Segmentation
- Invite the children to clap the syllables in *Fancy Nancy*. Ask, *Are there the same number of syllables in each word?*

Phonological Awareness
- Talk about the rhyming words *Fancy* and *Nancy*. Encourage the children to think of words that will rhyme with their names.

Print Awareness
- There are many examples of the uses of print in this story. Look at the page of bulletin board documents. Talk with the children about how people use message boards, and encourage the children to describe the messages on the board. Look at Nancy's sign on her refrigerator door. Read it to the children. Ask, *What is the purpose of the note on the refrigerator?* Talk about the print type on the page where Nancy is teaching her family to be fancy.

Letter Knowledge
- Show the children the cover to the book. Point to *Fancy* and then to *Nancy*, and ask the children the following questions, *Which letter is different in each word? Which letters are the same in each word?*

Special Activities
- Look at the first two pages of the book that show Nancy's room before and after she makes it fancy. Ask the children to point out differences. (Logical-Mathematical, Naturalist, Interpersonal, Intrapersonal)
- Have a Fancy Tea. Serve tea in small cups and serve fancy cookies. (Linguistic, Interpersonal)
- Sing "Frere Jacques." Explain that this is a French song. Remind the children that Nancy says French is a fancy language. (Linguistic, Musical, Naturalist)

Frere Jacques
Frere Jacques, Frere Jacques,
Dormez-vous, dormez-vous?
Sonnez les matines, sonnez les matines
Ding dang dong, ding dang dong.

Learning Activities

Art
(Spatial, Intrapersonal)
Provide fuchsia paint, paper, and brushes. Encourage the children to paint with Nancy's favorite color.

Music
(Bodily-Kinesthetic, Musical, Interpersonal)
Play classical music and invite the children to dance while balancing tiaras on their heads. Challenge them to curtsy and bow with the tiaras on their heads.

Dramatic Play
(Linguistic, Bodily-Kinesthetic, Interpersonal)
Provide fancy clothes for the children to use for dress up. Include boas, tiaras, sequined blouses and scarves, shoes, and other fancy accessories. Provide a mirror so the children can see themselves in fancy attire. Ask questions: *How does it feel to be a fancy dresser? Are the clothes comfortable?*

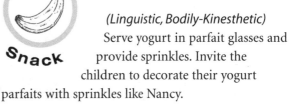

Snack
(Linguistic, Bodily-Kinesthetic)
Serve yogurt in parfait glasses and provide sprinkles. Invite the children to decorate their yogurt parfaits with sprinkles like Nancy.

Math
(Logical-Mathematical, Naturalist)
Make pretend pizzas by decorating and then cutting small, medium, and large pizza trays into pizza slices. Cut the small pizza into four slices, the medium into six slices, and the large into eight slices. Invite the children to put the pizzas together. Challenge them to count the number of pieces in each pizza.

Writing
(Linguistic, Bodily-Kinesthetic, Intrapersonal)
Invite the children to use a plume pen and fuchsia paint to print their names.

Let's Keep Reading

Eloise by Kay Thompson
Olivia by Ian Falconer

Thinking About What We Learned

1. Can you think of another word that means the same thing as *fancy*?
2. Do you like to be fancy or do you prefer to be plain? Why?

"Fire! Fire!" Said Mrs. McGuire

Author: Bill Martin, Jr. Illustrator: Richard Egielski

About the Book

A fire is raging, and in this rhyming text woman after woman spreads the word.

Learning Literacy

Oral Language

❍ Some of the characters in the story have names that relate to their jobs or the ways they are dressed. The character Mrs. Kopp, for example, is wearing a police uniform. As you read the book, invite the children to look carefully at the illustrations. Ask the children how many associations they can find. Because some of the associations are sophisticated, focus on those that are easier for the children to see, such as the kittens on the page with Mrs. Kitty.

Phonological Awareness/Print Awareness

❍ On chart paper, make a list of the characters in the book. Read the book again and encourage the children to say the rhyming words that go with the characters' names. Invite the children to think of rhyming words that might go with their own names.

Comprehension

❍ Ask the children the following questions: *Who is the first person to say there is a fire? What caused the fire? Is there really a fire? Have you ever seen a real fire?*

Print Awareness

❍ Help the children make a list of all the helpers/workers in the book.

❍ Show the children the cover of the book. Point out the quotation marks around "*fire.*" Discuss the use of quotation marks.

Special Activities

❍ Talk with the children about fire safety. Teach them to stop, drop, and roll if their clothing catches on fire. (Linguistic, Bodily-Kinesthetic)

❍ Bake cookies for your local firefighters to thank them for the work they do to protect the community. Give them to a visiting firefighter or take a field trip to a fire house to give the firefighters the cookies. (Linguistic, Logical-Mathematical, Interpersonal)

❍ Invite the children to make fire safety posters. Invite the children to brainstorm about different safety slogans. (Linguistic, Spatial, Intrapersonal)

❍ Read the "Firefighter" poem to the children. Encourage them to discuss times they have seen a fire truck. (Linguistic, Interpersonal)

Firefighter

Up onto their loud, loud truck
The firefighters climb.
They're in an awful hurry;
They move in quick, quick time,
They're going to put out a fire,
Help is on the way.
They'll get there with their water hose
And spray and spray and spray.

Learning Activities

Art *(Spatial)*
Invite the children to use paintbrushes; paper; brushes; and yellow, orange, red, and white paint to paint a blazing fire.

Language *(Linguistic, Intrapersonal)*
Collect objects to make rhyming pairs; for example, a rock and a sock, a twig and a plastic pig, a hat and a plastic cat, glue and a shoe, and so on. Mix them up. Encourage the children to name each of the objects, then match the items that rhyme. Challenge the children to find things that rhyme with their names.

Discovery *(Musical, Naturalist)*
Challenge the children to explore noisemakers, such as bells, alarms, whistles, drums, and megaphones, to determine which one would provide the loudest fire alarm. Ask questions: *Which noisemaker is easiest on the ears? Is it possible to make a warning that is melodic or at least rhythmic, for example, two fast beats and two slow beats?*

Water Table Water Play *(Logical-Mathematical, Interpersonal)*
Provide small buckets and hoses (or plastic tubing), and encourage the children to explore ways to carry water from one place to another.

Dramatic Play *(Linguistic, Interpersonal)*
Provide firefighter props, such as hoses, fire hats, coats, and boots. Invite the children to pretend to be firefighters.

Writing *(Linguistic, Bodily-Kinesthetic)*
Print *fire* on several sheets of paper. Provide orange fingerpaint and encourage the children to touch the paint with their fingertips, then trace over the letters of *fire*, making fingerprint letters.

Let's Keep Reading

Fire! Fire! by Gail Gibbons

Thinking About What We Learned

1. What rule should follow if your clothes catch on fire?
2. What did you learn today about firefighters?

Fish Wish

Author and Illustrator: Bob Barner

About the Book
A little boy takes a trip to an aquarium and begins to wonder just what it would be like to be a fish. His imagination sends him on a colorful journey through the coral reef as a clown fish that changes size depending on which sea creatures he meets: dolphins, sea turtles, octopi, squid, jellyfish, sea horses, shrimp, crabs, sea anemones, and starfish.

Learning Literacy

Comprehension
❍ Ask the children the following questions: *Which sea creatures do you like best? Why does the clown fish change its size? What do you think the little boy wishes for at the end of the story?*

Letter Knowledge/Phonological Awareness
❍ Show the children the cover of the book. Have them look at the letters in the title. Ask the children the following questions: *Which letters are the same in each word? Which letters are different? Do the words* fish *and* wish *rhyme? What are other words that rhyme with* fish *and* wish?

Special Activities

❍ Visit an aquarium or the aquarium area of the zoo. Bring a copy of *Fish Wish* along. Challenge the children to see how many of the sea creatures in the book they can find at the aquarium. (Linguistic, Logical-Mathematical, Naturalist, Interpersonal)
❍ Invite the children to swim like fish to a variety of different tempos of music. Suggest that they swim like happy fish, frightened fish, sleepy fish, and so on. (Bodily-Kinesthetic, Musical, Intrapersonal)

❍ Build a maze to represent a coral reef. Invite the children to pretend to swim through the maze without touching the "coral." (Spatial, Bodily-Kinesthetic, Interpersonal)
❍ Cut three pieces of yarn: one 30' long, one 28' long, and one 100' long. Take the yarn outdoors. Stretch each piece of yarn out across the playground; first the 100' piece, then the 30' piece, then the 28' piece. Explain to the children that the first piece of yarn represents the length of a blue whale (the largest whale). The 30' strip represents the length of a large dolphin and the 28' piece represents the distance of an octopus from one tentacle to the end of an opposite tentacle (note that 28' is one of the largest sizes an octopus can grow to; many octopi are only as large as a person's fist). Ask, *Which animal is the largest?* Have the children walk the pieces of yarn. (Logical-Mathematical, Bodily-Kinesthetic, Interpersonal)

Starfish
by Pam Schiller
Starfish, starfish, under the sea,
Starfish, starfish, grant this wish to me.

Learning Activities

Construction

(Spatial, Bodily-Kinesthetic)
Provide paper, pens, large sequins, and a construction paper template of a fish. Invite the children to trace the fish template onto their own paper and encourage them to add details, like an eye or a mouth, using the available materials. Help them glue the sequins onto their fish to make scales.

Listening

(Linguistic, Musical)
Provide tapes of ocean sounds. Encourage the children to identify the different sounds on the tape.

Language

(Linguistic, Spatial, Intrapersonal)
Give the children cutouts of starfish and teach them the "Starfish" poem on the previous page. Afterwards, encourage the children to think of wishes. Help the children copy their wishes onto their starfish, and encourage them to illustrate their starfish.

Math

(Logical-Mathematical)
Cut out several construction paper fish outlines, each one a little larger than the previous one. Invite the children to arrange the fish from the largest to the smallest, then shuffle and arrange them from the smallest to the largest. Ask, *What happens if you lay the fish on top of each other starting with the largest fish on the bottom and ending with the smallest fish?*

Library

(Linguistic, Intrapersonal)
Fill the center with books about sea creatures. Talk with the children about the animals in the books. If possible, bring a goldfish to the classroom for the children to observe.

Water Table

(Linguistic, Logical-Mathematical, Naturalist, Interpersonal)
Provide large rocks to create a shoreline in the water table, suction cups (to represent the suction cups on octopi), and items the children will be able to pick up with the suction cups, such as small blocks, play dishes, or anything with a flat, plastic surface.

Let's Keep Reading

A Swim Through the Sea by Kristin Joy Pratt
Swimmy by Leo Lionni

Thinking About What We Learned

1. What did you learn about the ocean today?
2. What do you think it would be like to live in the ocean?

Flower Garden

Author: Eve Bunting. Illustrator: Kathryn Hewitt

About the Book

A little girl and her father plan a birthday surprise for Mom. Simple text and large clean illustrations create an appealing combination for children.

Learning Literacy

Oral Language

❍ Define the words in the story that may be new for the children, such as *trowel, jamboree,* and *planting mix.*

❍ Talk with the children about birthday presents and birthday surprises.

Comprehension

❍ Ask the children the following questions: *How would the story be different if the little girl and her dad decided to buy a puppy for mom? Where would they have found it? How would they have brought it home? How would they have carried it up the stairs? How would they have surprised mom with it? What do you think your mom would like for a birthday present? What about your dad, grandmother, or grandfather?*

Special Activities

❍ Visit a florist. Ask the florist to demonstrate flower arranging for the children. (Naturalist, Interpersonal, Intrapersonal)

❍ Plant a flowerbed on the playground. Encourage the children to help decide how big the garden should be, what types of flowers to plant, and where to plant them. Involve the children in executing the plan. (Logical-Mathematical, Spatial, Bodily-Kinesthetic, Naturalist, Intrapersonal)

❍ Invite the children to dance to classical music, imagining that they are flowers swaying in the wind. (Bodily-Kinesthetic, Musical, Interpersonal Intrapersonal)

Learning Activities

Art *(Spatial)*
Encourage the children to use paper, brushes, and several bright paints to paint pictures of flowers. You may want to provide pictures of work from artists who specialize in painting flowers, such as Georgia O'Keeffe.

Math *(Logical-Mathematical, Spatial, Bodily-Kinesthetic)*
Provide playdough for making "birthday cakes" and candles for the cakes. Challenge the children to make five cakes, and to put one candle on the first cake, two on the second, and so on, up to five candles on the fifth cake.

Dramatic Play *(Logical-Mathematical, Spatial, Naturalist, Interpersonal, Intrapersonal)*
Provide artificial flowers, plastic vases, potter's clay, Styrofoam, order forms, play money, a cash register, and so on. Encourage the children to pretend they are opening a florist shop.

Science *(Spatial, Naturalist)*
Set out potting soil, plant mix, flowerpots, and flowers. Encourage the children to pick flowers to plant in their pots. Ask the children the following questions: *What color flowers are you going to plant? What goes into the flower pot first? What goes next? How often will we water the flowers?*

Gross Motor *(Bodily-Kinesthetic, Musical)*
Cut colorful flower shapes from felt squares. Cut a small hole in the center of each felt flower so that it can clasp snugly around the button on top of a service bell. Place the flowers on top of service bells. Use masking tape to mark a throw line on the floor. Encourage the children to toss beanbags onto the flowers to ring the bells.

Writing *(Linguistic, Spatial, Intrapersonal)*
Encourage the children to describe their favorite birthday presents and memories. Transcribe their stories onto sheets of construction paper and encourage them to illustrate the paper on which you copied the stories.

Let's Keep Reading
Peter's Chair by Ezra Jack Keats
Planting a Rainbow by Lois Elhert

Thinking About What We Learned
1. Which flower in the flower box did you like best?
2. What do flowers need to keep them growing?

Freight Train

Author and Illustrator: Donald Crews

About the Book
Through the day and into the night, a colorful train moves on and on until it is gone.

Learning Literacy

Oral Language

❍ Ask the children about each car mentioned in the book. *What is the car's purpose? What color is it?*

❍ Discuss words that might be new for the children, such as *trestle, track, hopper,* and *tank.*

❍ Talk with the children about the differences between a passenger train and a freight train.

Oral Language/Comprehension

❍ Create a KWL chart (see appendix page 228) about trains. Draw a chart with three columns on a piece of chart paper or bulletin board paper. Label the first column *What We Know,* the second column *What We Want to Know,* and the third column *What We Learned.* Talk with the children about crickets, and then fill in the first and second columns of the chart. At the end of the day or week if you continue studying trains, fill in the last column.

Comprehension

❍ Ask the children the following questions: *Have you ever seen a train before? Where? Did you count the cars? Which train car do you like best?*

Special Activities

❍ Take a trip to a train station. Encourage the children to find all the train cars mentioned in the book. Ask, *Is there a caboose? Do you see an engineer?* (Linguistic, Logical-Mathematical, Naturalist)

❍ Make a train snack. Give each child half a banana, ¼" slices of bananas for wheels, a large strawberry, and some yogurt. Help the children use the yogurt to attach the wheels to the body of the train (the half-banana), and place the smoke stack (strawberry) at the top of the train. (Logical-Mathematical, Spatial, Bodily-Kinesthetic)

❍ Reread the book as a rap. Ask the children if they like the book better when it is read or when it is recited as a rap. (Linguistic, Musical, Intrapersonal)

❍ Sing train songs with the children, for example, "Down by the Station" and "Little Red Caboose."

Learning Activities

Blocks

(Spatial, Bodily-Kinesthetic, Interpersonal)

Invite the children to build a train track with blocks. Talk with them as they work, using the appropriate vocabulary, such as *crosstie, trestle, track,* and so on. When the track is finished, encourage the children to build a town around it.

Language

(Linguistic, Spatial, Interpersonal)

Cut a train engine and several train cars from construction paper. Place the letters of the alphabet on each car. Challenge children to attach the trains by placing the letters in alphabetical order. Ask questions: *Which letter is on the first car? Which letter is on the last car?*

Construction

(Spatial, Intrapersonal)

Invite the children to use boxes, paints, construction paper, and glue to build a train. When the train is finished, encourage the children to pretend to take a trip. Ask them where they are going. *How long will it take you to get there?*

Listening

(Linguistic, Musical)

Provide a tape recorder and empty paper towel tubes. Encourage the children to use the paper towel tubes to make sounds like train whistles. Suggest that they also record the train whistle sounds that they make, and their attempts to copy the clacking sound of the train wheels on the track.

Fine Motor

(Spatial, Interpersonal)

Provide construction paper, scissors, glue, and rectangle and circle templates. Suggest that the children trace the templates to make train cars and wheels. Provide a sheet of butcher paper and black and brown strips of construction paper for a track. Encourage the children to make a track on the paper and then glue train cars onto the track.

Math

(Logical-Mathematical)

Make 15 train cars from construction paper. Use rectangles for the cars and small black circles for the wheels. Laminate. Attach a paper clip at the rear of each car. Provide cards with the numerals 1–5. Encourage the children to use the paper clips to connect the cars in correct numerical order.

Let's Keep Reading

The Little Engine That Could by Watty Piper
Train Song by Diane Siebert

Thinking About What We Learned

1. If you could ride in a train, where would you go?
2. What did you learn about trains today?

Gingerbread Baby

Author and Illustrator: Jan Brett

About the Book
This is a traditional tale with a little twist. A gingerbread baby leads Matti's mother, Matti's father, and a crew of others on a wild chase. Matti figures a clever way to end the chase.

Learning Literacy

Oral Language/Comprehension
❍ Invite the children to look at the illustrations on the side of each page. Ask what they think the images on the side panels indicate (they show what will happen next in the story). This is a technique that Jan Brett uses in many of her books. Find another Jan Brett book that uses this technique and show the children the side panels.

Comprehension
❍ Ask the children the following questions: *What do you think would have happened to the gingerbread baby if Matti hadn't made the gingerbread house? What do you think Matti will do with the gingerbread baby?*

Special Activities

❍ Visit a bakery. Watch the baker make gingerbread cookies. Invite the children to ask the baker questions: *How do you know which cookies to bake? How do you arrange the cookies? Where do you get your recipes? Where do you get your supplies?* (Spatial, Naturalist, Interpersonal)
❍ Sing "Gingerbread Men" to the tune of "Jingle Bells." Encourage the children to finish the second verse. (Linguistic, Musical)

Gingerbread Men
by Pam Schiller
Gingerbread, gingerbread,
Warming on the tray.
Oh, how good you smell to me
As I work and play.

Gingerbread, gingerbread,
Cooling on the tray.
Oh, how good you taste to me,
Fresh off the cooking tray.

Learning Activities

Blocks

(Spatial, Interpersonal, Intrapersonal)
Encourage the children to build a gingerbread house. Provide colorful paper to cut into "candy decorations" for the house and other decorative items, such as lace and pipe cleaners.

Math

(Logical-Mathematical)
Make a gingerbread baby outline on construction paper, and cut it in half. Show the children how to fold a sheet of paper in half, trace the gingerbread baby half on the fold, and cut out their gingerbread babies. Introduce the children to the word *symmetry*. Ask the children to think of other items that they could cut out on a fold, such as a heart shape or a ball.

Cooking

(Linguistic, Logical-Mathematical, Interpersonal)
Invite the children to help make gingerbread. Prepare the directions in rebus form, so that the children can follow the steps. While mixing the ingredients, stop long enough to let the children smell the ginger. When serving the gingerbread, talk with the children about how it tastes.

Music

(Musical, Interpersonal, Interpersonal)
Challenge the children to make up a rap or chant using words or lines of text from the book. Provide a drum or a tambourine to help the children establish a rhythm for their rap/chant.

Fine Motor

(Spatial, Bodily-Kinesthetic)
Provide brown playdough, gingerbread men cookie cutters, and plenty of decorative items, such as sequins, buttons, lace, and so on. Encourage the children to cut out and decorate gingerbread babies.

Writing

(Linguistic, Spatial)
Provide construction paper outlines of gingerbread babies. Encourage the children to trace the templates, and then use their crayons to decorate their gingerbread babies.

Let's Keep Reading
The Gingerbread Man by Paul Galdone

Thinking About What We Learned
1. Do you prefer gingerbread cookies, or gingerbread that is more like a cake?
2. What would you do with a gingerbread baby?

Guess Who?

Author and Illustrator: Margaret Miller

About the Book
This book is a photographic journey through the world of workers. Guessing the answers to the book's riddles adds to the fun.

Learning Literacy

Comprehension

○ Ask the children the following questions: *What do you want to be when you grow up? Why? What clues and objects would help someone guess your job?*

Print Awareness/Oral Language

○ Make a list of jobs that the people in the book do. After making the list, ask the children whether they have family members with the same jobs.

Special Activities

○ Visit a dance studio. Encourage the children to dance on the dance floor. Talk about the many different types of dance there are in the world. (Bodily-Kinesthetic, Musical)

○ Visit a library. Tour the different sections of the library. Sit and read a book in the children's section. (Linguistic, Naturalist, Interpersonal)

○ Visit a beauty salon. Watch the hair stylist work. (Spatial, Interpersonal)

○ Play worker charades. Invite one child to pantomime working at different jobs, while the other children guess which job is being pantomimed. (Bodily-Kinesthetic, Naturalist, Interpersonal, Intrapersonal)

○ Visit a construction site and watch the work. Encourage the children to discuss the various jobs. *Which ones look the most interesting? Which ones look dangerous?* **Safety Note:** Keep the children a safe distance from the construction work. (Spatial, Interpersonal, Intrapersonal)

○ Visit a bank. Help the children make a list of the many different jobs people do at the bank. (Logical-Mathematical, Naturalist)

Learning Activities

Art *(Spatial, Interpersonal, Intrapersonal)*
Invite the children to use art props, such as paints, easels, smocks, brushes, and other props, to pretend to be artists. Encourage the children to discuss the work of artists.

Library *(Linguistic, Naturalist)*
Provide books and shelves, and encourage the children to file the books away. Help them think of a filing system that will work.

Blocks *(Spatial, Bodily-Kinesthetic, Interpersonal)*
Provide blueprints and drafting tools for the children to pretend to be engineers, architects, and builders. Add the appropriate vocabulary as they build and encourage them to discuss their work.

Listening *(Bodily-Kinesthetic, Musical, Interpersonal, Intrapersonal)*
Provide props for dancers and singers, such as top hats, microphone, stage, and so on. Interact with the children and provide appropriate vocabulary as they play.

Dramatic Play *(Spatial, Interpersonal)*
Set out beauty salon props, such as brushes, curlers, ribbons, dryers (without cords), and so on. Interact with children as they play and introduce appropriate vocabulary.

Math *(Logical-Mathematical, Interpersonal)*
Suggest that the children use grocery store props, such as empty cans and boxes, cash registers, grocery bags, play money, baskets, and so on, to set up a grocery store. Encourage the children to describe the job of the grocery clerk as they play.

Let's Keep Reading
Jobs People Do by Christopher Maynard
Who Uses This? by Margaret Miller

Thinking About What We Learned
1. Which of the jobs did you like doing best today?
2. Do you think people can do more than one job?

Hello, Hello

Author: Miriam Schlein. Illustrator: Daniel Kirk

About the Book
This book illustrates the many ways animals and humans say "hello."

Learning Literacy

Oral Language
- Sing "Where Is Thumbkin?" Talk with the children about the way the fingers in the song say *hello* to one another.
- Teach the children to say *hello* in several languages: *Hola* (Spanish), *Aloha* (Polynesian), *Bonjour* (French), and so on.

Comprehension
- Ask the children the following questions: *How do you say* hello? *Have you ever watched animals say* hello?

Print Awareness/Oral Language
- Make a list of ways that children say *hello* to one another, such as nodding, hugging, waving, speaking, smiling, and so on. Discuss words people use to say *hello*, such as *good morning, hi, howdy, hey*, and so on.

Special Activities
- Invite people from other cultures to visit the classroom and describe ways that people from their cultures say *hello*. (Linguistic Naturalist, Interpersonal)
- Teach the children to say *hello* using the American Sign Language sign (see appendix page 236). (Linguistic, Bodily-Kinesthetic, Interpersonal, Intrapersonal)

- Encourage the children to try saying some of the greetings the animals in the book use. Ask them to face a partner toe-to-toe and flap their arms, imitating the way that the penguins flap their wings, rub heads together like the lions, and touch hands like chimpanzees. Encourage them to say *hello* to each other using their favorite way that humans say *hello*. (Linguistic, Spatial, Bodily-Kinesthetic, Naturalist, Interpersonal, Intrapersonal)
- Sing *hello* songs, for example, "Good Morning to You." (Linguistic, Musical, Interpersonal)

Good Morning to You
Good morning to you!
Good morning to you!
We're all in our places
With bright shining faces.
Oh, this is the way to start a great day!

- Say chants and rhymes that express *hello*. (Linguistic, Interpersonal)

Hello
by Pam Schiller
(Child's name, child's name) howdy-do,
Hello, good day, how are you?

Learning Activities

Art
(Spatial, Interpersonal, Intrapersonal)
Print *hello* in large block letters on a sheet of butcher paper. Invite the children to fill in the letters as they wish with dots, stripes, wiggle lines, circles, and so on. Display the finished sign outside the classroom door.

Listening
(Musical, Interpersonal)
When the children's family members drop them off at school, record them saying *hello*. Later, play the recordings and challenge children to identify the family members who are speaking.

Fine Motor
(Bodily-Kinesthetic, Interpersonal)
Demonstrate a few different and creative handshakes. Challenge the children to make up ways to shake hands. Supervise this activity so that the children don't get too silly.

Science
(Linguistic, Logical-Mathematical, Naturalist)
Provide photos of animals (as many as possible from those in *Hello, Hello*). Encourage the children to try to remember how each animal greets its friends. Classify the animals by those who have use an auditory greeting, those who touch to greet, and those who do both.

Language
(Linguistic, Interpersonal)
Provide puppets and encourage the children to interact with each other using the puppets. Suggest that they try different ways of having the puppets say *hello* to each other.

Writing
(Linguistic, Bodily-Kinesthetic)
Print *hello* on several index cards. Provide fingerpaint and encourage the children to make fingerprints over the letters.

Let's Keep Reading

Hello, Baby by Lizzy Rockwell
Hello Hello by Dan Zanes

Thinking About What We Learned

1. What did you learn today about saying *hello*?
2. How is saying *hello* like saying *goodbye*?

Henny Penny

Author and Illustrator: Paul Galdone

About the Book

A silly chicken that is hit in the head by an acorn believes that she has been hit by a piece of the falling sky. She stirs up all her animal friends as she races off to tell the king that "the sky is falling." Clever rhyming animal names add to the fun of the story.

Learning Literacy

Phonological Awareness/Letter Knowledge

❍ Create a rhyming name for each child in the classroom, such as *Michael–Tichael, Kathy–Tathy,* and so on. Print the names on chart paper and encourage the children to examine each part of the name to determine which letters are alike and which letters are different.

Comprehension

❍ Ask the children the following questions: *How would the story be different if the hen realized it was an acorn that hit her in the head? Which animal name in the story do you like best?*

❍ Invite the children to help you complete a story pyramid (see appendix page 229) for *Henny Penny.* Enlarge the pattern or copy it onto chart paper, and let the children help fill in the chart.

Letter Knowledge

❍ Print *Henny Penny* on a piece of chart paper. Encourage the children to look at the two parts of the name to determine which letters are the same and which letters are different. Help them notice that that the first letter is different. Encourage the children to think of other rhyming names for the animals. For example, *Henny Penny* might be *Henny Renny* and *Cocky Locky* might be *Cocky Rocky.*

Special Activities

❍ Visit a farm. Encourage the children to count the chickens on the farm. Ask questions: *Are there too many to count? Do any of the chickens look like Henny Penny?* After the trip, invite the children to draw pictures of their favorite parts of the trip. (Linguistic, Spatial, Naturalist)

❍ Do the "Chicken Dance." Music is available on *All-Time Favorite Dances* CD by Kimbo Educational, as well as on several other children's dance CDs. (Linguistic, Bodily-Kinesthetic, Musical, Interpersonal)

Learning Activities

Discovery *(Linguistic, Naturalist, Interpersonal)*

Crack an acorn open (adults only) and examine the inside with the children. Talk with them about what they see. *What color is the inside? What texture is the inside?*

Language *(Linguistic, Musical, Interpersonal, Intrapersonal)*

Challenge the children to make up rhyming chants. For example, *Henny Penny can't have any, even though she wants many.* This seems challenging, but you may be surprised to see how words come easily to young children. Nonsense chants are fine.

Dramatic Play *(Linguistic, Interpersonal, Intrapersonal)*

Encourage the children to use plastic farm animals to reenact the story. Do they remember the order in which the animals join Henny Penny?

Math *(Logical-Mathematical, Interpersonal)*

Provide a box of acorns. Divide the children into pairs. Ask each child to pick up a handful of acorns and drop them onto a paper plate. Ask the children to count their acorns to determine which partner has the most acorns. If the children are not able to count their acorns accurately, encourage them to match their acorns one-to-one with their partner to determine who has the most.

Gross Motor *(Bodily-Kinesthetic, Musical, Interpersonal)*

Place a box of acorns on the floor beside several different objects, such as an empty box, a pie tin, a vinyl placemat, a plastic bowl, and so on. Ask the children to take off their shoes and socks, and challenge them to use their toes to pick up the acorns, drop them onto the other objects, and then describe the sounds.

Writing *(Linguistic)*

Write the names of the story characters on index cards and hand them out to the children. Encourage the children to copy the names using magnetic letters. If the children are interested, encourage them to use the magnetic letters to spell their own names and then try to change the first letters of their names to make new rhyming names for themselves.

Let's Keep Reading

Henny Penny by Harriet Ziefert
Henny Penny by Jane Wattenberg

Thinking About What We Learned

1. Do you think Henny Penny is smart? What could she have done that might have saved her a lot of trouble?
2. Do you think the sky can fall? Why? Why not?

A House for Hermit Crab

Author and Illustrator: Eric Carle

About the Book

Hermit Crab moves out of his small shell in search of a new home. When he finds a bigger place, he also finds plenty of help from the sea community. A sea anemone, a starfish, and some coral agree to help decorate the plain shell. A snail offers to clean the house, and a sea urchin offers protection. A lantern fish offers lighting. Hermit lives happily for a while, until it is time to move again to an even larger place.

Learning Literacy

Oral Language

❍ Define vocabulary that may be new to the children, such as *floor of the ocean, sea anemone, starfish, coral, sea urchin, murky, gloomy, dim, prickly needles,* and *spiky.*

Phonological Awareness

❍ Talk with the children about the onomatopoeic phrase *scritch-scratch.* Explain that it serves as a predictable refrain in the story. Ask the children what the sound is describing.

Comprehension

❍ Create a KWL chart (see appendix page 228). Draw a chart with three columns on a piece of chart paper or bulletin board paper. Label the first column *What We Know,* the second column *What We Want to Know,* and the third column *What We Learned.* Talk with the children about hermit crabs and then fill in the first and second columns in the chart. You may find some of the information you are looking for at the beginning of the book. At the end of the day or week, fill in the last column.

❍ Ask the children the following questions: *What was Hermit Crab looking for? Why did he need a new home? Why was he afraid? How does the lantern fish help? Do you think Hermit Crab will outgrow his new shell again? Have you ever owned something and outgrown it? What was it?*

Special Activities

❍ Play Musical Shells. Use masking tape to make 2' diameter circles (to represent shells) across the floor. Make one less circle than the number of children playing the game. Play music. Explain to the children that when the music stops, it is a signal for them to step inside one of the "shells." It is okay for more than one child to stand inside a shell. After each round, remove one of the circles. In the final round, it will be necessary for all the children to find a way to fit inside the one remaining shell. In this game, the object is cooperation. (Bodily-Kinesthetic, Musical, Interpersonal)

❍ Place a hermit crab in a fish tank and add it to the science center. They are easy to keep and fun to watch. Allow the children to feed and care for their "guest." (Naturalist)

❍ Fill the library center with books about the ocean. Encourage the children to find hermit crabs in the illustrations. (Spatial, Intrapersonal)

Learning Activities

Art

(Spatial)
Provide paper, glue in squeeze bottles, and sand in salt shakers. Invite the children to create designs on their papers with the glue, then shake the sand over the glue designs to create sand pictures.

Listening

(Linguistic, Logical-Mathematical, Naturalist)
Discuss the sound a hermit crab might make as it walks on the ocean floor. Provide sandpaper and things to scratch it with, such as toothpicks, craft sticks, plastic forks, and so on. Challenge the children to test each item on the sandpaper and decide which items create a sound similar to the sounds Hermit Crab might make. Invite the children to make slow-walking sounds, fast-walking sounds, and running sounds.

Discovery

(Bodily-Kinesthetic, Naturalist)
Show the children how to rub the porous rocks together over paper plates to make sand. Talk with them as they work. Explain that sand forms as the shells and rocks in the ocean rub against one another.

Math

(Logical-Mathematical, Naturalist)
Provide a variety of shells for the children to explore. Encourage them to sort the shells by color, pattern, size, and shape. Ask whether they can find among the shells one that would make a good home for Hermit Crab. Encourage the children to find a favorite shell.

Dramatic Play

(Linguistic, Bodily-Kinesthetic, Interpersonal)
Provide boxes that the children can pretend to use as shells. Cut arches out of each end of the boxes so that the children can comfortably fit them over their backs. Ask them how it feels to crawl with a box on their backs. *Why do you think Hermit Crab feels safe in his shell? Why does he feel frightened when he is not in his shell?*

Music

(Musical, Intrapersonal)
Play ocean music. Encourage the children to name the sounds that they hear mixed in with the music; for example: ocean waves, birdcalls, splashing, and so on. Ask, *Do you think that Hermit Crab would like this music?*

Let's Keep Reading

Is This a House for Hermit Crab? by Megan McDonald

Thinking About What We Learned

1. Why do hermit crabs need shells?
2. Do you think that Hermit Crab cared what his house looked like on the inside? What was the most important thing to Hermit Crab about his new shell?

Hungry Hen

Author: Richard Waring. Illustrator: Caroline Jayne Church

About the Book

A hungry hen eats and eats and grows and grows. A watchful fox sits waiting on a nearby hill, hoping the hen's insatiable appetite will be a benefit when he eats her for dinner.

Learning Literacy

Oral Language

○ Show the children photos of a fox and a hen. Ask questions: *Which animal is larger? Do you think a hen could ever eat so much that she would be larger than a fox?*

Phonological Awareness

○ Show the children the cover of the book. Read the title, stressing the first letter of *Hungry* and *Hen*. Ask the children if there is a sound that repeats in both words. It is not as important that the children recognize that the sound belongs to the letter /h/ as it is that they hear the repeated sound. Explain to the children that repeated consonant sounds in a sentence or a phrase are examples of *alliteration*.

Comprehension

○ Ask the children the following questions: *Why was the fox waiting to eat the hen? What would have happened if the fox went right down and tried to eat the hen the first day he saw her?*

Letter Knowledge

○ Print *fox* and *hen* on a piece of chart paper. Ask the children to count the letters in each word. *Are any of the letters the same?* Show the children the cover of the book. Ask a volunteer to point out the two words that begin with the same letter. *Which letter is it?*

Special Activities

○ Visit a farm. Encourage the children to feed the chickens. Ask questions: *Are some chickens larger than others? What colors are the hens? Is there a hen here that is larger than a fox?* (Remind the children that a fox is about the size of a large dog.) (Linguistic, Naturalist, Interpersonal)

○ Do the "Chicken Dance." Music is available on *All-Time Favorite Dances* CD by Kimbo Educational, as well as on several other children's dance CDs. (Linguistic, Bodily-Kinesthetic, Musical, Interpersonal)

○ Fill the library with books about hens. Encourage the children to look for red hens in the illustrations. Ask, *Are there any other stories that have a hen and a fox as characters?* (*Hattie and the Fox, Rosie's Walk*) (Linguistic, Spatial, Intrapersonal)

Learning Activities

Art *(Spatial, Bodily-Kinesthetic, Naturalist, Intrapersonal)*
Invite the children to use feathers, paper, and glue to make feather collages. Talk about the feathers as the children work with them. Ask questions: *Are they heavy or light? Are they soft or hard? What happens when you drop them on the floor?*

Construction *(Logical-Mathematical, Spatial, Bodily-Kinesthetic, Interpersonal)*
Cut bulletin board paper into 1' x 3' strips. Invite the children to compare their hands. Provide brown fingerpaint. Show the children how to make an image of a chicken from a handprint (the thumb becomes the head and the finger the tail feathers). Invite the children to make handprint hens on the bulletin board paper, beginning with the smallest hand and working up to your hand.

Discovery *(Logical-Mathematical, Naturalist)*
Cut one hole 2", the second hole 4", and the third hole 8" in the bottom of a cardboard box. Provide a basket of items that will fit in each hole. Invite the children to sort the items by first trying to place them in the smaller hole, then the medium hole, and finally the large hole. Ask, *Which hole would the hen fit into at the beginning of the story? Which hole would she fit into at the end of the story?*

Fine Motor *(Bodily-Kinesthetic)*
Cut a penny-sized hole in the lid of a small box (stationery box size). Draw a chicken's head next to the hole. Provide kernels of corn and a pair of tweezers. Invite the children to feed the hen by using the tweezers to drop corn kernels into the box. **Safety Note:** Be sure children use child-safe tweezers. If child-safe tweezers are not available, encourage the children to use their fingers instead.

Listening *(Linguistic, Musical)*
Record the rhyme, "One, Two, Buckle My Shoe." Provide a drum. Invite the children to beat the drum to the beat of the rhyme.

Math *(Logical-Mathematical, Bodily-Kinesthetic)*
Make counting containers by cutting a 1" hole in the lid of margarine tubs. Print the numerals 1–5 on the tub lids. Provide kernels of corn and child-safe tweezers. Invite the children to use the tweezers to pick up kernels of corn and dropping them into the counting containers, putting the correct number of kernels in each container.

Let's Keep Reading

A Big Fat Hen by Keith Baker
Bob by Tracey Campbell Pearson
Fat Cat by Margaret Read MacDonald
Hattie and the Fox by Mem Fox
Rosie's Walk by Pat Hutchins

Thinking About What We Learned

1. Why do you think the hen was so hungry?
2. Do you think a hen can really eat a fox? How large is a fox?

Hurray for Pre-K

Author and Illustrator: Ellen B. Senisi

About the Book
Bright, colorful, multicultural photos show what to expect in a pre-k classroom. This is a great book for the first day of school and for family orientations.

Learning Literacy

Oral Language

❍ Write *school* in the center of a sheet of chart paper. Draw a circle around the word. Ask the children to talk about what they know about school. Write the information they provide on lines that extend from the circle.

Comprehension

❍ Ask the children the following questions: *What do the children in* Hurray for Pre-K *do at school? Does the classroom in the book look like our classroom? How?*

Print Awareness

❍ Encourage the children to read the words at the bottom of each page along with you. Point to the words as the children read them.

Special Activities

❍ Take a tour of the school. Ask people you meet on the tour about things they do at the school. (Linguistic, Spatial, Naturalist, Interpersonal)
❍ Sing songs about friends, such as "Good Morning to You." (See page 94 in *Hello, Hello.*) (Linguistic, Musical, Interpersonal)
❍ Ask the school principal to come to the classroom and read a story during story time. (Linguistic)
❍ Fill the library with books about school. (Linguistic, Intrapersonal)

❍ Use the tune to "Oh, Do You Know the Muffin Man" to create lyrics about the people who work at the school. (*Do you know the principal? Do you know the school nurse? Do you know the custodian?*). (Linguistic, Naturalist, Interpersonal)
❍ Encourage the children to draw a picture of something they like about school. (Linguistic, Spatial, Intrapersonal)
❍ Invite the school nurse to weigh and measure the children. Ask him or her to talk with the children about her job at school. (Logical-Mathematical, Bodily-Kinesthetic, Interpersonal)
❍ Suggest that the children help create a list of classroom rules. Write the rules on a large sheet of bulletin board paper, and encourage the children to illustrate each rule. Place the list of rules in a visible spot in the classroom. (Linguistic, Spatial, Interpersonal)

Learning Activities

Art

(Spatial, Intrapersonal)
Encourage the children to use tempera paint and easel paper to paint a picture of something they like about school, or show the children the flowers in the front of *Hurray for Pre-K* and suggest they paint their own colorful flowers.

Listening

(Linguistic, Intrapersonal)
Record a reading of *Hurray for Pre-K*, and place it and a copy of the book in the listening center.

Blocks

(Logical-Mathematical, Spatial)
Invite the children to build with the blocks.

Music

(Bodily-Kinesthetic, Musical, Interpersonal)
Put on some music, provide white fingerpaint, and encourage the children to fingerpaint directly on the tabletop.

Dramatic Play

(Linguistic, Interpersonal)
Provide puppets and encourage the children to create a puppet show.

Snack

(Interpersonal)
Provide pretzels and juice for snack. Suggest that the children eat their snack with a friend.

Let's Keep Reading

First Day, Hooray by Nancy Poydar
First Day Jitters by Julie Danneberg

Thinking About What We Learned

1. What did you like best about school today?
2. How is our classroom like the classroom in *Hurray for Pre-K*?

If You Give a Mouse a Cookie

Author: Laura Joffe Numeroff. Illustrator: Felicia Bond

About the Book
Giving a mouse a cookie turns into a humorous circular story of cause-and-effect relationships.

Learning Literacy

Oral Language

❍ Talk with the children about cause-and-effect relationships. Demonstrate cause-and-effect relationships with such items as a jack-in-the box, a flashlight, and a music box. Encourage the children to think of things that have a cause-and-effect relationship; for example, turning on the water or light, turning a door knob, and so on.

❍ Give the children a story starter that will enable them to write their own cause-and-effect story. For example, *If you give a child a crayon…*

Comprehension

❍ Ask the children the following questions: *How would the story be different if the little boy gave the mouse a piece of cheese instead of a cookie? What kind of cookie did the little boy give the mouse? How do you know?*

❍ Look through the book page by page. Ask the children questions such as, *Can you tell what the characters are feeling on each page? Which character is most expressive?*

Special Activities

❍ Find a simple recipe and make chocolate chip cookies with the children. Create a rebus recipe so the children can see the steps in baking the cookies. (Linguistic, Logical-Mathematical, Spatial, Interpersonal, Intrapersonal)

❍ Play Who Took the Cookies From the Cookie Jar? with the children. (Linguistic, Bodily-Kinesthetic, Interpersonal)

Who Took the Cookies From the Cookie Jar?

Who took the cookies from the cookie jar?
(child's name) took the cookies from the cookie jar.
Who me?
Yes, you.
Not me.
Then who?
(next child's name) took the cookies from the cookie jar.
(continue until all children have had a turn)

Learning Activities

Art *(Spatial, Intrapersonal)*
Invite the children to use paper, crayons, markers, or paints to draw pictures they can take home and place on their refrigerators, just as the mouse in the story did. Be sure to provide pens so the children can sign their names.

Fine Motor *(Linguistic, Bodily-Kinesthetic, Interpersonal)*
Encourage the children to use playdough and cookie cutters to make cookies. Ask the children questions as they work. *What kind of cookie are you making? How do you make that kind of cookie?*

Discovery *(Logical-Mathematical, Naturalist, Interpersonal, Interpersonal)*
Provide several cause-and-effect items, such as a music box, rhythm band instruments, portable radio, and a flashlight for children to explore. Challenge the children to organize the items by *cause*. Categories can include things that must be shaken, turned, pushed, pulled, and so on.

Listening *(Logical-Mathematical, Musical, Intrapersonal)*
Provide musical cause-and-effect items, such as music boxes, stuffed animals that sing, a jack-in-the-box, and so on. Invite the children to explore the musical toys. Create a graph that shows each item. Ask the children to choose the toys they like best. Chart the results. After all the children vote, ask them which toy was the most popular.

Dramatic Play *(Linguistic, Bodily-Kinesthetic, Interpersonal)*
Provide story retelling props such as a play cookie, milk glass (non-breakable), napkin, mirror, and so on. Encourage the children to re-enact the story.

Math *(Logical-Mathematical)*
Cut large cookie shapes (4" diameter) from brown felt or construction paper. Provide either penny-sized circles of darker brown felt or construction paper to represent chips. Write the numerals 1–5 on index cards. Place a numeral card by each cookie and instruct children to place that number of chips on the cookie.

Let's Keep Reading

If You Give a Moose a Muffin by Laura Joffe Numeroff
If You Give a Pig a Pancake by Laura Joffe Numeroff

Thinking About What We Learned

1. Why did the mouse need a glass of milk at the end of the story?
2. How are chocolate chip cookies different from sugar cookies?

Imogene's Antlers

Author and Illustrator: David Small

About the Book
Imogene wakes up with antlers on her head. Her mom and dad, the doctor, the principal, and everyone else she meets can't figure out what caused the antlers to grow. Imogene spends the day learning to live with her new antlers. When she wakes up the following day, the antlers are gone, but something new has appeared.

Learning Literacy

Oral Language
❍ Discuss the new vocabulary in the story, such as *encyclopedia, rare, miniature, elk, decked,* and *milliner.*
❍ Explain to the children the meaning of the non-English words used in the story: *voilà, bravo,* and *bravissimo.*

Oral Language/Print Awareness
❍ Encourage the children to think about what will happen to Imogene after the book ends. Ask the children questions, such as, *How do you think Imogene will like her peacock tail? What problems might she encounter?* Challenge the children to help write a "what happens next" story.

Comprehension
❍ Ask the children the following questions: *Which days of the week are mentioned in the story? Could this story really happen or is it make-believe? Would you like to wake up with antlers? Why? Why not?*

Special Activities

❍ Visit the zoo. Encourage the children to look for animals with antlers, and be sure to visit the peacocks. Tell the children to watch for other animal body parts that Imogene might acquire, such as a monkey's tail or elephant's trunk. After returning to the classroom, encourage the children to write a story about Imogene acquiring some of these new animal body parts. (Linguistic, Bodily-Kinesthetic, Naturalist, Interpersonal, Intrapersonal)
❍ Show the children how to strut like a peacock. Play some strutting music like "Let Me Entertain You" (from *Gypsy* by Stephen Sondheim) and encourage the children to strut. (Bodily-Kinesthetic, Musical, Intrapersonal)
❍ Provide a large sun hat. Let the children take turns putting it on their heads, and then trying to hug friends without knocking it off. (Logical-Mathematical, Spatial, Bodily-Kinesthetic)

Learning Activities

Art *(Spatial, Interpersonal)*
Set out crayons, paper, yarn, lace, ribbon, glue, and a tree branch that resembles antlers. Invite the children to decorate the antlers with pictures, bows, and so on.

Listening *(Linguistic, Musical)*
Record the story on cassette tape, leaving spaces, where appropriate, for sound effects. Place the tape and the book in the center, and encourage the children to listen to the story and add their own sound effects. For example, they might add sound effects to the scene where mother faints, or the sounds of birds chirping when they are eating the donuts.

Cooking *(Linguistic, Logical-Mathematical)*
Make donuts. Give each child a refrigerator biscuit. Show them how to punch a hole in its middle using a soda bottle lid. Drop the donuts into a fryer for six minutes—three minutes on each side (adults only). (**Safety Note:** Keep the children a safe distance from the fryer.) Drain the donuts and let the children shake a little powdered sugar over them. Hang the donuts on a tree branch that looks like antlers to let them cool.

Math *(Logical-Mathematical, Intrapersonal)*
Provide a large tree branch to represent a pair of antlers, crayons, and paper. Encourage the children to look at the "antlers" closely and draw hats that might cover them.

Gross Motor *(Spatial, Bodily-Kinesthetic, Intrapersonal)*
Build a maze by stacking boxes to create the walls of the maze. Provide a wide-brimmed sun hat. Encourage the children to place the hat on their heads and crawl through the maze. Ask questions: *Can you make it through the maze without knocking over any boxes? Do you think this is how Imogene felt with the antlers on her head?*

Science *(Naturalist)*
Provide photos of deer, elk, moose, and peacocks. If you have access to a real pair of antlers or real peacock feathers, place them in the center. Encourage the children to examine the photos. Ask, *Do any of the antlers look like Imogene's?*

Let's Keep Reading

I Wish That I Had Duck Feet by Dr. Seuss
Wacky Wednesday by Dr. Seuss

Thinking About What We Learned

1. What did you find out today about having a pair of antlers?
2. What might be good about having antlers on your head?

In the Tall, Tall Grass

Author and Illustrator: Denise Fleming

About the Book

The insects, bugs, animals, reptiles, and birds are busy in the tall, tall grass. The caterpillars munch, the bees hum, and the ants tug. The rhyming text of this simple story is filled with wonderfully onomatopoeic and descriptive vocabulary.

Learning Literacy

Phonological Awareness

❍ Invite the children to find the rhyming words on each page of the book.

❍ Identify for the children the *onomatopoeic* words that appear in the story, such as *crunch*, *munch*, *hum*, and *flap*.

Comprehension

❍ Show the children the cover of the book. Ask the children what insects they have seen in the grass before. *What would you do in the tall, tall grass?*

Special Activities

❍ Take the children outdoors. Have them select a partner. Give each pair of children a 24" piece of yarn and two magnifying glasses. Show them how to lay the yarn on the ground in a circle. Encourage them to look inside the circle for bugs. (Naturalist, Interpersonal)

❍ Make a start line and a finish line using strips of masking tape or pieces of yarn. Split the children into pairs. Ask each of them to imitate the style of movement of their favorite animals or bugs from *In the Tall, Tall Grass* as they race their partners to the finish line. (Logical-Mathematical, Bodily-Kinesthetic, Interpersonal, Intrapersonal)

❍ With the children, write a song about life in the tall, tall grass. Use the tune to "Wheels on the Bus." Below is a start. (Linguistic, Musical, Interpersonal)

The Ants in the Grass
by Pam Schiller

The ants in the grass go pull, tug, lug.
Pull, tug, lug! Pull, tug, lug!
The ants in the grass go pull, tug, lug,
All through the day.

Additional verses:
The birds overhead go dart, dip, sip…
The bees in the grass go strum, drum, hum…

Learning Activities

Art *(Spatial)*
Encourage the children to use green tempera paint, brushes, and easel paper to paint images of the tall, tall grass. The illustrations in the book itself are simple, and some children may like looking at them while they paint.

Language *(Linguistic, Musical, Naturalist)*
Provide band instruments, kitchen utensils, paper, plastic bottles, and other objects the children might be able to use to create some of the sounds described in the book. Ask questions about the sounds: *What makes a crunching sound? Drumming sound? Humming sound? Flap? Snap?*

Discovery *(Logical-Mathematical, Naturalist)*
Provide photographs of insects and animals. Encourage the children to count the legs on each animal and bug. Ask, *Which creature has the most legs?* If you don't have photos, use the illustrations in the book.

Listening *(Linguistic, Musical)*
Record the story on cassette tape and place it in the center along with a copy of the book. Encourage the children to identify the onomatopoeic words as they listen to the story.

Gross Motor *(Bodily-Kinesthetic, Interpersonal, Intrapersonal)*
Challenge the children to slither like a snake, glide like a bird, scratch like a mole, tug like an ant, hop like a rabbit, and dart like a bat. Comment on the children's movements as they create them. Ask the children, *Do all the creatures move in the same way?*

Sand Table *(Naturalist, Interpersonal)*
Hide plastic bugs in the sand table and encourage the children to use a strainer to find the hidden bugs. Talk with them about the bugs: *What is that bug called? What sound does it make?*

Let's Keep Reading
In the Small, Small Pond by Denise Fleming

Thinking About What We Learned
1. Which animal in the grass makes the most noise? Which animal makes the least noise?
2. What did you find in the grass?

It Looked Like Spilt Milk

Author and Illustrator: Charles Shaw

About the Book
The white shape silhouetted against a blue background changes on every page. Is it a rabbit, a bird, or just spilt milk?

Learning Literacy

Book Knowledge and Appreciation
❍ Read the book again and have the children join in on the predictable phrases. Try letting the children play a xylophone or tambourine in time with the meter of the verse.

Comprehension
❍ Ask the children the following questions: *Did you know it was a cloud before we got to the end of the book? Have you ever spilled milk? Did the milk make an interesting shape on floor or the table?*

Special Activities

❍ Take the children outdoors on a nice day and encourage them to lie in the grass and watch the clouds roll by. Ask, *Can you find any shapes in the clouds?* (Linguistic, Spatial, Naturalist)

❍ Make a class book. Invite the children to tear paper into shapes and then paste them on blue construction paper. Gather the papers and place them in a baggie book or staple them together to create a book (see directions on page 38). Encourage each child to dictate a sentence that describes or highlights the page of the book that he made. (Linguistic, Spatial, Interpersonal, Intrapersonal)

❍ Play classical music and invite the children to dance like clouds in the sky. (Bodily-Kinesthetic, Musical, Intrapersonal)

Learning Activities

Art *(Linguistic, Spatial, Bodily-Kinesthetic, Intrapersonal)*
Provide blue construction paper and white paint. Encourage the children to explore the paint on the blue surface. Ask the children to describe their creations. Some children will paint a design or shape. Others will try to paint an actual picture.

Discovery *(Spatial, Bodily-Kinesthetic, Interpersonal, Intrapersonal)*
Provide an overhead projector and scrap paper. Show the children how to tear the paper into a shape. Invite them to place their torn paper shapes on the projector and look at the silhouettes on the wall. *What does it look like?*

Fine Motor *(Spatial, Bodily-Kinesthetic, Interpersonal, Intrapersonal)*
Cover the top of a table with a black or blue vinyl tablecloth. Spray non-menthol shaving cream on top of the tablecloth. Let the children make designs. **Safety Note:** Minimize the amount of time children spend handling shaving cream, and caution them to keep the shaving cream out of their mouths and eyes.

Language *(Linguistic, Spatial)*
Give the children a folded piece of construction paper. Help them place a blob of tempera paint on half of the paper, then close the paper and rub the blob around inside the folded paper. Then, encourage them to open the paper and describe the designs. As they dictate descriptions of their designs to you, write them on the backs of their artwork.

Math *(Logical-Mathematical, Bodily-Kinesthetic)*
Fold several sheets of paper in half. Coming out from the fold, draw dotted lines that show half of an image, such as a heart, a triangle, a circle, and so on. Challenge the children to cut along the dotted lines and then open and describe the shapes. Provide folded paper without dotted lines and encourage the children to cut freeform shapes.

Snack *(Linguistic, Spatial, Interpersonal)*
Give each child a slice of bread. Invite the children to take bites around the edges of the bread and then look at the resulting shapes. Encourage the children to describe their shapes. Suggest that they take more bites and then look at the bread again. Ask, *What does it look like now?*

Let's Keep Reading

The Cloud Book by Tomie dePaola
Clouds by Marion Dane Bauer

Thinking About What We Learned

1. What shapes did you create today?
2. Which shape in the story did you like best?

The Itsy Bitsy Spider

Author and Illustrator: Iza Trapani

About the Book
The Itsy Bitsy Spider struggles with more than the rain and a waterspout, but she does finally get her day in the sun.

Learning Literacy

Oral Language
❍ Discuss *persistence*. Point out how persistent and determined the spider is each time she meets an obstacle or challenge. Encourage the children to talk about things that they have been persistent about, such as learning to blow a bubble, walk, catch a ball, tie shoelaces, and so on.

❍ Sing "The Itsy Bitsy Spider" using a small voice. Sing it again, changing the words *itsy bitsy* to *super enormous*. Encourage the children to change their voices to match the new adjectives. Challenge them to come up with other new adjectives.

Phonological Awareness
❍ Make a list of the rhyming words in the story, such as *waterspout/out, blow/go, pail/tail, tree/me, stop/hop,* and *spun/sun.*

Comprehension
❍ Ask the children the following questions: *What are some of the things that happened that stopped the spider from getting where she wanted? What did the Itsy Bitsy Spider do when she finished spinning her web? Would the story be different if the Itsy Bitsy Spider was a Big Gigantic Spider?*

Special Activities

❍ Sing "Itsy Bitsy Spider," using the new verses introduced in the book. Create hand or body motions for the new verses. (Linguistic, Bodily-Kinesthetic, Musical)

❍ Show the children how to bend at the waist and touch the floor with their hands, and invite them to pretend they have four legs. Play music and encourage the children to dance like spiders. (Bodily-Kinesthetic, Musical, Interpersonal)

❍ Create a spider web maze. Encourage the children to navigate the maze while walking on all fours like spiders. (Spatial, Bodily-Kinesthetic)

❍ Fill the library with books about spiders and other bugs. Make certain that some of the books are nonfiction and that there are at least a few reference books. Encourage the children to attempt to use the reference books to identify the kind of spider Itsy Bitsy might be. (Logical-Mathematical, Naturalist, Intrapersonal)

Learning Activities

Art

(Linguistic, Spatial, Intrapersonal)
Encourage the children to draw pictures of things that are challenging for them to do. Invite them to describe their pictures. With the children's permission, write their stories on the backs of their artwork.

Language

(Linguistic, Interpersonal)
Provide a basket of several objects made up of rhyming pairs, such as socks and rocks, a shoe and a plastic number two, a plate and a plastic number eight, and so on. Encourage the children to match the rhyming pairs.

Discovery

(Logical-Mathematical, Interpersonal)
Make spider toys by twisting black pipe cleaners together. To make the spiders small, cut the pipe cleaners into 2" lengths before twisting them. Place the spiders on a table and encourage the children to attempt to blow them off the table. Provide straws and empty toilet paper tubes for the children to use to direct the air.

Listening

(Linguistic, Musical)
Sing and record the words to *The Itsy Bitsy Spider* as they appear in the book. Place the book and the tape in the center for listening.

Fine Motor

(Bodily-Kinesthetic)
Draw a waterspout on the inside of a small box (stationery size). Glue a strip of magnetic tape on the underside of a plastic spider or one of the pipe cleaner spiders. Place the spider at the base of the waterspout drawing and encourage the children to hold a magnet under the box and use it to move the spider up the spout.

Science

(Logical-Mathematical, Naturalist)
Provide photos of spiders and a magnifying glass. Encourage the children to look at the details in the photos. Ask questions: *How many legs do the spiders have? How many body parts? What are the spiders doing?*

Let's Keep Reading

The Little Engine That Could by Watty Piper

Thinking About What We Learned

1. How do you know that the Itsy Bitsy Spider is persistent?
2. Which activity was your favorite today? Why?

Jump, Frog, Jump

Author: Robert Kalan. Illustrator: Byron Barton

About the Book

A frog chasing a fly sets off a humorous chain of events. This is perfect story to have children read along to by chiming in.

Learning Literacy

Phonological Awareness

❍ Talk with the children about the sounds that the frog in the book makes. Explain that these sounds are *onomatopoeic* words—words that imitate the sounds they are describing. Sing "Hear the Lively Song."

Hear the Lively Song

Hear the lively song
Of the frogs in yonder pond:
Crick, crick, crickety-crick,
Burr-ump!

Comprehension

❍ Ask the children the following questions: *Would the story have been different if the frog had left the fly alone? Do you think the frog was tired at the end of the story? Why?*

Letter Knowledge/Print Awareness

❍ Print *Jump, Frog, Jump* on a piece of chart paper. Ask a volunteer to find the two words that look alike. Talk about the letters in each word. Point out the sound of the first letter in the word *jump*. Encourage the children to say *jump*, emphasizing the initial sound. Ask, *Do any of the letters in* jump *show up in* frog? Clap the syllables in *jump, frog, jump*. Print *hop, frog, hop* (use lowercase letters) on the chart paper. Ask the children questions, such as, *Which words are alike? What does the first letter of the word* hop

sound like? Say the phrase again, emphasizing the sound of the /h/. Ask the children, *Do any of the letters in* hop *show up in* frog? *Which letter?* Clap the syllables of *hop, frog, hop* with the children.

Special Activities

❍ Play Leap Frog. Select one child to be the "frog." Ask the other children to stand in a line and crouch down on their hands and knees. Invite the frog to leap over the children by placing her hands on each child's back and "hopping" over. After the frog jumps over the first child, that child stands up and follows the frog, and so on. When the frog leaps over the last child, the frog crouches down on her hands and knees, continuing the line. (Bodily-Kinesthetic, Interpersonal)

❍ Visit a pond or another watery spot where frogs might live. Ask the children questions: *Can you find a frog? Why do you think frogs like water and ponds? What things around the pond would be interesting to the frog?* (Linguistic, Naturalist, Intrapersonal)

Learning Activities

Dramatic Play

(Interpersonal, Intrapersonal)
Provide a large laundry basket or box, and encourage the children to take turns pretending to be the frog hiding under the basket. Ask questions: *How do you think the frog felt under the basket? Do you think he was frightened? Is it dark under the basket? Is it crowded?*

Games

(Logical-Mathematical, Bodily-Kinesthetic, Interpersonal)
Play Catch the Fly. Twist black pipe cleaners into small balls that resemble flies (or use small plastic flies). Give each child a paper cup and one fly. Show the children how to toss their flies in the air and then catch them in their cups. When the children are ready, help them find partners. Give the pairs one fly and two cups, and encourage them to toss the fly to each other.

Gross Motor

(Logical-Mathematical, Bodily-Kinesthetic, Interpersonal)
Teach the children how to play Frog Jumps. Make a start line by placing a strip of masking tape on the floor. Invite the children to squat beside the start line and jump as far as they can. Mark the distances of their jumps by placing beanbags where they land. Measure the length of each jump using a piece of yarn.

Math

(Logical-Mathematical, Spatial, Bodily-Kinesthetic, Interpersonal)
Cut empty toilet paper tubes into 1" and 2" segments. Paint (or cover with construction paper) the 1" segments gold, the 2" segments red, and full-length tubes green. Pinch together the end of one of the green tubes to make a "snake head." Glue eyes on the snake head. Challenge the children to use the colored segments of tubing to make a snake that looks like the one in the book.

Music

(Musical, Interpersonal, Intrapersonal)
Provide a tape recorder. Encourage the children to record frog sounds and then play them back to themselves. Ask, *Can you identify who made these sounds?*

Writing

(Linguistic)
Print *Jump, Frog, Jump* on a piece of chart paper. Encourage the children to copy the book title using magnetic letters.

Let's Keep Reading

Hop Jump by Ellen Stoll Walsh
In the Tall, Tall Grass by Denise Fleming
Tuesday by David Wiesner

Thinking About What We Learned

1. Have you ever tried to catch a frog? What happened?
2. What was it like under the basket?

Koala Lou

Author: Mem Fox. Illustrator: Pamela Lofts

About the Book
Koala Lou is loved by everyone, but it is her mother who loves her most of all. She often tells her daughter, "Koala Lou, I DO love you." As the family grows and her mother gets busier, Koala Lou yearns to hear those words again. She sets out to win the Bush Olympics as a way to gain her mother's attention. This is a sweet story about the important love between mother and child.

Learning Literacy

Oral Language
- Discuss the words in the story that may be new for the children, such as *bush*, *emu*, and *platypus*.
- Teach the children how to say *I love you* in American Sign Language (see appendix page 236).

Comprehension
- Ask the children the following questions: *Why does Koala Lou want to win the Bush Olympics? Why did Koala Lou hide when the Olympics were over? Have you ever felt left out like Koala Lou did?*

Letter Knowledge
- Print *Koala Lou* on a sheet of chart paper. Encourage the children to identify the letters in Koala Lou's name. Ask the children to point out the letters that show up in *Koala Lou* more than once.

Special Activities
- Host an Olympic Games. Set up broad jumps, races, and ball tosses. (Logical-Mathematical, Bodily-Kinesthetic, Interpersonal)
- Sing "Kookaburra." This song is about another Australian animal that also likes gum trees. Encourage the children to look at the illustration in *Koala Lou* to find the kookaburra. (Linguistic, Musical, Naturalist, Interpersonal)
- Fill the library with books written by Mem Fox, such as *Wombat Devine*, *Night Noises*, *Wilfrid Gordon McDonald Partridge*, and with books by other Australian writers. Encourage the children to identify similarities in the books' illustrations. (Spatial, Intrapersonal)

Learning Activities

Art
(Spatial)
Explain to the children that the illustrations in *Koala Lou* were made with colored pencils. Encourage the children to use paper and colored pencils to draw their own illustrations.

Math
(Linguistic, Logical-Mathematical, Naturalist)
Provide items that can be sorted into categories such as *soft and round*, or *hard and round*. For example cotton balls, pompoms, tennis balls, blocks, beads, pennies, and so on. Encourage the children to test each item to determine which items are soft and round.
Safety Note: Supervise this activity closely.

Construction
(Spatial, Bodily-Kinesthetic, Intrapersonal, Interpersonal)
Challenge the children to use feathers, paper plates, ribbons, rickrack, lace, netting, and paper and silk flowers to make hats like those worn by Koala Lou's friends. Give each child a paper plate with the center removed to use as a base for their creations, or provide old hats to use as the foundations.

Science
(Naturalist)
Place photos of Australian animals in the science center. Encourage the children to name the animals they see in the photos. Ask the children if they see any of the animals that are in *Koala Lou.*

Gross Motor
(Bodily-Kinesthetic, Musical, Interpersonal)
Prepare props for a workout area, including light weights, music, and mats. Show the children how to do push-ups and toe touches. Remind them of all the things Koala Lou does to prepare for the Olympics.

Writing
(Linguistic)
Print *I* _____ *U* on a sheet of chart paper. Encourage the children to copy it using pencils and pens, then add a heart to the center of the text.

Let's Keep Reading

Guess How Much I Love You by Sam McBratney
Mama, Do You Love Me? by Barbara Joosse

Thinking About What We Learned

1. What were your favorite activities today?
2. Why did Koala Lou's friends toss their hats into the air?

Listen to the Rain

Authors: Bill Martin, Jr. and John Archambault
Illustrator: James Endicott

About the Book
This is a lyrical story about the rain. The authors use rhythmical and onomatopoeic language to describe the sound of rain, from its slow, soft, sprinkly beginning, into its dynamic crashing crescendo, and to its slow, slow stopping. This is a great book to use to teach children about weather, onomatopoeia, and/or sounds.

Learning Literacy

Oral Language
○ Encourage the children to describe rainstorms they have experienced. Ask the children questions, such as, *Which sounds do you remember? Was it a hard rain or a soft rain? What is the difference between a hard and soft rain?*

Phonological Awareness/Print Awareness
○ Make a list of all the *onomatopoeic* words (words that imitate the sounds they are describing) in the story. Challenge the children to use new onomatopoeic words to describe the rain.

Comprehension
○ Ask the children the following questions: *How were the sounds at the beginning of the rainstorm different from those in the middle of the story? Which of the rain sounds did you like the best? Why? What is the difference between a thunderstorm and a rainstorm? How do you feel on a rainy day?*

Special Activities

○ Encourage the children to catch raindrops in cups. Show the children how to measure the amount of rain they catch by putting craft sticks in the cups and marking the height of the water with markers. (Bodily-Kinesthetic, Logical-Mathematical)
○ Show the children how to make mud pies. (Spatial, Interpersonal)
○ Invite the children to jump over and in rain puddles, or jump over a drawing of a rain puddle. (Bodily-Kinesthetic)

Learning Activities

Art

(Spatial, Intrapersonal)
Invite the children to draw pictures of things they can do on a rainy day. Encourage them to describe their drawings. With their permission, write their ideas on the backs of their drawings.

Listening

(Linguistic, Naturalist)
Make a recording of yourself reading the book in two different voices. Make one recording with an almost monotone voice. Make the second recording in a dynamic voice that emphasizes the changes in the text. Encourage the children to listen to both recordings and then vote for the type of reading they enjoyed the most.

Gross Motor

(Bodily Kinesthetic, Intrapersonal)
Challenge the children to dance like raindrops to a variety classical music. Ask the children, *How does the dance change as the rain moves from a light sprinkle to a driving rain?*

Math

(Logical-Mathematical)
Cut five large clouds (4" x 6" or larger) from white construction paper. Number the clouds 1–5. Cut 15 raindrops from light blue construction paper. Make each drop about the size of a quarter. Encourage the children to place the number of raindrops on each cloud that corresponds with the numeral printed on the cloud.

Language

(Linguistic, Musical)
Ask the children to think of as many different ways as they can to describe the rain. Copy their ideas onto chart paper, and invite the children to choose their favorite descriptive word and make an illustration of it.

Music

(Musical, Interpersonal)
Invite the children to use spray bottles of water and a cookie sheet to imitate the sound of rain as it would hit the tin roof of a house. Challenge them to use the varied levels of spray intensity of the bottles to create "rain music." For example, one child might spray two quick sprays on high intensity, one soft spray, and a third four soft sprays.

Let's Keep Reading

Cloudy With a Chance of Meatballs by Judi Barrett
Rain by Robert Kalan

Thinking About What We Learned

1. Do you like rainy days? Why? Why not?
2. Which of the rainy day sounds do you like best? Why?

The Little Engine That Could

Author: Watty Piper. Illustrator: George and Doris Hauman

About the Book
When a little red engine runs out of steam, it is rescued by a little blue engine that uses the power of positive thought to pull the first engine over a mountain.

Learning Literacy

Oral Language
○ Talk about the meaning of words in the story that may be new to the children, such as *rumbled, jolly, jerk, passenger train, dingy, rusty,* and *chugging.*
○ Talk with the children about the power of believing in yourself.

Comprehension
○ Ask the children the following questions: *Why did the little red train stop? What sounds does the train make when it rolls down the track? Which thing on the train do you like best? Have you ever seen a real train? Have you ever ridden on a train?*

Letter Knowledge/Print Awareness
○ Print *I think I can* on a piece of chart paper. Print *I thought I could* just below the first phrase. Ask the children to look at both phrases. Ask, *How are they alike? How are they different? Which letters are the same? Which letters are different?*

Special Activities

○ Visit a train station. Invite the children to talk about the different types of train cars. Ask questions: *What colors are the cars? What do the words on the cars say?* Encourage the children to count the number of train cars they see. (Linguistic, Logical-Mathematical, Naturalist, Interpersonal)
○ Invite the children to do the following action rhyme. Point out the patterns in the rhyme and rhythm. Talk with the children about the experience of riding in a train. *How do you think it feels? Does the train sway? Can you feel it when it is moving fast?* (Linguistic, Bodily-Kinesthetic, Musical, Interpersonal, Intrapersonal)

Clickey, Clickety, Clack
Clickety, clickety, clack,
Clickety, clickety, clack,
Clickety, clickety, clickety, clickety,
Clickety, clickety clack.

(Make a train with the children by inviting a few of them to walk around the room holding each other's hips while reciting the poem. Add more children to the train at the end of each verse.)

Learning Activities

Construction

(Logical-Mathematical, Spatial, Bodily-Kinesthetic, Interpersonal)
Encourage the children to create a train out of several large boxes. Make sure the boxes are large enough to hold one child. Large laundry baskets also work. Provide an engineer's hat, tickets, and other props to enhance play. If you can't obtain boxes large enough to hold the children, provide stuffed animals and dolls to be the passengers. **Safety Note:** Make sure that only one child sits in each box.

Discovery

(Logical-Mathematical, Bodily-Kinesthetic, Naturalist)
Make an inclined plank. Give the children items to roll down the plank. Provide some rolling toys, such as cars and trucks and even trains, if available. Encourage the children to roll the vehicles up and down the plank. Ask, *Which way is easier—up or down?*

Dramatic Play

(Linguistic, Interpersonal)
Provide costumes that will encourage the children to dress like some of the passengers on the train, such as clowns, dolls, soldiers, and so on.

Language

(Linguistic, Spatial, Interpersonal)
Cut a train engine and 26 train cars from construction paper, and write one letter of the alphabet on each car. Challenge the children to arrange the trains by placing the letters in alphabetical order. Ask questions: *Which letter is on the first car? Which letter is on the last car?*

Listening

(Logical-Mathematical, Naturalist, Musical, Intrapersonal)
Record four tracks of chugging train sounds on a cassette. Vary the chugging sounds from fast to slow and place them in random order on the tape. Give the children four index cards with numerals 1–4 printed on them. Challenge the children to listen to the tape and assign numbers to the train sounds according to their speed—1 being slowest and 4 being fastest.

Writing

(Linguistic, Spatial)
Print *I can* on a piece of chart paper. Encourage the children to use magnetic letters or felt letters to copy the phrase.

Let's Keep Reading

Freight Train by Donald Crews
The Itsy Bitsy Spider by Iza Trapani

Thinking About What We Learned

1. Have you ever tried to do something that was difficult for you to do? What was it? Did you keep reminding yourself that you could?
2. Would you rather fly in an airplane or travel in a train? Why?

The Little Red Hen

Author and Illustrator: Paul Galdone

About the Book
This is the classic tale of an industrious hen and her lazy friends, a cat, a dog, and a mouse. The hen asks each friend for help while she is growing wheat and converting it into a cake, but the three lazy friends refuse to help. Will she share her cake when she is finished working?

Learning Literacy

Book Knowledge and Appreciation
○ Write, *Who will help me?* and *Not I!* on chart paper. Talk with the children about these phrases as predictable lines in the story. Brainstorm a list of responses that the animals could have made to the hen's question, such as *I'm busy, I don't want to, I can't help you now,* or *Maybe later.*

Comprehension
○ Ask the children the following questions: *Which friends did the hen ask for help? How would the story be different if the animals had helped when they were asked? Do you think it is okay that the little red hen didn't share her bread with the animals that didn't help?*
○ Encourage the children to re-enact the story. Select children to be the hen, the dog, the cat, and the mouse. Provide simple costumes. The little red hen can wear an apron and a red bandana. The dog, cat, and mouse can wear felt ears glued to headbands. Read the story, prompting children to fill in the dialogue for the hen and her friends.
○ Invite the children to help you create a story pyramid (see appendix page 229). Enlarge the pattern or copy it onto chart paper and encourage the children help fill in the chart.

Special Activities

○ Take a field trip to bakery. Encourage the children to pay attention to the steps required to turn flour or wheat into bread. Suggest that the children be "Sense Detectives." Encourage them to pay special attention to sensory experiences, such as how the bread smells when it is cooking, what the bread tastes like, what the dough feels like, what they see as they watch the process of making bread, and what sounds are heard during the baking process. (Logical-Mathematical, Bodily-Kinesthetic, Naturalist)

Suggested Versions
The Little Red Hen by Paul Galdone
The Little Red Hen by J. P. Miller
The Little Red Hen by Carol Ottolenghi

Learning Activities

Art

(Spatial, Intrapersonal)
Encourage the children to use tempera paints, brushes, and paper to paint their favorite characters from the story.

Discovery

(Logical-Mathematical, Naturalist)
Provide barley, wheat grain, and oats in separate plastic bags for the children to observe. Help the children correctly identify each item. Talk about their textures, colors, and sizes. Explain to the children how these ingredients become foods.

Blocks

(Spatial, Interpersonal)
Provide various farm props and "terrain" (a section of an old sheet sprayed with earth-tone colors, such as brown, green, gray, and gold). Encourage the children to build a farm on the terrain.

Music

(Bodily-Kinesthetic, Interpersonal)
Show the children how to do the Chicken Dance. Provide the music and let them dance away. Challenge the children to make up new dances to celebrate the other characters in the story; for example, a Dog Jog, Cat Scat, or Mouse Rouse.

Cooking

(Linguistic, Logical-Mathematical, Interpersonal)
Invite the children to make bread using the banana quick bread recipe on appendix page 233. Create a rebus recipe so that the children can follow the steps.

Writing

(Linguistic, Spatial)
Write *hen, dog, mouse,* and *cat* on index cards. Draw a picture of each animal on the cards. Provide tracing paper and crayons. Encourage the children to use crayons to trace over the letters on each card: *hen* in red, *dog* in brown, *mouse* in gray, and *cat* in black. Invite the children to illustrate each word they copy.

Let's Keep Reading

The Little Red Hen Makes a Pizza by Philemon Sturges
With Love, Little Red Hen by Leslie Tyron

Thinking About What We Learned

1. Has anyone asked you to help to do something that you didn't want to do? What was it? What happened?

Make Way for Ducklings

Author and Illustrator: Robert McCloskey

About the Book

Mr. and Mrs. Mallard search for a place to raise their family. They select a cozy spot in the bushes along the Charles River in Boston. Mrs. Mallard hatches eight ducklings and begins teaching them survival skills.

Learning Literacy

Oral Language/Print Awareness

❍ Explain to the children that baby ducks are called *ducklings*. With the children, create a list of mother and baby animals (cow and calf, cat and kitten, and so on).

Comprehension

❍ Ask the children the following questions: *Fron which animals was Mrs. Mallard trying to protect her babies? What almost ran over Mr. and Mrs. Mallard in the Public Garden? Why didn't the big bird on the boat in Public Garden speak to Mrs. Mallard? Why did Mr. and Mrs. Mallard like to visit with Michael every day?*

Letter Knowledge/Phonological Awareness

❍ Print the names of the baby ducks on chart paper, one after the other. Invite the children to look at the names and determine which letter is different in each name. Point out the consecutive letters used in the names. Discuss rhyming words with the children. *Do you think the author selected the baby duck names because they all rhyme with quack?* Challenge the children to make up names for the ducklings that rhyme with *peep.*

Special Activities

❍ Take a field trip to feed ducks. Ask questions: *Do any of the ducks have babies? How many babies? Do any of the ducks look like Mr. and Mrs. Mallard?* (Logical-Mathematical, Interpersonal)

❍ Create a maze that represents Mrs. Mallard's trip across the St. Charles River, across the street to Mt. Vernon Street, through town to the corner of Beacon Street, and into Public Park. Select one child to be Mrs. Mallard. Invite the other children to line up like the baby ducklings. Encourage "Mrs. Mallard" to lead the ducklings through the maze. Invite the "ducklings" to move in their own ducky ways; for example, swimming, waddling, or floating behind Mrs. Mallard. (Spatial, Bodily-Kinesthetic Intrapersonal)

❍ Sing "Five Little Ducks." Change the number of ducks in the song to eight to reflect the number of ducks in the story. (Linguistic, Logical-Mathematical, Musical, Interpersonal)

Learning Activities

Art *(Spatial)*
Provide drawing paper and a variety of hues of brown crayons. Encourage the children to draw a sepia picture. As they are drawing, talk with the children about using only one color to make a picture. Ask, *Does your picture look like the illustrations in the book?*

Math *(Logical-Mathematical)*
Fill each of eight plastic eggs with one plastic duck. Suggest that the children match one duck to each egg. Place a strip of masking tape down the center of the table. Invite the children to take the ducklings from the eggs and use them to create two families of different sizes by putting various combinations of ducks and eggs on either side of the line.

Gross Motor *(Linguistic, Spatial, Bodily-Kinesthetic, Interpersonal)*
Provide a 20' piece of ribbon or yarn. Help the children arrange the ribbon or yarn in a creative path design. Suggest that the children take turns being the "mother duck" and lead the "ducklings" along the path. Remind the ducklings to walk in a straight line behind their mother.

Science *(Linguistic, Logical-Mathematical, Naturalist)*
Encourage the children to look at photos of mother and baby animals and then to match the mothers with their babies. Discuss the matches they make, and encourage the children to name the baby animals.

Listening *(Linguistic, Musical, Interpersonal, Intrapersonal)*
Record songs about ducks, such as "Five Little Ducks," "Six White Ducks," and "Little Ducky Duddle." Invite the children to listen to the songs. If appropriate, suggest that they quack along with the songs. Ask which duck song they like the best and why. Have them make up a new duck song.

Writing *(Linguistic, Bodily-Kinesthetic)*
Print the names of the ducklings on chart paper. Provide crayons and pencils and encourage the children to write the names. Beginning writers may prefer to use magnetic letters.

Let's Keep Reading
Three Ducks Went Wandering by Paul Galdone

Thinking About What We Learned
1.   Which duck's name do you like best? Why?
2.   Why did the policeman help the ducks?

Matthew and Tilly

Author: Rebecca Jones. Illustrator: Beth Peck

About the Book
Matthew and Tilly are best friends. They do everything together. One day they have a disagreement and go their separate ways. Soon Matthew and Tilly realize that they enjoy each other's company too much to let a little disagreement come between them.

Learning Literacy

Oral Language/Print Awareness
❍ Encourage the children to think of things that they like to do with their friends. Make a list of the things they discuss. Talk about the things they enjoy doing with friends that are not nearly as much fun to do alone.

Comprehension
❍ Ask the children the following questions: *What kind of games do Matthew and Tilly play? What games do you play with your friends? Why did Matthew and Tilly get angry with each other? Have you ever been angry with a friend?*

Special Activities
❍ Play a game of Matthew and Tilly, similar to Hide and Seek. Select a few children to be "Matthews" and others to be "Tillies." Give the Matthews red headbands and the Tillies white headbands. Encourage the Tillies to hide, and the Matthews to find them. Once all the Tillies have been found, encourage the Matthews to hide and the Tillies to seek. (Bodily-Kinesthetic, Interpersonal)
❍ Use chalk to draw a hopscotch grid on the sidewalk. Teach the children how to play hopscotch. (Logical-Mathematical, Bodily-Kinesthetic, Interpersonal)

❍ Help the children set up a lemonade stand. Encourage them to sell the lemonade to their families. (Linguistic, Logical-Mathematical, Interpersonal)

❍ Fill the library with books about friends. Challenge the children to find a story that has a pair of friends like Tilly and Matthew, a girl and a boy. Ask, *Are there more books about two girls who are friends, two boys who are friends, or friends who are like Matthew and Tilly?* (Linguistic, Logical-Mathematical, Spatial, Intrapersonal)
❍ Sing songs about friends, such as "Make New Friends" and "The More We Get Together." (Linguistic, Musical, Interpersonal)

Learning Activities

Art

(Spatial, Intrapersonal)
Provide crayons and paper, and encourage the children to draw pictures of activities they enjoy doing with their friends. Talk with them as they work. Ask, *What is your friend's name? Where did you meet your friend?*

Music

(Linguistic, Musical, Interpersonal)
Provide rhythm band instruments. Invite the children to break into pairs. Hand each pair two identical musical instruments and ask them to sit back-to-back. One child in each pair makes a musical pattern while their partners listen carefully. Then the listening partners copy the patterns with their own instruments. Switch roles and play again.

Dramatic Play

(Linguistic, Logical-Mathematical, Naturalist, Interpersonal)
Set up a grocery store. Provide a cash register, play money, empty cans, and boxes to stock the shelves, and so on. Encourage the children to add signs. Invite them to play grocery store.

Snack

(Interpersonal, Intrapersonal)
Serve ice cream for snack. Encourage the children to pick a partner to sit with while they eat. Ask, *Does having a friend to share the experience make the ice cream taste better?*

Math

(Logical-Mathematical)
Make counting jars by printing the numerals 1–5 on plastic baby food jars. Cut out several different colored construction paper circles to represent gumballs, and encourage the children to drop the correct number of "gumballs" into each jar.

Water Table

(Logical-Mathematical, Bodily-Kinesthetic, Interpersonal)
Place a quarter in the bottom of a small tub filled halfway with water. Give the children a cup of pennies and invite the children to take turns tossing pennies into the tub. Encourage them to try to completely cover the quarter with the pennies. Ask questions: *How many pennies does it take to cover the quarter?*

Let's Keep Reading

Best Friends by Steven Kellogg
Chester's Way by Kevin Henkes

Thinking About What We Learned

1. Where do Matthew and Tilly live? Do they live in the country or in the middle of town?
2. Who is your best friend? What do you like about your friend?

Max Found Two Sticks

Author and Illustrator: Brian Pinkney

About the Book
A young boy sitting on his front steps finds two heavy twigs and begins to use them as drumsticks. He uses his sticks on buckets, boxes, bottles, and cans. The beats match the beats Max hears in the wind, the pumping of birds' wings, church bells, and rain. Then a real band passes by and Max gets a real pair of drumsticks.

Learning Literacy

Comprehension

◯ Ask the children the following questions: *What is different each time Max changes the object he is drumming? Do you think the real drumsticks sound different than the twigs? How would the story be different if Max was ringing bells instead of drumming with sticks? Have you ever had a day when you didn't feel like speaking?*

Print Awareness

◯ Challenge the children to make a list of other things Max might have be able to do with his sticks.

Print Awareness/Phonological Awareness

◯ Make a list of sounds that Max creates with his sticks. Explain that words that imitate the sounds they are describing are *onomatopoeic* words.

Special Activities

◯ Visit a high school band. Encourage the children to identify the instruments and find a name for the sounds that they make. (Linguistic, Musical, Intrapersonal)

◯ Provide rhythm band instruments and encourage the children to play the instruments along with band music. Talk about the instruments with the children. (Bodily-Kinesthetic, Musical, Naturalist, Interpersonal)

◯ Take the children outdoors for a listening walk. Challenge them to listen for the rhythms of nature's music, such as wind blowing through the trees, animals moving through the air and on the ground, the sounds of water or rain, and so on. (Musical, Naturalist, Intrapersonal)

◯ Talk about all the ways the children can make music with their bodies, such as whistling, humming, clapping, tapping, snapping, blowing, clucking, smacking, and stomping. Play music and invite the children to use their bodies to keep time with the music. (Musical, Interpersonal, Intrapersonal)

◯ Provide a variety of drumsticks of varying lengths and colors. Encourage the children to match the sticks into pairs. (Logical-Mathematical, Spatial)

Learning Activities

Art

(Spatial, Musical)

Provide tempera paint, paper, and sturdy coat hanger tubes or paper towel tubes. Turn on some music and encourage the children to dip one end of the coat hanger tubes in tempera paint and then drum them on their papers to create pictures. Ask the children to describe the pictures they are making.

Language

(Linguistic, Musical, Interpersonal)

Provide items the children can use to create sounds, such as rhythm band instruments, spray bottles of water and pie tins, and sandpaper and wooden blocks. Encourage the children to make sounds with the various items and then make up names for the sounds.

Construction

(Logical-Mathematical, Spatial)

Give the children glue, rubber bands, and craft sticks and encourage them to make anything they wish with the sticks.

Math

(Logical-Mathematical, Spatial, Interpersonal)

Give the children drumsticks (or sturdy coat hanger tubes) and encourage them to use the sticks as measuring devices. Challenge the children to find objects in the classroom that are the same size as their drumsticks.

Games

(Bodily-Kinesthetic, Musical, Interpersonal, Intrapersonal)

Separate the children into pairs. Provide two sets of drums (or boxes) and drumsticks (or stiff cardboard coat hanger tubes). Invite one child to play a beat and a second child to copy the beat.

Music

(Logical-Mathematical, Musical, Naturalist, Intrapersonal)

Give the children drumsticks, sturdy coat hanger tubes, or dowels. Provide boxes, pans, bottles, and buckets. Encourage the children to beat their drumsticks on each item, and then arrange the items in order from lowest sound to highest sound. Ask the children which objects they most enjoy drumming on.

Let's Keep Reading

If I Only Had a Horn by Roxane Orgill
Zin! Zin! Zin! A Violin by Lloyd Moss

Thinking About What We Learned

1. What are some of the names you gave to the sounds you heard today?
2. What instrument would you like to play? Why?

Miss Polly Has a Dolly

Retold by Pamela Duncan Edwards
Illustrator: Elicia Castaldi

About the Book
This is an extension of the popular children's jump rope rhyme and song. Miss Polly's dolly is sick but the doctor comes and helps Miss Polly make her all better.

Learning Literacy

Phonological Awareness

❍ Print *Polly* and *Dolly* on chart paper. Discuss which letters are the same and which letters are different. Point out that the words *Polly* and *Dolly* are rhyming words. Make a list of other rhyming words in the story.

❍ Print *rat-a-tat-tat* on chart paper. Explain that *rat-a-tat-tat* is an *onomatopoeic* word, which means a word that imitates the sound it is trying to describe. Ask the children what *rat-a-tat-tat* describes.

Comprehension

❍ Ask the children the following questions: *What does Miss Polly do when her dolly gets sick? What does the doctor say Miss Polly's dolly needs to do? Where does Miss Polly take her dolly when she gets well?*

Special Activities

❍ Ask a doctor to visit the classroom. Have the doctor talk about things that are important for staying healthy, such as keeping hands clean, eating right, and so on. (Linguistic, Interpersonal)

❍ Invite the children to jump rope as they recite the rhyme, "Miss Polly Has a Dolly." With young children, let them jump over a rope swung low to the ground. (Linguistic, Bodily-Kinesthetic, Interpersonal)

❍ Sing the song, "Miss Polly Has a Dolly." (The words are on the inside cover of the story book.) (Linguistic, Musical)

❍ Talk with the children about how they feel when they are sick. Design "get-well cards" for Miss Polly's dolly or for a sick friend. (Spatial, Intrapersonal)

❍ Invite the children to discuss medicine safety, which includes only taking medicine when administered by an adult. Talk about the differences between medicine and candy. (Logical-Mathematical)

Learning Activities

Art *(Spatial)*
Encourage the children to draw pictures of dolls and name them. Challenge them to give their dolls names that rhyme with their own names.

Games *(Bodily-Kinesthetic, Musical, Interpersonal)*
Challenge the children to create their own hand-clapping game to the rhythm of the "Miss Polly Has a Dolly" rhyme.

Cooking *(Linguistic, Logical-Mathematical, Bodily-Kinesthetic, Interpersonal)*
Make Baggie Ice Cream. For each serving: Mix ½ cup milk, one tablespoon sugar, ¼ teaspoon vanilla in a small resealable plastic bag. Place the small bag, three tablespoons of rock salt, and ice cubes in the large bag and seal. Shake.

Language *(Linguistic, Intrapersonal)*
Invite the children to make a list of all the different ways that they might feel ill, such as sore throat, stomachache, headache, runny nose, cough, and so on. Ask the children to describe each illness, and encourage them to talk about times that they have been ill. Ask, *What makes you feel better when you are ill?*

Dramatic Play *(Linguistic, Interpersonal)*
Encourage the children to use dolls, doctor supplies, bedding, and so on to re-enact the story.

Writing *(Linguistic)*
Print *Polly* and *Dolly* on chart paper. Provide magnetic letters for the children to use to copy the words.

Let's Keep Reading
Five Little Monkeys Jumping on the Bed by Eileen Christelow

Thinking About What We Learned
1. When is the last time you were sick? Who took care of you?
2. What do you think was wrong with Miss Polly's dolly?

Miss Tizzy

Author: Libba Moore Gray. Illustrator: Jada Rowland

About the Book

Miss Tizzy is eccentric and peculiar to all of her neighbors. She is, however, beloved by the children who come to her house each day for games and activities. When Miss Tizzy becomes ill, the children find one way for each day of the week to let Miss Tizzy know that they care about her.

Learning Literacy

Oral Language

❍ Talk with the children about the meaning of words that may be new, such as *bagpipes* and *peculiar.*

Book Knowledge and Appreciation

❍ Ask the children to think of other stories they know that follow a "days of the week" format, such as *The Very Hungry Caterpillar* by Eric Carle, *Today Is Monday, Boss for a Week* by Libby Handy, and *A Week of Raccoons,* by Gloria Whelan. Make a list of the stories.

Comprehension

❍ Ask the children the following questions: *Why do the children love Miss Tizzy? Can you think of some other things the children could do to help Miss Tizzy feel better? What do you think caused Miss Tilly to become ill?*

❍ Invite the children to describe Miss Tizzy's clothing.

Special Activities

❍ Plant a garden with the children. Invite them to help pick out the flowers to plant, plan a design, and measure the garden. (Linguistic, Logical-Mathematical, Naturalist, Interpersonal)

❍ Sing songs and recite poems about the moon, such as "Hey Diddle, Diddle," or "Mister Moon," as Miss Tizzy does on Sundays. (Linguistic, Musical)

❍ Play bagpipe music and encourage the children to dance. (Bodily-Kinesthetic, Musical, Interpersonal, Intrapersonal)

❍ Encourage the children to make get-well cards for children or elderly people who are in the hospital. (Spatial, Interpersonal, Intrapersonal)

Learning Activities

Art *(Spatial, Interpersonal, Intrapersonal)*
Provide crayons and paper, and encourage the children to draw "sunshines" and butterflies for people who have forgotten how to smile. Print *Thursday* on a 5" x 7" index card and place it, along with paper and crayons, in the art center for the children to use as a model for copying.

Language *(Linguistic, Interpersonal)*
Provide sock puppets for the children to play with, as Miss Tizzy does on Tuesday. Encourage the children to copy the word *Tuesday* (written on a 5" x 7" index card) on a piece of paper.

Dramatic Play *(Linguistic, Interpersonal)*
Provide dress-up clothes and serve pink lemonade, as Miss Tizzy does on Friday. Print *Friday* on a 5" x 7" index card and place it in the dramatic play center for the children to use as a model for copying.

Math *(Logical-Mathematical)*
Cut circles from light brown construction paper to represent cookies. Cut dark brown smaller circles to represent raisins. Write the numerals 1–5 on the "cookies," and challenge the children to place the correct number of raisins on each cookie. Print *Monday* on a 5" x 7" index card and encourage the children to copy it on a piece of paper.

Gross Motor *(Logical-Mathematical, Bodily-Kinesthetic, Interpersonal)*
Cut sun shapes from yellow poster board. Show the children how to roll the suns like they are wheels. Cut quarter moons, half moons, and full moons from white poster board, and invite the children to roll the moons. *Do all of the moons roll? Which is the easiest to roll?*

Music *(Musical)*
Provide bagpipe music on CDs or tapes. Invite the children to listen to the music. Print *Wednesday* on a 5" x 7" index card and encourage the children to copy it on a piece of paper.

Let's Keep Reading

Flower Garden by Eve Bunting
Old Henry by Joan Blos
Today Is Monday by Eric Carle

Thinking About What We Learned

1. Do you know anyone like Miss Tizzy? Who?
2. Which of Miss Tizzy's games do you think you would enjoy the most?

The Mitten

Author and Illustrator: Jan Brett

About the Book
Nicki begs his grandmother to knit him a pair of mittens that are white as snow. When Nicki loses one of his mittens, animals begin to use it as a shelter. The mitten accommodates an amazing number of creatures!

Learning Literacy

Oral Language

❍ Introduce words that may be new for the children, such as *prickles, jostled, commotion, glinty, talons, investigate, lumbered, plumped,* and *silhouetted.* Explain to the children that *Baba* is the Ukrainian word for *grandmother,* and discuss other foreign language words for grandmother, including *abuela* (Spanish), *mormor* or *farmorola* (Swedish), *nonna* (Italian), *lola* (Filipino), and so on.

❍ Ask the children how many animals fit inside the mitten. With the children, go back and count them.

Oral Language/Comprehension

❍ Compare Jan Brett's story with Alvin Tresselt's version of the story.

Comprehension

❍ Ask the children the following questions: *Why did Nicki's grandmother not want to knit white mittens? Was she right? How would the story have been different if the mitten were red? Which parts of the story might be true? Which parts are make-believe?*

❍ Reread the book. Call attention to the illustrations that are on the borders of the pages. Ask the children what the book's borders predict.

Special Activities

❍ Play a recording of "Peter and the Wolf" for the children. Afterwards, ask the children questions: *Which instrument was used to represent Peter? Why do you think the composer chose a string instrument? Why do you think the composer used a percussion instrument to represent the wolf?* (Bodily-Kinesthetic, Musical, Interpersonal, Intrapersonal)

❍ Cut large mittens from bulletin board paper. Use them to play games. (Spatial, Bodily-Kinesthetic, Naturalist, Interpersonal)

1. Place the mittens on the floor to make a path. Encourage the children to jump from mitten to mitten until they reach the end of the pathway.

2. Play a color game. Again, place the mittens on the floor, this time in a random pattern. Ask all the children to stand on a red mitten. More than one child can occupy a mitten. Then have them change colors to blue and so on until the children identify and stand on all the colors.

Learning Activities

(Logical-Mathematical, Spatial) Invite the children to use paper, paintbrushes, and white paint to paint snow pictures. Provide several mittens cut from different colors of construction paper, including white. Invite the children to test each color of mitten against their pictures. Ask, *Which color is the easiest to see?*

(Logical-Mathematical, Naturalist) Encourage the children to match a variety of mittens of different sizes, shapes, and patterns into pairs. Discuss the patterns of the mittens and the many colors. Ask the children, *Which colors might be easy to see in the snow?*

(Logical-Mathematical, Bodily-Kinesthetic, Interpersonal) Provide a sleeping bag and encourage the children to use it as the animals use the mitten in the book. Ask, *How many children can fit inside the sleeping bag?* **Safety Note:** Supervise this activity closely to ensure no one is hurt.

(Logical-Mathematical) Provide a mitten and several small plastic animals. Encourage the children to see how many animals they can fit inside the mitten. Next, dump out the contents when the mitten is full, and count the animals by making tally marks on a piece of paper for every animal that was inside the mitten. Help the children add up the tally marks.

(Logical-Mathematical, Bodily-Kinesthetic) Show the children how to finger crochet: tie yarn around your index finger to make a circle. Give the circle to the child. Show the child how to make a loop with the yarn and then pull the loop through the circle to start the crochet chain. Form another loop and pull that loop through the loop you have just created. Tighten each loop as you pull the next loop through.

(Musical, Intrapersonal) Invite the children to listen to a recording of "Peter and the Wolf," such as Sergei Prokofiev's *Peter and the Wolf: a Fully-Orchestrated and Narrated CD*. Explain to the children that the music comes from the same part of the world from which the story, *The Mitten* originated.

Let's Keep Reading

The Mitten by Alvin Tresselt
Mushroom in the Rain by Mirra Ginsburg
The Red Umbrella by Robert Bright

Thinking About What We Learned

1. Have you ever lost something? What was it? Did you find it?
2. What is your favorite color of mitten?

Mouse Paint

Author and Illustrator: Ellen Stoll Walsh

About the Book

Three white mice find three jars of paint, one red, one blue, and one yellow. The three mice climb right in the paint. They find out some amazing things about colors as they jump in and out of the paints and dance in the puddles left behind.

Learning Literacy

Oral Language

❍ Teach the children the action rhyme, "Little Mouse."

Little Mouse

Walk little mouse, walk little mouse. (tiptoe around)

Hide little mouse, hide little mouse. (cover eyes with hands)

Here comes the cat! (look around)

Run little mouse, run little mouse! (walk quickly to the circle area and sit down)

Comprehension

❍ Ask the children the following questions: *Why did the mice jump into the paint? Why couldn't the cat see the mice when they were hiding on the white paper at the beginning of the story? Why did the mice leave a white stripe on the paper they painted with the paints?*

Letter Knowledge

❍ Print *red, blue,* and *yellow* on chart paper. Print each word using a marker of that color. Ask the children to look at each word and to identify the letter that appears in all three words.

Special Activities

❍ Visit a pet store to observe the white mice. Ask questions: *What do the mice eat? How large are they? Where do they sleep?* (Linguistic, Naturalist)

❍ Create a "Mouse Maze." Encourage the children to maneuver the maze by crawling and by reading color-coded directions. For example, when they see a red circle, they should turn left. When they see a blue circle, they should turn right. When they see a yellow circle, they should go straight. (Logical-Mathematical, Spatial, Intrapersonal)

Learning Activities

Art

(Logical-Mathematical, Spatial, Bodily-Kinesthetic)

Set out white easel paper; brushes; and jars of red, blue, yellow, orange, green, and purple paint. Invite the children to paint stripes of each color on their white paper. Encourage the children to try making different patterns and use different sizes of brushes to make different-sized stripes.

Music

(Logical-Mathematical, Musical, Interpersonal, Intrapersonal)

Help the children create a rhyme that retells the story of *Mouse Paint*. For example:

Three White Mice

Three white mice in paint did play.
It turned out to be a colorful day.
Red, yellow, blue here and there,
Here and there and everywhere.

Discovery

(Spatial, Bodily-Kinesthetic)

Provide fingerpaints in red, blue, and yellow. Invite the children to explore mixing the paints. Ask, *What happens when you mix all the colors?*

Science

(Logical-Mathematical, Spatial, Intrapersonal)

Provide 4" x 4" squares of red, yellow, and blue cellophane, and an overhead projector. Invite the children to create colored shadows on the wall. Ask, *What happens when you overlap two colors of cellophane? What interesting designs can be made? What color combination is your favorite?*

Gross Motor

(Linguistic, Logical-Mathematical, Bodily-Kinesthetic, Naturalist)

Invite the children to step their bare feet into yellow, red, or blue paint and then step onto a 12' strip of butcher paper that is taped to the floor. Ask a child who stepped into yellow paint to step on blue footprints. What happens? Ask a child who stepped into red paint to step on yellow footprints. Talk about what happens. Provide pans of water and towels for the children to wash and dry their feet. **Safety Note:** Supervise closely.

Writing

(Linguistic, Bodily-Kinesthetic)

Print *red*, *blue*, and *yellow* on index cards. Provide tracing paper and red, yellow, and blue crayons. Suggest that the children trace the names of the colors using crayons of the same color.

Let's Keep Reading

Little Blue and Little Yellow by Leo Lionni

Thinking About What We Learned

1. Which color is your favorite? Why?
2. Were the mice having fun playing in the paint? How do you know?

Mr. Gumpy's Outing

Author and Illustrator: John Burningham

About the Book

When Mr. Gumpy decides to take a boat ride, two children, a rabbit, a dog, a pig, a cat, a sheep, some chickens, a calf, and a goat ask to go along. He agrees to allow each character to come along, but warns them that they must behave. He gives special instructions to each passenger. Of course, misbehavior abounds and all the characters end up in the water.

Learning Literacy

Oral Language

❍ Invite the children to demonstrate the action words Mr. Gumpy uses when he is telling each passenger what they are not to do; for example, *squabble, hop, chase, tease, muck about, bleat, flap, trample,* and *kick.*

❍ Invite the children to discuss the meaning of *outing.*

Comprehension

❍ Ask the children the following questions: *What does Mr. Gumpy tell the animals they have to do to ride in his boat? How does Mr. Gumpy's boat move? Which is the first animal to misbehave? What happens when the boat tips over?*

Special Activities

❍ Sing "Row, Row, Row Your Boat." Encourage the children to pretend to row as they sing, or stand up and pole the boat the way Mr. Gumpy does. If the children choose to pretend they are poling the boat, change lyrics to *push, push, push your boat,* or *pole, pole, pole your boat.* (Linguistic, Bodily-Kinesthetic, Musical)

❍ Fill the library with books about boats. Encourage the children to see if they can find another boat like Mr. Gumpy's boat. (Spatial, Intrapersonal)

❍ Visit a marina. Ask questions: *What kind of boats do you see? How do the boats move? Do any of the boats use a pole to move them?* (Linguistic, Logical-Mathematical, Naturalist, Interpersonal)

Learning Activities

Blocks

(Linguistic, Logical-Mathematical, Spatial, Interpersonal)
Cut blue bulletin board paper into long, narrow, and angular shapes, similar to rivers. Encourage the children to build houses for Mr. Gumpy beside the rivers. Provide boats and plastic animals and encourage the children to re-enact the story.

Listening

(Musical, Interpersonal)
Make a recording of *Mr. Gumpy's Outing* and place the recording and the book in the listening center. Challenge the children to add sound effects to the tape as they listen to the story. Leave plenty of space between lines for their sounds. After the children have practiced their sound effects, re-record the story with the children's sound effects.

Construction

(Logical-Mathematical, Spatial)
Give the children clay and encourage them to shape the clay into small boats. Provide a tub of water and invite the children to test the seaworthiness of their boats.

Math

(Logical-Mathematical)
Encourage the children to arrange several plastic animals of various sizes from the smallest to the largest. Ask, *Which animals would cause the most trouble when misbehaving on a boat, the big animals or the small animals?*

Dramatic Play

(Linguistic, Interpersonal)
Set out cups and saucers, pretend cookies, and napkins, so the children can have a tea party. Offer several stuffed animals to represent the characters in the story, and include the animals as guests.

Water Table

(Linguistic, Logical-Mathematical)
Provide several toy boats that can float on the water. Invite the children to play with the boats, splashing them through rough waters. Ask, *What does it take to tip the boats over?* Provide plastic animals to ride in the boats.

Let's Keep Reading
Who Sank the Boat? by Pamela Allen

Thinking About What We Learned

1. How would the story be different if the animals on the boat had behaved?
2. What did you learn about boats today?

Mrs. Goose's Baby

Author and Illustrator: Charlotte Voake

About the Book
Mrs. Goose finds an egg and protects it against all kinds of threats. When the egg hatches, the little bird inside looks different from what Mrs. Goose expects—but she continues her diligent protection. As it turns out, Mrs. Goose's egg belonged to a chicken.

Learning Literacy

Oral Language/Comprehension
❍ Draw a Venn diagram (two large overlapping circles—see appendix page 227) on chart paper. Encourage the children to discuss and compare chickens and geese. Write things that both birds have in common in the overlap of the two circles. Write things that are exclusive to chickens inside the circle to the left and things that are exclusive to geese in the circle on the right.

Phonological Awareness
❍ Talk with the children about the sounds that geese make, like *honk*, and the sounds that chickens make, like *cheep* and *cluck*. Print each sound word on chart paper. Tell the children that words that imitate the sounds they are describing are *onomatopoeic* words. Invite the children think of other onomatopoeic words they know. Remind the children of the sound that Mrs. Goose makes when she scares the cat away (*hiss*). Ask the children if this is an *onomatopoeic* sound.

Comprehension
❍ Ask the children the following questions: *Where did Mrs. Goose find the egg? What things did Mrs. Goose do to protect her egg? Is Mrs. Goose's baby a gosling? Do you think Mrs. Goose will keep her baby if she finds out it is a chicken? Why does Mrs. Goose not know that her baby is a chicken?*

Special Activities

❍ Visit a farm. Spend time observing the chickens and the geese. Ask the children the following questions: *How are chickens and geese different? How are they alike?* (Linguistic, Logical-Mathematical, Naturalist, Interpersonal)
❍ Play Chicken, Chicken, Goose as you would Duck, Duck, Goose. Children sit in a circle. One child—IT—walks around the outside of the circle, tapping each player on the head and saying *Chicken*. Eventually IT taps a player and says *Goose* instead. The tapped player gets up and chases IT around the circle. If she taps IT before they get around the circle, she gets to go back to her place. If she doesn't, she becomes the new IT and the game continues. (Bodily-Kinesthetic, Interpersonal)
❍ Do the Chicken Dance. Music is available on *All Time Favorite Dances CD* by Kimbo Educational as well as on several other children's dance CDs. (Linguistic, Bodily-Kinesthetic, Musical, Interpersonal)
❍ Create a maze. Provide a large plastic egg and invite the children to push the egg through the maze by crawling on the floor and using their elbows as goose wings. (Spatial, Intrapersonal)

Starting With Stories

Learning Activities

Art *(Spatial)*
Cut easel paper into egg shapes. Encourage the children to use the egg-shaped paper, tempera paint, and brushes to paint their own special eggs.

Math *(Logical-Mathematical, Musical)*
Place jingle bells inside several plastic eggs. Place one bell in one egg, two in the next, three in the next, and so on, up to eight bells. Invite the children to shake the eggs and then arrange them in order from quietest to loudest.

Discovery *(Naturalist, Interpersonal)*
Provide a balancing scale and a bag of feathers (available from a craft store or teacher supply store). Suggest that the children weigh the feathers on the scale. *How is weighing feathers different from weighing blocks?* Provide a block so that the children can make a comparison.

Snack *(Bodily-Kinesthetic, Interpersonal)*
Help the children make Bird Nest Candies. Melt a bag of butterscotch chips in the microwave. Add chow mein noodles to the butterscotch and mix them together until the noodles are coated. The children scoop spoonfuls of the mixture, drop them on wax paper, and then press their spoons into the mixture, creating bird nests. Let cool before serving.

Games *(Logical-Mathematical, Interpersonal)*
Hide eggs and invite the children to find them.

Writing *(Linguistic, Bodily-Kinesthetic)*
Provide a goose feather to use as a writing tool. Show the children how to dip the shaft of the feather into the tempera paint and then use it to write. Talk with the children as they write. *Is it easier to write with the feather or a pencil? Why?*

Let's Keep Reading

Are You My Mother? by P.D. Eastman
The Ugly Duckling by Hans Christian Andersen

Thinking About What We Learned

1. What did Mrs. Goose's baby look like when he pecked his way out of the egg?
2. Would you rather have a chicken or a goose? Why?

The Napping House

Author: Audrey Wood. Illustrator: Don Wood

About the Book
A sleeping granny is joined by a cast of characters who eventually wake her up, and then no one is sleeping.

Learning Literacy

Oral Language

❍ Go through the pages on the book slowly. After the first couple of pages, ask the children to predict which sleeper is going to get on the bed next. *How do you know?* Go through the book another time, this time paying attention to the colors the illustrator uses. Ask the children the following questions: *What colors are the pages when everyone is asleep? What colors are the pages when everyone wakes up?*

❍ Read the book slowly. On each page, invite the children to change the descriptive word in the sentence. Ask, *Does the new word change the story?*

❍ Invite the children to brainstorm a list of words related to sleep, such as *nap, snooze, doze, rest, forty winks,* and so on.

Phonological Awareness/Oral Language

❍ Sing songs about sleeping, such as "Are You Sleeping?" "Lazy Mary," and "Rock-a-Bye Baby." Invite the children to discuss their sleeping habits and routines.

Comprehension

❍ Ask the children the following questions: *Have you ever had to share your bed with someone? Who? When? What happened?*

Special Activities

❍ Take a trip to the zoo. Visit the nocturnal animals. Make a list of the nocturnal animals. (Linguistic, Naturalist)

❍ Play lullaby music. Invite the children to lie on the floor and pretend to be asleep. Encourage them to snore if they want to. Challenge the children to do this activity without laughing. (Bodily-Kinesthetic, Musical, Interpersonal, Intrapersonal)

❍ Separate the children into groups of four. Encourage them to arrange themselves in order from the largest to the smallest. (Logical-Mathematical, Spatial, Interpersonal)

❍ Play CDs or tapes of lullabies. Ask the children questions, such as, *How is a lullaby different from a song we dance to? Which lullaby do you like best?* (Musical, Intrapersonal)

Learning Activities

Art

(Spatial, Intrapersonal)
Provide blue paint, paper, and brushes so the children can paint sleepy blue pictures. Talk with the children about how the color blue makes them feel. Later on or on another day, suggest that the children use yellow paint, paper, and brushes to paint a yellow *good morning* picture. Ask, *How does the color yellow make you feel?*

Blocks

(Logical-Mathematical, Spatial, Bodily-Kinesthetic, Naturalist, Interpersonal)
Encourage the children to stack several sizes of boxes from largest on the bottom to smallest on the top, and then to try stacking the boxes on top of one another, from the smallest on the bottom to the largest on the top. Ask, *Which is easier?*

Dramatic Play

(Linguistic, Interpersonal)
Provide a sleeping bag the children can pretend is a bed, and several stuffed animals that can represent the animals in *The Napping House*. Encourage the children to re-enact the story. Ask questions: *Can you remember who comes to bed next? How do you remember who comes next?*

Gross Motor

(Bodily-Kinesthetic, Interpersonal, Intrapersonal)
Group the children in pairs. Provide several small boxes, and invite one child in each pair to lie on the floor on his back. Challenge each partner to stack the boxes on the partner's tummy. Ask, *How many can you stack before the boxes tumble down? What makes the boxes tumble? What happens if your partner laughs?*

Language

(Linguistic, Naturalist, Interpersonal, Intrapersonal)
Provide pictures illustrating activities that people do during the day, as well as activities that people do at night. Ask the children to sort the pictures into *day* and *night* categories. Ask, *How do you know which pictures are showing nighttime activities? Are any of the activities in the pictures things you might do both during the day and at night?*

Listening

(Musical, Naturalist, Interpersonal, Intrapersonal)
Invite the children to use a tape recorder to record their best "granny" snores. Play the recordings. Invite the children to select the snore they like best. Ask questions, *Who has the funniest snore? Who has the loudest snore? Can you identify your snore?*

Let's Keep Reading

The Mitten by Jan Brett
Roll Over by Mordecai Gerstein

Thinking About What We Learned

1. What do you think is the funniest part of *The Napping House*?
2. Do you have a special animal or blanket that you take to bed with you? What does the child in the story take to bed with him?

Noisy Nora

Author and Illustrator: Rosemary Wells

About the Book
No one is paying attention to Nora. Mum is taking care of Jack, and Dad is busy with Kate. Nora gets attention the only way she knows how…she makes noise, lots of noise.

Learning Literacy

Oral Language
- Discuss words that may be new to the children, such as *monumental, mum, cellar, felled, sifted,* and *shrub.*

Phonological Awareness
- Reread *Noisy Nora* to the children. Stop for the second word in each set of rhyming words and encourage the children to say them aloud.

Comprehension
- Ask the children the following questions: *Why was Nora making so much noise? Is there a way that Nora might get attention without making noise? How do you think Nora feels about being called* dumb? *Where was Nora hiding?*

Print Awareness
- Make a list of all the things Nora did to make noise. *Can you think of other ways Nora might make noise?*

Special Activities

- Encourage the children to sort through all the books in the classroom and find those that are about a mouse or mice. Encourage them to create a Mouse Library. (Linguistic, Naturalist, Interpersonal)
- Create a maze. Invite the children to creep and sniff through the maze like mice. (Spatial, Bodily-Kinesthetic, Interpersonal)
- Hide a stuffed or plastic mouse in the classroom and challenge the children to find it. (Interpersonal)
- Take the children outdoors. Provide noisemakers such as clickers, rattles, bells, whistles and so on, and turn the children loose to make noise . Describe the sounds that each item makes. Ask questions: *Which noisemaker is the loudest? Do the noises hurt your ears? What would happen if we used the noisemakers indoors?* (Linguistic, Bodily-Kinesthetic, Musical, Interpersonal)
- Sing songs about mice, such as "Three Blind Mice," "Hickory Dickory Dock," "Little Bunny Foo-Foo" and "Mickey Mouse." (Linguistic, Musical, Interpersonal)

Learning Activities

(Musical, Naturalist, Intrapersonal)
Provide a basket of items that will make a noise when dropped, such as marbles, washers, pennies, and spools, and another basket full of items that will not make noise, such as cotton balls, feathers, tissues, and Band-Aids. Mix the items together on the table and ask the children to sort the items into the *noisy* and *quiet* baskets.

(Logical-Mathematical, Interpersonal)
Use masking tape to make 3" diameter circles on the floor. Show the children how to flick marbles with their thumbs and middle fingers so they roll into the circle. Ask the children questions about the sounds the marbles make when they roll on different surfaces. **Safety Note:** Be sure the children do not put marbles in their mouths.

(Interpersonal, Intrapersonal)
Encourage the children to bathe a "baby" (a baby doll, or even better, a rubber mouse!) using a tub of water, soap, a rubber ducky, washcloth, and towel.

(Linguistic)
Encourage the children to choose books from the library and read them to Kate (Nora's sister). Provide a stuffed mouse to represent Kate. Ask, *What kind of book does a mouse like?*

(Spatial)
Provide fingerpaint and paper. Show the children how to turn their thumbprints into mouse profiles by adding eyes and tails with fine-point pens. Help the children add pink noses to make the mice look like Nora.

(Linguistic, Musical, Interpersonal, Intrapersonal)
Play lullabies. Encourage the children to listen and select the lullabies they think might help Mum put Jack to sleep so she will be able to pay attention to Nora.

Let's Keep Reading

Night Noises by Mem Fox
The Very Quiet Cricket by Eric Carle

Thinking About What We Learned

1. Have you ever had a difficult time getting attention? What did you do?
2. How did Nora's family know she was gone?

Nonsense

Author and Illustrator: Sally Kahler Phillips

About the Book

Rhyming text and whimsical illustrations present example after example of nonsense scenarios including a rhino with wings, a bat with a hat, and a book-reading bunny. The author's purpose is to help children understand that the cutting remarks of others are another form of nonsense. Her goal is to help children realize that only they can decide who they are.

Learning Literacy

Comprehension

❍ Ask the children the following questions: *Which nonsense thing mentioned in the book did you think was the funniest? Why? Has anyone ever said something to you that hurt your feelings? How did it make you feel? What did you do?*

Oral Language

❍ Talk with the children about the meaning of *nonsense.* Encourage the children to brainstorm a list of nonsense things. You might help them by giving them a *what if* starter. Discuss *sense. How is it different from nonsense?*

Segmentation

❍ Invite the children to clap the syllables in *nonsense.* Clap the syllables in *sense. Which word has more syllables?*

Phonological Awareness

❍ Help children find the rhyming words in the text.

Print Awareness

❍ Look at the type of print used in the book. Ask the children, *How is this type of print different from the print normally found in books?*

Letter Knowledge

❍ Show the children the cover of the book. Point to the word *nonsense.* Ask questions: *Which letter does* nonsense *start with? Which letter is in the word three times? Which letters are in the word twice? Are any of the letters in* nonsense *made with straight lines? What is the symbol at the end of the word?*

Special Activities

❍ Have a "Nonsense Day" at school. Invite the children to wear their clothes inside out and backwards. Do silly things during center time. Hang stuffed animals in outdoor trees. Serve lunch backwards. Ask *what if* questions all day. *What if cars had square wheels? What if dogs could fly? What if red was the only color we had?* (Logical-Mathematical, Naturalist, Interpersonal, Intrapersonal)

❍ Have a "Turtle Tea." Serve green punch and turtle-shaped cookies. (Linguistic, Interpersonal)

❍ Provide stilts. Encourage the children to try walking on stilts like the fish in the books. Ask questions: *Is it easier for a child to walk on stilts or a fish to walk on stilts? Why would it be impossible for a fish to walk on stilts?* (Spatial, Bodily-Kinesthetic)

Learning Activities

Art
(Spatial, Intrapersonal)
Cut block letters from different types of paper, such as wrapping paper, wallpaper, and foil. Encourage the children to glue the letters to paper to spell *nonsense*.

Music
(Linguistic, Musical, Intrapersonal)
Record some nonsense songs such as "There Was an Old Lady Who Swallowed a Fly" and "Willaby, Wallaby, Woo" and invite the children to listen to the songs. Ask, *Which nonsense song do you like best?*

Construction
(Linguistic, Bodily-Kinesthetic)
Give the children playdough, chenille stems, feathers, lace, small branches, and so on. Encourage them to shape the various items to make the letters in the word *nonsense*. Ask, *Can you spell* nonsense *with the letters you make?*

Snack
(Linguistic, Bodily-Kinesthetic)
Provide letter cereal for snack. Invite the children to find the letters that spell *nonsense* before they eat their handful of cereal.

Math
(Logical-Mathematical, Spatial, Naturalist, Interpersonal, Intrapersonal)
Cut wallpaper into 4" x 4" squares. Use plaids, stripes, and polka dot patterns. Invite the children to pretend they are pigs sewing quilts as they put the squares together to create a colorful quilt. When they are finished making their quilt, invite them to glue the pieces to a sheet of butcher paper.

Writing
(Linguistic, Bodily-Kinesthetic, Naturalist, Intrapersonal)
Provide small silk flowers and leaves, glue, and sheets of drawing paper with *nonsense* written on them. Invite the children to glue the flowers on top of the letters to create a decorative sign. Show them the page in the book that uses flowers to spell *nonsense*.

Let's Keep Reading

There Was an Old Woman Who Swallowed a Fly by Simms Taback
Tuesday by David Wiesner
Wacky Wednesday by Dr. Seuss, writing as Theodore LeSieg

Thinking About What We Learned

1. Can you think of another word that means the same thing as nonsense?
2. What will you say if someone says something about you that is not true?

Oh Lord, I Wish I Was a Buzzard

Author: Polly Greenberg. Illustrator: Aliki

About the Book
A little girl harvests cotton with her family during the sweltering crop season. Imagining her way through the endless day, she wishes she could be anything else—from a snake curled up and cool to a buzzard going round and round in the sky.

Learning Literacy

Oral Language
- Talk with the children about the uses of cotton. Point out fabrics that are made of cotton. Discuss cotton fillings in pillows and bedding.
- Look at the illustrations in the story. Ask the children, *Why do the white pages turn gray as the day fades into night?*

Comprehension
- Ask the children the following questions: *Why does the little girl keep wishing she was something else? At the end of the day, does the little girl feel good about what she has accomplished? How do you know?*

Special Activities

- If geographically possible, visit a cotton field. If a cotton field is not possible, but another type of field is available, arrange to visit it. Talk with the children about working in a field, the different crops that grow in fields, and so on. (Linguistic, Logical-Mathematical, Naturalist, Interpersonal)
- Play music and encourage the children to fly like buzzards across the sky. Remind the children about the buzzard's wingspan. Encourage the children to stretch their arms out wide. Ask them to imagine a cool breeze on their faces as they soar through the air all alone and high above the hot cotton fields. (Spatial, Bodily-Kinesthetic, Musical, Intrapersonal)

Learning Activities

Art *(Spatial)*

With the children, make white Puff Paint by mixing ⅓ cup white glue, 2 tablespoons white tempera paint, and 2 cups of shaving cream. Invite the children to use brown paper and the white Puff Paint like fingerpaint to make cotton balls on their brown "dirt" paper. Ask, *Do the pictures look like the pictures in the book.*

Gross Motor *(Logical-Mathematical, Bodily-Kinesthetic, Interpersonal)*

Provide a box and some cotton balls. Use masking tape to create a throw line. Invite the children to stand behind the throw line and then toss cotton balls into the box. Ask questions: *Is it easy to get the cotton balls into the box? Is it harder to toss a beanbag or a cotton ball?*

Language *(Linguistic, Intrapersonal)*

Invite the children to finish the sentence, *I wish I were _____.* Transcribe their answers onto drawing paper and invite them to make illustrated versions of their responses.

Math *(Logical-Mathematical, Interpersonal)*

Use four pieces of brown paper to represent four fields of cotton. Lay 20 cotton balls on each sheet. Give four children a sack and assign each child to one of the four "fields." The children take turns rolling die, looking at the numbers on their dice, and removing from their "fields" that many pieces of cotton. The child who removes all the cotton balls from his field first is the winner.

Music *(Linguistic, Musical, Naturalist, Intrapersonal)*

Invite the children to think of a list of songs and chants that the little girl in *Oh Lord, I Wish I Was a Buzzard* might have sung to keep her mind off the heat; for example, "Frosty the Snowman," "Jingle Bells," "You Scream, I Scream," and so on. Encourage the children to make tapes of the songs.

Science *(Naturalist)*

Provide cotton and cotton items for the children to explore. Provide photos of real cotton fields, if possible.

Let's Keep Reading

Dream Carver by Diana Cohn and Amy Cordova

Thinking About What We Learned

1. What do you do to help your family at home?
2. What kind of things do you wish for when you are hot?

The Old Man and His Door

Author: Gary Soto. Illustrator: Joe Cepeda

About the Book

This is the story of an old man who is good at working in his garden but not so good at listening to his wife. He makes a listening error one day that results in a humorous adventure. The story introduces several Spanish words.

Learning Literacy

Oral Language

❍ Discuss the words in the story that may be new for the children, such as *plump, heaved, shabby, gurgled, peephole, wriggled, tinkled,* and *blushed.*

❍ Teach the children additional Spanish words, such as *hola* (hello), *adios* (goodbye), *amigo/amiga* (friend), and so on.

❍ Cut a 6" x 9" rectangle of cardboard. Ask the children to brainstorm a list of things for which they could use the rectangle.

Comprehension

❍ Ask the children the following questions: *What does the old man do well? What does he do not so well? What did the old man's wife ask for? What did the old man think she asked for? Would the story be different if the old man thought his wife asked him to bring a bicycle to the neighbors? Why do you think the old man didn't listen to his wife?*

Print Awareness

❍ Make a list of all the different things the old man was able to do with his door.

Special Activities

❍ Take a walk through the school, or, if possible, the neighborhood. Ask the children questions about what they see: *How many different kinds of doors do you see? How many wooden doors? How many glass doors? How many garage doors? Doggie doors? What other kinds of doors are there? Car doors? Cellar doors?* Make a list of all the kinds of doors the children find. (Linguistic, Logical-Mathematical, Naturalist)

❍ Play Kick the Rock during outdoor play. Provide wadded brown paper bags for rocks and encourage the children to kick the "rocks" across the playground. (Bodily-Kinesthetic, Interpersonal)

❍ Provide a piñata and Mexican music. Invite the children to break the piñata. Discuss the use of piñatas at fiestas. Point out the piñata in the story. **Safety Note:** Supervise closely. Make sure the children all stand a safe distance away from the child swinging at the piñata. (Bodily-Kinesthetic, Musical, Interpersonal)

❍ Show the children a brick. Ask them to think of all the ways they might be able to use the brick. (Linguistic, Logical-Mathematical, Spatial, Naturalist, Intrapersonal)

Learning Activities

Art
(Linguistic, Spatial, Intrapersonal) Give each child a manila folder to use as a door. Cut off the tab to make the doors more symmetrical. Give the children crayons and markers and encourage them to decorate their doors, then imagine and describe what places their doors might open into.

Gross Motor
(Bodily-Kinesthetic, Musical, Interpersonal) Encourage the children to play Ring the Doorbell by tossing a beanbag at a service bell. Ask, *Was a doorbell mentioned in the story?*

Discovery
(Logical-Mathematical, Bodily-Kinesthetic, Interpersonal) Provide an inclined plank (to represent a door) as well as several cars, trucks, and balls to roll down the plank. Talk with the children about the speed that each item gathers on its way down the plank. Try rolling the items up the plank. *How did the old man use his door to help move furniture?*

Language
(Linguistic, Logical-Mathematical, Spatial) Glue a large magazine picture or photo inside a manila folder. Cut five small doors (2" x 3") on the cover of the folder. Number the doors 1–5. The children open the doors one at a time and describe what they see behind them. After all the doors have been opened, guess what is pictured behind the all doors.

Games
(Bodily-Kinesthetic, Interpersonal) Invite the children to use drawing paper, crayons, and markers to draw pictures. Encourage them to use their pictures as places to hide their faces behind while playing Knock, Knock, Who's There? Encourage the children to play Peek-a-Boo with younger children by hiding behind their artwork.

Water Table
(Interpersonal) Set out a bottle of soap (labeled *Dog Shampoo*), a scrub brush, small towels, and several plastic or rubber dogs, and invite the children to bathe the dogs. Encourage the children to name the dogs, and then give them baths. Talk with the children while they play. Ask questions: *How do you keep the dog in the tub? How do you dry the dog?*

Let's Keep Reading

The Old Woman and Her Pig by Eric Kimmel

Thinking About What We Learned

1. Have you ever misunderstood something someone asked you to do?
2. Which activity did you like best today? Why?

On the Go

Author: Ann Morris. Illustrator: Ken Heyman

About the Book
Beautiful photographs and simple text describe the many ways people around the world travel from one place to another.

Learning Literacy

Oral Language
❍ Discuss walking as a means of travel. Talk with the children about places that they walk to, such as parks, school, neighbors' homes, and so on. Teach the children "Walk, Walk, Walk Your Feet" to the tune of "Row, Row, Row Your Boat."

Walk, Walk, Walk Your Feet
by Pam Schiller
Walk, walk, walk your feet
Everywhere you go.
Walk 'em fast, walk 'em slow,
* Walk them heel to toe.*

Comprehension
❍ Ask the children the following questions: *What animals are in the story? What things do animals carry on their heads? What things in the book move on tracks? How do people travel to the moon?*

Print Awareness
❍ Encourage the children to help make a list of all the different ways people in the story travel.

Special Activities

❍ Visit a train station, an airport, a bus station, or any place that provides transportation. (Linguistic, Naturalist, Interpersonal)
❍ Sing songs about transportation vehicles, such as "Wheels on the Bus," "Little Red Caboose," "Row, Row, Row Your Boat," and so on. (Linguistic, Bodily-Kinesthetic, Musical, Interpersonal)
❍ Fill the library with books about transportation. Encourage the children to look at books about a type of vehicle that they would like to ride. (Linguistic, Spatial, Intrapersonal)
❍ Teach the children "Put Your Little Foot." (Bodily-Kinesthetic, Musical)

Put Your Little Foot
(Tune: Traditional)
Put your little foot, put your little foot,
Put your little foot right there.
Put your little foot, put your little foot,
Put your little foot right there.
Walk and walk, walk and turn.
Walk and walk, walk and turn.
Walk and walk, walk and turn.
Walk and walk, walk and turn.

Learning Activities

Construction *(Spatial, Bodily-Kinesthetic)*
Teach the children how to make paper airplanes. Encourage them to decorate their paper before folding their planes. Take the children outdoors to fly their airplanes.

Gross Motor *(Bodily-Kinesthetic)*
Use masking tape to make a line on the floor. Provide baskets, books, and tin cups for the children to balance on their heads as they walk the masking tape line.

Discovery *(Logical-Mathematical, Musical, Naturalist)*
Provide a basket of toys with wheels, such as cars, bicycles, trucks, motorcycles, and so on. Create an inclined plank for the children to use to roll the vehicles downhill. Place an upside down tricycle in the center so the children can explore the wheels.

Music *(Linguistic, Musical, Interpersonal)*
Encourage the children to look through the book and create sounds for each type of transportation.

Dramatic Play *(Linguistic, Interpersonal)*
Encourage the children to carry the babies in various carriers such as strollers, buggies, walkers, and slings. Give them a task to do so they can get the feel for the different carriers. Talk with them as they play. *What do you think it would be like to carry your baby on your back all day while you worked in a field picking berries or cotton?*

Water Table *(Logical-Mathematical, Interpersonal)*
Provide a variety of boats for the children to float in the water table. Show the children how to push the water and fan the boats to make them move.

Let's Keep Reading
Freight Train by Donald Crews
I Go With My Family to Grandma's by Riki Levinson

Thinking About What We Learned
1. What did you learn about travel today?
2. Children can't drive cars or fly planes, but they can travel. Name some ways that children travel.

Once Upon MacDonald's Farm

Author and Illustrator: Stephen Gammell

About the Book

MacDonald shows his lack of knowledge about farming when he tries to run his farm with an elephant, a baboon, and a lion. When the animals rebel and leave, MacDonald's neighbor gets him a chicken, a cow, and a horse. Unfortunately, MacDonald messes up again, and the mistake is one that makes everyone laugh out loud.

Learning Literacy

Segmentation

❍ Clap the syllables in each of the animal's names, both the first group and the second group of animals. Ask the children which animal has the longest name.

Comprehension

❍ Ask the children the following questions: *What was wrong with the first group of animals that MacDonald had on his farm? When they ran away, where do you think they went? How do you think people learn how to run a farm?*

Print Awareness

❍ Invite the children to look at the print in the book. Ask them how it is different from the print they are used to seeing in books.

❍ Help the children write a letter to Old MacDonald from the first group of animals he has on his farm, explaining why they are leaving.

Special Activities

❍ Take a trip to the zoo. See how many farm animals you can find in the zoo. Take a trip to a farm. Ask, *Which farm animals are also found at the zoo?* (Linguistic, Logical-Mathematical, Naturalist)

❍ Sing "Old MacDonald Had a Farm" using zoo animals in place of farm animals. (Linguistic, Musical, Naturalist)

❍ Fill the library with books about farms. (Linguistic, Intrapersonal)

❍ Sing and play The Farmer in the Dell, substituting the names of the first group of animals for the traditional verses. (Linguistic, Bodily-Kinesthetic, Musical)

❍ Provide several books that have been written and illustrated by Stephen Gammell, such as *Old Henry, Twigboy Finds a Friend,* and *Is that You, Winter?* Mr. Gammell always puts himself in the illustrations, so invite the children to compare the books to see if they can figure out what Stephen Gammell looks like, and then find him in *Once Upon MacDonald's Farm.* (Linguistic, Logical-Mathematical, Spatial, Interpersonal)

Learning Activities

(Spatial)
Provide pencils and paper and invite the children to draw pictures. Point out that the illustrations in *Once Upon MacDonald's Farm* are done in pencil, and are not color images. Ask the children how they like drawing without colors. Show them how to use a tissue to rub the pencil lines and create a smudged look.

(Bodily-Kinesthetic, Interpersonal)
Make Sand Combs for the children to explore in the sand table. To make Sand Combs, cut poster board into 4" x 8" strips and them cut a pattern in one of the ⅛" sides. Point out that the plow makes tracks in the earth in the same way that the combs make tracks in the sand.

(Logical-Mathematical, Bodily-Kinesthetic)
Ask the children to look at magazines that contain several images of animals, and cut out as many farm animals as they can find. Help the children separate the animals by type and ask the children whether the animals they selected could stock MacDonald's farm.

(Naturalist)
Provide plastic farm and zoo animals. Challenge the children to sort the animals into two categories: *zoo animals* and *farm animals*. Ask the children to name the animals that belong in both groups.

(Linguistic, Musical, Intrapersonal)
Suggest that the children listen to a tape of farm songs. Ask them if they think listening to the songs would help MacDonald be a better farmer.

(Linguistic)
Print the names of the animals that appear on MacDonald's farm on 4"x 6" index cards. Provide tracing paper and crayons and encourage the children to trace the names.

Let's Keep Reading

Farming by Gail Gibbons
Mrs. Wishy-Washy's Farm by Joy Cowley

Thinking About What We Learned

1. What did you learn about farming today?
2. Do you think that MacDonald's new animals will run away, too?

One Cow Moo Moo

Author: David Bennett. Illustrator: Andy Cooke

About the Book

A parade of animals runs past the narrator, who wonders why until he sees what's at the end of the parade.

Learning Literacy

Phonological Awareness

❍ Discuss the sounds that each animal in the book makes. These sounds are *onomatopoeic*. Ask the children to make up *onomatopoeic* sounds for the monster.

❍ Challenge the children to brainstorm a list of words that rhyme with *moo*. Print their words on chart paper and, with the children, count how many total rhyming words they can name.

Comprehension

❍ Help the children make a Venn diagram (two large overlapping circles—see appendix page 227) comparing this story and Denise Fleming's *Barnyard Banter*. In the overlapping area, write what both stories have in common. In the separate portion of one circle, write information that is unique to *One Cow Moo Moo*, and in the separate portion of the other circle, write information that is unique to *Barnyard Banter*.

❍ Ask the children the following questions: *Why was everyone running? Why was the monster chasing the animals? Which numbers are mentioned in the book?*

Special Activities

❍ Visit a farm. Make a list of the animals that are in the story. Try to locate each animal on the list. (Linguistic, Naturalist, Interpersonal)

❍ Invite the children to run in ways that mimic the way the animals in the story run. Ask, *How does running like a cow differ from running like a hen or a pig?* (Linguistic, Logical-Mathematical, Bodily-Kinesthetic, Naturalist, Interpersonal)

❍ Fill the library with other books about monsters. (Intrapersonal)

❍ Fold four sheets of drawing paper into three equal parts. Draw monster heads on the top third of each page, monster torsos in the middle third, and monster legs in the bottom third. Cut each picture apart, mix up the pieces, and invite the children to create their own monsters by choosing a head, body, and legs, and assembling the parts. (Logical-Mathematical, Spatial, Naturalist)

Learning Activities

Art *(Spatial)*

Set out drawing paper, markers, and crayons. Invite the children to draw monsters like the one in *One Cow Moo Moo* or any kind of monster. Remind them that monsters are make-believe, so their creatures don't have to have two eyes, one nose, one mouth, and so on. Monsters don't have to be scary, either!

Discovery *(Spatial, Bodily-Kinesthetic, Musical, Interpersonal, Intrapersonal)*

Set out an overhead projector or other light source. Play monster music for added effect. Show the children how to create animal shadows on the wall, and encourage the children to invent their own creatures. If possible, provide a book about shadow hand puppets.

Language *(Linguistic)*

Put out photographs of the animals in *One Cow Moo Moo*, as well as a drawing of the monster. Invite the children to retell the story using the photos.

Listening *(Musical, Naturalist)*

Record actual animal sounds for each animal in the story, and make up a sound for the monster. Encourage the children to identify the sounds that belong to each animal.

Math *(Logical-Mathematical, Naturalist)*

Provide several similar-sized images of the different animals that appear in *One Cow Moo Moo*. Challenge the children to arrange the animals in the pictures by size from the smallest to the largest.

Water Table *(Logical-Mathematical, Interpersonal)*

Provide spray bottles, magic dust (glitter or confetti), and a few watered down extracts. Challenge the "research scientist" children to create a monster spray by combining a few aromas with water and the "magic dust." The children to fill the bottles with their concoctions, give the concoctions names, and label them.

Let's Keep Reading

Abiyoyo by Pete Seeger
Barnyard Banter by Denise Fleming
The Judge by Harve Zemach
The Old Woman and Her Pig by Rosanne Litzinger

Thinking About What We Learned

1. What do you think might have happened if the animals all turned around and started chasing the monster?
2. Which activity did you most enjoy today? Why?

Over in the Meadow

Traditional. Illustrator: Ezra Jack Keats

About the Book
This text in this book is based on a traditional Southern Appalachia counting song, which is more than 100 years old.

Learning Literacy

Oral Language
○ Discuss the words in the book that may be new vocabulary, such as *reeds, shore, muskrat, burrowed, glen*, and so on.

Comprehension
○ Ask the children the following questions: *Which of the animals in the meadow do you like best? Why? Which animals dig? Which animals say caw? How many numbers are mentioned in the book?*
○ Assign the children to represent each animal group and re-enact the story.

Print Awareness
○ Ask the children how many colors are mentioned in the song, and help them make a list of the colors.
○ Invite the children to help you write a new verse for the song. Ask them to select an animal not mentioned in the story, a cat and kitten, for instance, then select a number, two, for instance, that has several options for rhyming words, such as *dew, few, who*, and *knew*.

Special Activities

○ Sing "Over in the Meadow" with the children. (Musical)
○ Assign each child to be one of the animals from the book, and invite them to act out the story. (Linguistic, Naturalist, Interpersonal)
○ Visit a park or a nature preserve. Ask, *How many animals mentioned in the book do you find in the park or preserve?* (Linguistic, Logical-Mathematical, Naturalist)
○ Play music and challenge children to dance and move like their favorite animals from the story. Challenge the children to identify the animals their classmates are imitating. (Bodily-Kinesthetic, Intrapersonal)
○ Build a paper meadow. Make a pond from blue bulletin board paper or with blue cellophane. Create trees and grass with crepe paper and construction paper. Make terrain by using spray paint in earth tone colors. Spray the paint randomly on an old bed sheet. Provide plastic animals and place them where they go in the meadow, according to the story. (Spatial, Bodily-Kinesthetic, Naturalist)

Learning Activities

Art *(Spatial, Intrapersonal)*
Suggest that the children use paints, paper, and brushes to paint their favorite animals from the story. Challenge them to paint both the mother animal and the appropriate number of babies she has with her.

Math *(Logical-Mathematical, Naturalist)*
Give the children plastic animals to count, such as one frog, two fish, three birds, and so on. Keep the number of animals consistent with the numbers mentioned in the book, even if you have to skip some numbers because you do not have enough of a particular type of animal.

Gross Motor *(Bodily-Kinesthetic, Naturalist, Interpersonal)*
Find photos to represent each animal mentioned in the story. Glue the photos to 4" x 6" index cards. Lay the cards face down. Invite the children to draw one card at a time, and then imitate the movements of the animals on their cards.

Sand Table *(Interpersonal)*
Encourage the children to bury plastic turtles in the sand. Talk with the children as they play. Discuss how turtles bury themselves in the sand to stay cool. Ask, *Does anyone have a turtle at home?*

Listening *(Linguistic, Musical)*
Place a recording of the song version of "Over in the Meadow," along with a copy of the book itself in the center. Encourage the children to listen to the song while looking through the pages of the book.

Science *(Linguistic, Naturalist, Logical-Mathematical)*
Provide photographs of all of the animals mentioned in the story. Encourage the children to sort the animals by *large* and *small, flies* and *doesn't fly, insect* and *non-insect*, and so on. Talk with the children about all the different ways to sort the animals.

Let's Keep Reading

In the Small, Small Pond by Denise Fleming
In the Tall, Tall Grass by Denise Fleming

Thinking About What We Learned

1. Can you think of animals that might be in a meadow, but were not mentioned in the book?
2. Which activity did you enjoy most today?

Owl Babies

Author: Martin Waddell. Illustrator: Patrick Benson

About the Book

Three baby owls wake up to find their mother owl gone. Their anxiety grows as they wait for her to return. This is great story about a common childhood fear. The predictable language and beautiful illustrations are comforting to children.

Learning Literacy

Oral Language

❍ Ask the children questions about times when they had to wait for their mothers. *How do you feel when you have to wait for your mother to come home?*

Comprehension

❍ Ask the children the following questions: *How would the story be different if mother owl had been in the nest when the babies woke up? What was the mother owl doing?*

❍ Create a KWL chart (see appendix page 228). Draw a chart with three columns on a piece of chart paper or bulletin board paper. Label the first column *What We Know*, the second column *What We Want to Know*, and the third column *What We Learned*. Discuss owls with the children and then fill in the first and second columns in the chart. At the end of the day or week, after you have studied owls, fill in the last column.

Print Awareness

❍ Point out the quotation marks in the book. Explain that the quotation marks indicate words someone is speaking.

Letter Knowledge

❍ Talk with the children about the use of uppercase letters in some of the words and phrases in the book. *Why does the author use all uppercase (big) letters?*

Special Activities

❍ Visit the zoo or wildlife center to see the owls. Ask the children to keep track of how many different kinds of owls they find at the zoo. Ask, *Can you find the owls like those in* Owl Babies? (Logical-Mathematical, Naturalist, Interpersonal)

❍ Provide paper or plastic plates for wings, and invite the children to dance, bounce, flap, and fly like baby owls. Play music to inspire an owl dance. (Linguistic, Intrapersonal, Interpersonal, Bodily-Kinesthetic, Musical)

❍ Invite the children to spread their wings (arms) and "fly" like owls between a light source (overhead projector) and the wall. Ask questions: *Do you look like an owl? How wide can you spread your wings?* (Spatial, Bodily-Kinesthetic, Interpersonal)

Learning Activities

 Construction *(Spatial, Bodily-Kinesthetic, Naturalist)*
Provide a box to represent a tree trunk, with a hole cut in the side for an owl nest. Provide twigs, feathers, and leaves so the children can build an owl nest.

 Listening *(Logical-Mathematical, Musical, Interpersonal)*
Invite the children to "*whoo*" like owls. Encourage them to "*whoo*" into a box, inside a plastic cup, inside a paper bag, through a paper towel tube, and so on. Ask questions: *How does the sound change with each item? Which sounds most like an owl* whooing *at night in the woods?*

 **Gross Motor** *(Logical-Mathematical, Bodily-Kinesthetic, Interpersonal)*
Encourage the children to stand or walk on a balance beam like the baby owls balance on the branch of a tree. Provide paper plates for wings and challenge the children to stand on the balance beam while flapping their "wings."

 Math *(Logical-Mathematical)*
Provide three different branches, one small, one medium, and one large. Invite the children to arrange the branches from largest to smallest and then from smallest to largest.

 **Language** *(Linguistic, Intrapersonal)*
Encourage the children to describe times they waited for their mothers or someone else to come back and pick them up. Ask questions. *How did you feel? Were you frightened?* After the children have told their stories, encourage them to illustrate their stories.

 Writing *(Linguistic, Bodily-Kinesthetic)*
Print *Sarah*, *Percy*, and *Bill* on chart paper. Invite children to use magnetic letters to copy the owl names.

Let's Keep Reading

Owl Moon by Jane Yolen
Owly by Mike Thaler

Thinking About What We Learned

1. How did the owls feel when they finally saw their mother?
2. Which owl activity did you like best today? Why?

Owl Moon

Author: Jane Yolen. Illustrator: John Schoenherr

About the Book

A young girl and her father go owling late one winter night. The two walk along in silence waiting to see an owl. When finally an owl appears, the little girl is at a loss for words at the wonder of the hunt and joy of the find.

Learning Literacy

Oral Language

❍ The story is filled with imagery. Explain to the children that *imagery* is the use of imaginative words to describe something. Tell the children that many authors like to use imagery, and show the children some of the following examples from *Owl Moon*: *whiter than milk in a cereal bowl, the trees stood as still as giant statues,* and *I could feel the cold as if someone's icy hand was palm-down on my back.* Talk with the children about what each example describes.

❍ Show the children photographs of owls. Invite them to talk about the owls—the colors of the feathers, their size, their behavior, and diet. The owl in the book is a great horned owl. Share details about this type of owl with the children.

❍ Discuss unusual phrases used in the story, such as *pumped his wings; like a sad, sad song; made his face into a silver mask*; and so on.

Comprehension

❍ Ask the children the following questions: *Why does Pa say, "…all you need is hope"? Have you ever seen an owl? Where?*

Special Activities

❍ Visit the zoo. Read books about owls before the trip, such as *Owl Babies* by Martin Waddell, *Goodnight, Owl* by Pat Hutchins, and *Owly* by Jane Thaler. Make a list of the different kinds of owls discussed in the books. At the zoo, see how many different kinds of owls the children can find. Look for other animals mentioned in *Owl Moon.* Encourage the children to try calling to the owls. *Do they return the call?* (Linguistic, Logical-Mathematical, Musical, Naturalist, Interpersonal)

❍ Play classical music and invite the children to pretend they are soaring like owls. Remind the children that owls are large, graceful birds that seem to float through the air. (Bodily-Kinesthetic, Interpersonal, Intrapersonal)

Learning Activities

Art *(Spatial)*
Put out containers of white tempera paint, paper, and several feathers the children can use as brushes or pens. Invite the children to use their unusual brushes to make snowy pictures.

Language *(Linguistic, Spatial, Intrapersonal)*
Suggest that the children dictate stories about special events they have enjoyed with family members or friends. Write down their stories and invite the children to illustrate them.

Discovery *(Logical-Mathematical, Naturalist, Interpersonal, Intrapersonal)*
Encourage the children to look at photos of different types of owls. Talk with them as they look through the photos. Ask questions: *How many different colors of owls do you see? How many different sizes?*

Listening *(Linguistic, Musical, Interpersonal, Intrapersonal)*
Encourage the children to practice owl calling, *Whoo-whoo-whoo-whoo-whoo-whooooooooo.* Ask the children to find partners and practice calling and echoing one another. Ask the children the following questions: *What does the call sound like? Is it scary? Is it soothing? Is it different if you whisper it?*

Dramatic Play *(Bodily-Kinesthetic, Interpersonal, Intrapersonal)*
Provide a light source and some items that will make interesting shadows—a branch, crumpled paper, stuffed animals, and toy cars and trucks. Encourage the children to make shadows. Remind them of the shadows discussed in the story.

Science *(Bodily-Kinesthetic, Naturalist, Interpersonal)*
Provide paper cutouts in the shapes of feathers. Encourage the children to drop the feathers in the air, and watch them float to the ground. Provide other items such as pennies, tissues, and cotton balls. Encourage the children to work in pairs to race the feathers against all the other items.

Let's Keep Reading

The Polar Express by Chris Van Allsburg

Thinking About What We Learned

1. If you could stay up past your bedtime, what would you want to do?
2. Would you like to go owling? Why? Why not?

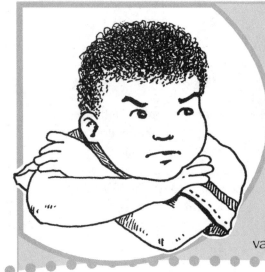

Peter's Chair

Author and Illustrator: Ezra Jack Keats

About the Book
Peter is feeling sad when he sees that all the things that used to be his are now being painted pink for his new baby sister. Peter decides to run away with his chair before his family paints it for his sister, too. Peter learns a valuable lesson about growing up and moving on.

Learning Literacy

Oral Language

❍ Talk with the children about the use of pink for girls and blue for boys. *Do you think that using blue for boys and pink for girls is a good idea? Why? Why not?*

Comprehension

❍ Ask the children the following questions: *Why is Peter feeling sad? What does Peter learn about his chair? Have you ever felt like Peter? What did you do?*

Print Awareness/Oral Language

❍ Encourage the children to help make a list of ways they know they are growing up. For example, their old clothes don't fit, they can reach things they couldn't reach before, and so on.

Special Activities

❍ Encourage the children to wash the chairs in the classroom. Play lullaby music while they work. (Musical, Interpersonal)

❍ Invite the children to bring in baby pictures of themselves. Make a bulletin board of "Beautiful Babies," or put the photos in a baggie book (see page 38). Invite the children to help you arrange the photos on the board or in the baggie book. (Spatial, Interpersonal)

❍ Ask the children's families to bring in clothes that their children have outgrown. When the children have a substantial collection, help them sort and classify the clothing by size and season. Find an organization that can distribute the clothing to children and make a class donation. Discuss the experience with the children. *How does it make you feel to help others? Do you think other children will be glad to have some new clothes to wear?* (Linguistic, Logical-Mathematical, Naturalist, Interpersonal, Intrapersonal)

❍ Teach the children the rhyme, "When I Was One." Encourage them to suit their actions to the words. (Linguistic, Logical-Mathematical, Bodily-Kinesthetic, Intrapersonal)

When I Was One

When I was one, I was so small, (hold up one finger)
I could not speak a word at all. (shake head)
When I was two, I learned to talk. (hold up two fingers)
I learned to sing, I learned to walk. (point to mouth and feet)
When I was three, I grew and grew. (hold up two fingers)
Now I am four and so are you! (hold up four fingers)

Learning Activities

Art *(Spatial)*
Provide pink paint and paper and encourage the children to paint a pink picture. Talk with the children about their artistic creations.

Dramatic Play *(Linguistic, Interpersonal, Intrapersonal)*
Provide a variety of dress-up clothes, including some items that are too small for the children. Talk with them as they try the clothing items on. Ask questions: *Does that fit? How old do you think you would have to be for that to fit?*

Blocks *(Bodily-Kinesthetic, Interpersonal, Intrapersonal)*
Encourage the children to stack blocks as high as they are tall.

Listening *(Musical)*
Encourage the children to use a tape recorder to record lullabies for Peter's baby sister. You may want to record a few lullabies on the tape in case the children prefer to listen instead of sing.

Discovery *(Linguistic, Logical-Mathematical, Naturalist)*
Cut a hole in the center of a plastic lid of a 5-pound coffee can. Provide a collection of items, some of which will fit through the hole and some of which will not fit. Invite the children to look at the items, guess if the items will fit in the hole, and test their predictions.

Science *(Logical-Mathematical, Interpersonal, Intrapersonal)*
Weigh and measure each child. Record their height and weight and keep the information in a safe place. In a couple of months, weigh and measure children again, and invite them to compare the differences.

Let's Keep Reading
A Chair for My Mother by Vera B. Williams

Thinking About What We Learned

1. Do you have a younger brother, sister, relative, or friend? What can you do that the younger person cannot do?
2. What did you paint with the pink paint?

The Pig in the Pond

Author: Martin Waddell. Illustrator: Jill Barton

About the Book
One hot summer day, a pig sits by a pond and wishes he could swim. After a while, it just doesn't matter if he can swim. He's so hot, he just jumps in. Before long, others join the pig in the cool water.

Learning Literacy

Oral Language/Print Awareness
❍ Ask the children, *How do you cool off on a warm day?* Make a list of the ideas that the children name.

Phonological Awareness
❍ Read the book a second time and ask the children to raise their hand each time they hear an *onomatopoeic* sound (words that imitate the sounds they are trying to describe) in the story.

Comprehension
❍ Ask the children the following questions: *Why did the pig not go in the water right away? Why did he finally jump in? Have you ever seen a pig swim? Why are pigs not built for swimming?*

Letter Knowledge
❍ Show the children the cover of the book. Read the title. Invite a volunteer to show you those words in the title that begin with the same letter. Ask someone to name the letter.

Special Activities

❍ Plan a water play day. Have parents bring the children to school in their bathing suits. Provide bubbles, a wading pool, sprinkler, body paint, sponges and soap to wash chairs, a tub of soapy water and a hose to wash tricycles, spray bottles of water and surfaces to spray, and so on. Read *The Pig in the Pond* under a tree outside, or somewhere that provides a good seating area. (Linguistic, Logical-Mathematical, Spatial, Bodily-Kinesthetic, Musical, Naturalist, Interpersonal, Intrapersonal)

❍ Visit a farm. Show the children the pigs. Ask the children why they might not make good swimmers. *Do they have fins? Webbed feet? Are they graceful? Do they appear energetic?* (Logical-Mathematical, Naturalist, Interpersonal)

❍ Make a list of the animals in the story. Sing "Mr. Neligan Had a Farm," making sure to include all the animals in the story. (Linguistic, Musical)

Learning Activities

(Spatial)
Fill an ice tray with water and place in the freezer. When the cubes begin to freeze, place a craft stick in each section. When the cubes freeze around the sticks, remove them from the tray and give them to the children to use as paintbrushes. Place a small amount of flavored powdered juice on a sheet of fingerpaint paper and encourage the children to use the "ice brushes." After they finish painting, invite them to eat their brushes if they like.

(Linguistic, Spatial, Bodily-Kinesthetic, Interpersonal)
Provide several plastic farm animals. Cut blue bulletin board paper in an irregular shape to represent a pond. Encourage the children to build a farm around the pond. Invite the children to retell the story using the plastic animals. Encourage them to use the animals' sounds as part of their story.

(Linguistic, Logical-Mathematical, Interpersonal)
Help the children prepare lemonade. Allow them to slice the lemons with a plastic knife and squeeze the juice through a strainer. Encourage them to pour the sugar and add it to the lemons and water. Invite the children to add ice and serve the cool lemonade to their friends.

(Logical-Mathematical, Naturalist, Interpersonal)
Provide summer clothing and encourage the children to figure out the best outfits to wear when it is hot outside. Ask the children to explain the differences between winter and summer clothing. *Which type of clothing has the heaviest fabric? Which type of clothing has longer sleeves?*

(Linguistic, Spatial, Bodily-Kinesthetic)
Encourage the children to use paper and crayons to draw "cool" pictures, and then show them how to fold the paper to make a fan. Ask, *Does the fan keep you cool?*

(Linguistic, Musical, Interpersonal)
Select one child to represent each animal group in the story. Read the story, stopping to allow the children to fill in the animal sounds. When it is time for the water to splash, invite all the children say *splash* or make splashing sounds. After practicing a couple of times, read the story again and record it with the children making the sound effects.

Let's Keep Reading

The Old Woman and Her Pig by Eric A. Kimmel

Thinking About What We Learned

1. Why did Mr. Neligan jump in the pond?
2. Do you think the pig was smart or not smart for jumping in the water?

The Pigeon Finds a Hot Dog!

Author and Illustrator: Mo Willems

About the Book
Pigeon finds a hot dog, but before he can enjoy it he is joined by a very clever, very hungry duckling. Who will eat the hot dog?

Learning Literacy

Oral Language

❍ Introduce words that may be new to the children, such as *sensation, morsel,* and *splendor.*

❍ Encourage the children to discuss the expressions the pigeon uses to describe the hot dog, such as *taste sensation* and *celebration in a bun.*

❍ Show the children pictures of real pigeons and ducks. Ask, *How may toes do pigeons have? How many toes do ducks have? How are pigeons like ducks? How are they different?*

Comprehension

❍ Ask the children the following questions: *Have you ever eaten a hot dog? When? What does a hot dog taste like? What do you eat on your hot dog? Do you think the duckling has ever eaten a hot dog before? How does he know it might taste better with mustard?*

Special Activities

❍ Visit a hot dog stand. Ask the children the following questions: *How do the cooks prepare the hot dogs? What do the customers like on their hot dogs?* (Linguistic, Interpersonal, Intrapersonal)

❍ Go somewhere to watch pigeons. Ask the children, *How do they walk? What do they eat?* (Linguistic, Bodily-Kinesthetic, Naturalist)

❍ Invite the children to sing duck songs, such as "Six White Ducks," "Little Ducky Duddle," or "Five Little Ducks." (Linguistic, Musical, Interpersonal)

❍ Create a maze using furniture, such as chairs, or classroom materials, such as blocks. Provide a small plastic egg (pigeon egg). Challenge the children to roll the egg through the maze using their toes. Provide an empty toilet paper tube covered in red paper to represent a hot dog. Challenge the children to roll the hot dog through the maze using only their toes. (Spatial, Bodily-Kinesthetic, Interpersonal)

Learning Activities

Art

(Spatial, Bodily-Kinesthetic)
Make a pigeon leg and foot by twisting two pipe cleaners together in the middle, then bending the pipe cleaners in half and twisting them together until they are an inch from the bottom. Spread the four pipe cleaner ends to make a pigeon foot. Provide tempera paint and paper and invite the children to make bird footprints using the pipe cleaner feet.

Dramatic Play

(Linguistic, Logical-Mathematical, Interpersonal)
Provide props such as hats, pretend buns and wieners, empty condiment jars, a cash register, play money, and so on, for a hot dog stand. Encourage the children to make signs for the stand, and pretend to buy and sell hot dogs.

Games

(Logical-Mathematical, Naturalist)
Place six large, black wiggle eyes (to represent the pigeon's eyes) and six smaller blue wiggle eyes (to represent the duck's eyes) in a bowl. The children reach in the bowl pick up a few eyes, and drop them onto a mat. Encourage them to match the black eyes and the blue eyes one to one. Ask, *Are there more blues eyes or black eyes?*

Listening

(Musical)
Suggest that the children use a cassette recorder to record birdcalls. Provide a commercial tape of birdcalls, and encourage the children to listen to the tape. Ask questions: *Which bird makes the loudest sound? Do any of the birds sound like pigeons? Do any of the birds sound like ducks? Do ducks* quack *or do they* peep? *Do pigeons* quack *or* peep?

Snack

(Linguistic, Intrapersonal)
Serve hot dogs for snack. Encourage the children to help prepare the hot dogs. Introduce the word *condiment*, and ask the children which condiments they like on their hot dogs.

Writing

(Linguistic, Spatial, Intrapersonal, Interpersonal)
Invite the children to describe their ideal hot dogs. Write their descriptions on sheets of drawing paper and encourage the children to draw images of those hot dogs and their favorite condiments.

Let's Keep Reading

Don't Let the Pigeon Drive the Bus! by Mo Willems
The Little Mouse, the Red Ripe Strawberry, and the Big Hungry Bear by Don and Audrey Wood

Thinking About What We Learned

1. Do you think the pigeon did the right thing when he decided to share his hot dog?
2. Do pigeons really eat hot dogs? Which part of the hot dog would the pigeon like best? Do ducks really eat hot dogs?

Right Outside My Window

Author: Mary Ann Hoberman. Illustrator: Nicholas Wilton

About the Book
There are wonders galore right outside the window. This book explores the many wonders of each season.

Learning Literacy

Oral Language

❍ Ask the children what they might see if they went outside and looked through the window from the other side.

❍ Discuss windows with the children. *Where do we see windows? Why do houses have windows? Why do cars have windows? Are our eyes windows?* Help the children make a list of all the different kinds of windows they can think of. Make a note of the function of each type of window; for example, store windows are for displays, car windows are for safety, home windows are for letting in light, envelope windows are for displaying an address, and so on.

❍ Introduce the children to window vocabulary, for example, *windowpane, windowsill, window frame, screen, locks*, and so on.

Comprehension

❍ Ask the children the following questions: *What do you see right outside the window? What is outside your window at home?*

Print Awareness

❍ Look out the classroom window with the children. Make a list of the things they see outside the window. Challenge them to think about the changes that might take place outside the window during a different season.

Special Activities

❍ Take a walk around the school and see how many different kinds of windows you can find. *What shapes are the windows? Are there windows in doors? Are the windows high or low? What is the purpose of a window if it is so high you can't see outside?* (Linguistic, Logical-Mathematical, Naturalist)

❍ Fly a kite with the children. Invite the children to discuss how the kite must feel as it soars above. Ask the children what they think they would be able to see if they were up with the kite. Invite the children to make their own kites—decorated lunch bags tied to pieces of yarn make simple kites. (Spatial, Bodily-Kinesthetic, Intrapersonal)

❍ Sing the song and play the game, Go In and Out the Windows. (Bodily Kinesthetic, Musical, Interpersonal)

Go In and Out the Windows

Go in and out the windows. (IT walks around the circle, weaving in and out between children)
Go in and out the windows,
Go in and out the windows,
As we have done before.

Additional verses:
Stand and face your partner... (IT chooses a partner)
Now follow her/him to London... (IT and partner weave through circle)
Bow before you leave her/him... (IT leaves partner [new IT] and joins circle)

Learning Activities

Art

(Linguistic, Spatial, Intrapersonal)
Give the children paper, crayons, markers, and paint, and encourage them to draw what they see outside their bedroom windows or outside the classroom window. Ask them to describe their pictures. With their permission, transcribe their descriptions on the backs of their pictures.

Dramatic Play

(Spatial, Bodily-Kinesthetic)
Help the children use scissors, rolls of tape, and several squares of cellophane to create designs on the windows. Let them cut cellophane into any shape they like and then tape them to the windows. Ask questions: *How does the cellophane change the way things look inside the room? Does the sun coming in make colored shadows on the floor?*

Blocks

(Spatial, Bodily-Kinesthetic, Interpersonal, Intrapersonal)
Challenge the children to use blocks to build a house, leaving spaces for windows. Provide toy animals and shrubbery and suggest that the children create a special scene just outside one of the windows.

Listening

(Musical, Interpersonal, Intrapersonal)
Make a tape of the story and place it in the center with the book. Provide a spray bottle of water (for rain), a fan (for wind), some dry leaves, and a whistle. Encourage the children to use the items and their own voices and bodies to create sound effects as you reread the book.

Discovery

(Linguistic)
Give each child an 8" square of poster board with a 6" square window cut in it. Provide various colors of cellophane cut in 7" square sheets. Have them select single sheets of cellophane and tape them to the backs of their windows. Ask the children to describe what they see when they look through their windows.

Science

(Linguistic, Logical-Mathematical, Naturalist)
Provide a collection of items that represent each season; for example, dried leaves, dried flowers, acorns, sand, glitter, moss, feathers, seasonal confetti, and so on. Provide several clean ½-liter soda bottles and help the children create observation bottles for each of the four seasons.

Let's Keep Reading

Flower Garden by Eve Bunting

Thinking About What We Learned

1. Does the scene outside your window change with time?
2. Which activity did you enjoy most today? Why?

Rosie's Walk

Author and Illustrator: Pat Hutchins

About the Book
A fox is after Rosie, but she is totally unaware of its presence. She walks across the farmyard and home again, leading the fox into one catastrophe after another. In the end, she makes it home safely.

Learning Literacy

Oral Language

○ Ask a volunteer to demonstrate all of the spatial vocabulary used in the book (*across, through, around, over,* and *under*). Help the children see that each of these words refers to a location. Tell the children, *These words tell us where Rosie is walking.*

○ Invite the children to identify the farm buildings and objects in the illustrations. *Which farm animals are in the illustrations?*

○ Discuss the illustrations with the children. *Why do you think the illustrator uses only warm colors such as red, brown, orange, and gold? Which items in the book might be blue or green?*

Comprehension

○ Ask the children the following questions: *What happened to the fox at the end of the story? Why is he not behind Rosie anymore? Does Rosie know the fox is behind her? How would the story be different if it happened in a jungle instead of a farm?*

○ Look through the pages of the book again. See if the children can tell the story by just looking at the pictures, or if they can tell the story from the fox's point of view.

Special Activities

○ Visit a farm. Try to take the same walk Rosie took across the yard. Ask, *Do you see any beehives?* (Bodily-Kinesthetic, Naturalist, Interpersonal)

○ Do the Chicken Dance. Music is available on *All Time Favorite Dances CD* by Kimbo Educational as well as on several other children's dance CDs. (Linguistic, Bodily-Kinesthetic, Musical, Interpersonal)

○ Play Fox and Chicken as you would play Cat and Mouse. This is a simple game of chase. Choose one child to be the Fox, and tell the rest of the children they are chickens. The Fox chases the chickens. When the Fox tags a chicken, the chicken then becomes the Fox. (Linguistic, Bodily-Kinesthetic, Interpersonal)

○ Create a maze that goes from the hen house around the farmyard and back to the hen house. Outline the pathway with masking tape. Make some "hazards" along the way, such as a tub of water (pond), a bucket of beads (representing bees), ropes to step over, and so on. Invite the children to strut through the maze the way Rosie does, hands tucked under arms to make wings. (Linguistic, Logical-Mathematical, Spatial, Bodily-Kinesthetic, Interpersonal)

○ Fill the library with books about hens. Challenge the children to find other stories about a hen and a fox, such as *Big Fat Hen* by Keith Baker and *The Hungry Hen* by Richard Waring. (Linguistic, Intrapersonal)

Learning Activities

Art

(Linguistic, Spatial)
Make an audio recording of directions for drawing a house. Ask children to place a sun over the house, a tree next to the house, a chicken under the tree, and a fox behind the tree. Leave about 45 seconds of space between each direction. Challenge children to follow the directions as they draw.

Art

(Spatial, Naturalist, Intrapersonal)
Encourage the children to paint a picture using only warm colors, like those that Hutchins uses in the book. Ask questions: *How does it feel to use only warm colors? What happens when you use warm colors to paint something that is usually blue, green, or purple?*

Blocks

(Spatial, Bodily-Kinesthetic, Interpersonal)
Encourage the children to use farm and story props to build a farm. Provide a plastic hen and fox, a rake, bag of flour, beehive (box), hay, and so on. Challenge the children to re-enact the story using these materials.

Discovery

(Logical-Mathematical)
Hang a pulley in the classroom. Compare it to the pulley in the book that holds a bag of flour. Place a bucket at one end of the rope and run the other end through the pulley. Demonstrate how the pulley works. Show the children what happens if you let go of the rope. Provide items to place in the bucket. **Safety Note:** Supervise closely.

Music

(Musical, Interpersonal)
Provide several different suspenseful pieces of music, such as music from the *Lord of the Rings* or *The Polar Express* soundtracks. Invite the children to choose a piece of music that would make good sneaky music for the fox, and encourage them to dance around as though they were the sneaky fox.

Writing

(Linguistic)
Print *Rosie* on an index card. Provide magnetic letters and encourage the children to copy the name.

Let's Keep Reading

Hattie and the Fox by Mem Fox
The Hungry Hen by Richard Waring
The Wolf's Chicken Stew by Keiko Kasza

Thinking About What We Learned

1. How would the story have been different if Rosie knew the fox was behind her?
2. Would you rather be a fox or a hen? Why?

Silly Sally

Author and Illustrator: Audrey Wood

About the Book
Silly Sally walks on her hands to town. Along the way, she is joined by many creatures who add to the silliness of this story.

Learning Literacy

Oral Language

○ Discuss words in the story that may be new for the children, such as *jig, leaping, loon,* and *tune.* Encourage the children to demonstrate the meaning of *backwards, forwards, upside down,* and *right side up.*

Phonological Awareness

○ Write *Silly Sally* on a sheet of chart paper. Point out the /s/ sound in both of Sally's names. Explain that the repetition of beginning sounds is called *alliteration.* Ask the children if anyone in class has an alliterative name. Help the children think of ways to make their names alliterative.

Comprehension

○ Ask the children the following questions: *How would the story be different if Sally had just walked to town on her feet? How did Neddy Buttercup wake the group of sleeping animals and Silly Sally? Do you think it is difficult to walk upside down? Have you ever tried it?*

Special Activities

○ If possible, take the children to a circus. Talk about the circus acts they will see before the trip so that children will know what to expect. Discuss the circus when you return to the classroom. Encourage the children to make a list of the performers. Invite them to talk about the equipment that the performers use, such as the trapeze, trampoline, tightrope, and so on. Ask the children which acts they enjoyed the most. (Linguistic, Naturalist, Intrapersonal)

○ Create a circus in the dramatic play center. Hang fabric from the ceiling so the room has the feel of a tent. Provide costumes, stuffed animals and other props, such as balls, hoops, and homemade dumbbells (lunch bags filled with paper, attached to a cardboard tube and painted black). Encourage the children to sell tickets and to perform circus acts. Don't forget to play circus music as the children perform. (Linguistic, Logical-Mathematical, Spatial, Musical, Interpersonal, Intrapersonal)

○ Teach the children to play Leap Frog like the silly dog in the story. (Bodily-Kinesthetic, Interpersonal)

Learning Activities

Art *(Spatial)*

The illustrations in the book are done in watercolor. Provide watercolor paints, brushes, and paper, and encourage the children to paint watercolor pictures. Talk with the children about the experience of using watercolors. Ask questions: *How are watercolors different from tempera paint? How can you keep the colors from running together?*

Gross Motor *(Bodily-Kinesthetic)*

Place a strip of masking tape on the floor. Give the children beanbags. Show them how to walk on "all fours." Challenge them to place the beanbags on their heads and then walk the masking tape line on "all fours." Ask, *Is it difficult to walk in this upside-down position?*

Blocks *(Linguistic, Logical-Mathematical, Spatial, Bodily-Kinesthetic, Interpersonal)*

Invite the children to use blocks to build a town and a road leading to the town. Provide plastic animals and cars the children can push along the road.

Music *(Bodily-Kinesthetic, Musical)*

Encourage the children to dance a "pig jig." Challenge the children to dance their jig backwards. Encourage the children create a song for Silly Sally to sing with the loon, and challenge them to sing that backwards, too.

Discovery *(Spatial, Bodily-Kinesthetic)*

Provide crayons and drawing paper. Invite the children to stand, bend over, and look through their legs. Challenge them to draw a picture of something they see while looking at things in this upside-down position.

Writing *(Linguistic, Naturalist)*

Place several sets of magnetic letters and a copy of *Silly Sally* in the center. Challenge the children to use the letters to spell *Silly Sally*. Talk with the children about the letters in *Silly Sally*. Ask, *Which letters are the same in each part of Silly Sally's name? Which letters are different in each part of her name?*

Let's Keep Reading

Circus Fun by Becky Radtke
I Went Walking by Sue Williams

Thinking About What We Learned

1. How long do you think it would take to get to the playground if you had to walk on your hands?
2. Which of the animals that joined Silly Sally do you like best?

"Stand Back," Said the Elephant, "I'm Going to Sneeze!"

Author: Patricia Thomas. Illustrator: Wallace Tripp

About the Book

An elephant announces he is going to sneeze and all the animals beg him not to, reminding him of what happened the last time. A mouse scares him out of his sneeze, but causes him to laugh, which brings about the same results.

Learning Literacy

Oral Language

❍ Point out the way each animal in the story exaggerates the outcome of the sneeze. Find some examples of exaggeration statements; for example, *I told you a thousand times,* or *I could eat a horse.* Ask the children what might really happen if the elephant sneezed. *Would the story be as much fun without the exaggeration?*

Phonological Awareness

❍ Point out the *onomatopoeic* words (words that imitate the sounds they are describing), such as *thumping, he-he,* and so on.

❍ Read the book a second time, stopping to let the children fill in the rhyming words and predictable text. Reread the book again at another time, and point out the many examples of *alliteration,* repetition of beginning sounds, such as *ho-hoed, ha-haed, giggled and gaffed, chortled and chuckled,* and so on.

Comprehension

❍ Ask the children the following questions: *Why did the animals not want the elephant to sneeze? How did the animals know what would happen? What made the elephant laugh? What happened? Where does this story take place? How would it be different if it happened in the desert?*

Print Awareness

❍ Show the children the cover of the book. Talk with the children about the quotation marks in the title.

Special Activities

❍ Visit the zoo. Encourage the children to find the animals that are in the story. Keep a count of how many animals the children find. Ask the zookeeper if the elephant ever sneezes. (Linguistic, Logical-Mathematical, Naturalist, Interpersonal)

❍ Play Tummy Ticklers. Invite children to lie on the floor on their backs with their heads on someone else's tummy. Do something silly to make the children start laughing. Ask the children what is making their heads jiggle. This activity should cause contagious laughing. Ask, *Do you think the elephant could stop himself from laughing?* (Interpersonal, Intrapersonal)

❍ Invite the children to think of items in the classroom they might us as an elephant's trunk, such as a piece of ribbon, an empty paper towel tube, or their arms, and encourage them to pretend that they are elephants announcing things to the other children. (Logical-Mathematical, Spatial, Naturalist)

Learning Activities

Blocks

(Linguistic, Spatial)
Suggest that the children use trees, plastic animals, and ground cover (an old bed sheet sprayed with earth-tone paints) to re-enact the story.

Construction

(Spatial, Bodily-Kinesthetic)
Give each child an 8" paper plate, an empty toilet paper tube (for a trunk), construction paper (for ears), two wiggle eyes, and gray paint to make elephant faces. After they paint the plates and toilet paper tubes, help them cut big ears from construction paper and glue to the plates, and then glue on the wiggle eyes and trunks (toilet paper tubes).

Discovery

(Logical-Mathematical, Naturalist, Interpersonal)
Give the children a hand-held fan, paper plate, straws, empty paper towel tubes, and a baster. Place a leaf on the floor and invite the children to move the feather with air created using the various items. Ask, *Which item works best?* Change the leaf to a twig. Ask, *Is moving the twig more difficult? Why?*

Dramatic Play

(Linguistic, Naturalist, Interpersonal, Intrapersonal)
Make cards with the names of each animal in the story on them, give them to the children, and invite them to re-enact the story. Help them remember each animal's objections and exaggerations. Ask the children which animals in the book are their favorites.

Gross Motor

(Bodily-Kinesthetic, Interpersonal)
Place an elephant face (see construction activity) on the floor. Challenge the children to stand over the plate and drop unshelled peanuts (held waist high) into the trunk. After this activity, invite the children to eat the peanuts. **Allergy Warning:** Check for peanut allergies before proceeding with this activity.

Listening

(Musical, Intrapersonal)
Record the story with jungle sounds playing quietly in the background. Encourage the children to listen to the recording of the story, and ask them how they think the music works with the story. *What animal sounds do you hear in the background?*

Let's Keep Reading

The Camel Who Took a Walk by Jack Tworkov
Elephants by Norman Barrett
Jungle Animals by Dorling Kindersley

Thinking About What We Learned

1. Do you think the elephant could stop himself from laughing?
2. Which animal in the story is your favorite?

Stone Soup

Author and Illustrator: Marcia Brown

About the Book
Three hungry soldiers stop by a French village and ask for food. The townspeople all refuse to share. The hungry soldiers decide to make soup from stones. The cunning soldiers soon manage to get contributions to the soup from everyone. The soup bubbles and boils and the townspeople lick their lips. When the soup is served, everyone agrees it is the best soup ever. This is a great telling of a traditional tale.

Learning Literacy

Oral Language

❍ Discuss the words and phrases in the story that may be new to the children, such as *spare, curiosity, peasants, bit of beef, quilts, splendid, loft,* and *cellar.*

❍ Talk with the children about how Marcia Brown used only red and brown in her illustrations. *What other colors could she have used? Would you like the pictures better if they were in full color? Why do you think the author chose red and brown?*

Comprehension

❍ Ask the children the following questions: *Do you think the stones added any flavor to the soup? Why did the people tell the soldiers that they had no food? What did the children bring to put into the soup?*

❍ Read *Fox Tale Soup* by Tony Bonning. Ask the children, *How are the stories alike? How are they different?* Make a Venn diagram (two large overlapping circles—see appendix page 227). Write the things the stories have in common in the overlap of the circles. Write things that are different about each story in the two portions of the circles that do not overlap.

Special Activities

❍ Make Stone Soup. Send a letter home to families requesting that children bring a vegetable to contribute to the soup. Provide the broth, meat (optional), and of course, the (clean) stone. Help the children peel and slice the vegetables. Ask questions about the textures of the vegetables as you add them to the soup. Point out the changes of state that occur in the textures of the vegetables as you eat them. Ask the children to describe the taste of each vegetable. *Which vegetable do you like best? Can you find the vegetable that you contributed? What makes the soup taste so good? Can you taste the stone?* You will probably need to cook on one day and serve on the next. (Linguistic, Logical-Mathematical, Bodily-Kinesthetic, Interpersonal)

Stone Soup
3 clean stones
water
salt and pepper
3 carrots
1 head of cabbage
3 large potatoes
barley
beef

❍ Give each child a large stone. Provide acrylic paint and invite the children to decorate their stones any way they choose. (Spatial, Intrapersonal)

Learning Activities

Art *(Logical-Mathematical, Spatial)*
Shuck an ear of corn, cut off all the kernels, and put them away to add to the classroom soup (see Special Activities on page 178). Provide tempera paint and paper and encourage the children to make prints with the cobs. Ask questions: *What happens when you roll the cob on your paper? What happens when you press it onto your paper?*

Gross Motor *(Bodily-Kinesthetic, Interpersonal)*
Provide crumpled brown paper to represent "stones." Provide a soup pot or a bucket. Use masking tape to mark a start line, and place the soup pot 4' to 6' away. Invite the children to toss their "stones" into the soup pot.

Blocks *(Linguistic, Spatial, Interpersonal)*
Invite the children to build a village using the blocks and other props, including stones of several different sizes. Ask the children questions as they build. *Are stones as easy to stack as blocks? Can you use the stones to build a road? Is a stone road more or less bumpy than a block road?*

Music *(Logical-Mathematical, Musical)*
Provide stones, a box, a can, a plastic bag, a plastic bowl, and a paper sack. Encourage the children to put the stones inside the different containers and shake them to see what kind of noises they make. Ask questions: *Do you think the stones would make any noise in the soldier's backpack?*

Dramatic Play *(Linguistic, Bodily-Kinesthetic, Naturalist, Interpersonal)*
Encourage the children to use props, such as backpacks, logs for a fire, stones, a pot, salt and pepper shakers, and plastic vegetables, to reenact the story. Talk with them as they play. Ask, *Can you remember the order in which the vegetables went into the soup?*

Writing *(Linguistic, Logical-Mathematical, Bodily-Kinesthetic, Intrapersonal)*
Print a recipe for Stone Soup on chart paper (see previous page). Provide pencils or crayons and paper. Challenge the children to copy the recipe. Talk with the children as they write. Ask them how they feel about the different ingredients.

Let's Keep Reading
Fox Tale Soup by Tony Bonning
The Great Big Turnip (Traditional)

Thinking About What We Learned
1. What is your favorite soup? Have you ever helped to make your favorite soup?
2. How does soup smell when it is cooking?

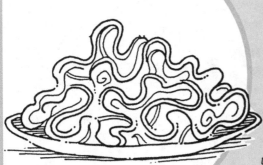

Strega Nona

Author and Illustrator: Tomie dePaola

About the Book
Strega Nona, Grandma Witch, helps everyone with their problems. When she hires Big Anthony to help her keep her house and take care of her yard, she has no idea how much trouble one man can cause.

Learning Literacy

Oral Language

○ Read the spells that start and stop the pasta pot. Ask the children, *Do the spells sound like the chant in any other story you have read? Snow White? The Three Little Pigs?*

○ Discuss how to say *grandmother* in other languages: *nonna* (Italian), *abuela* (Spanish), *vovó* (Portuguese), *amma* (Icelandic), *großmutter* (German), and *bedstemor* (Danish).

○ Talk with the children about cause-and-effect relationships. Present sentences that state a cause, and help the children identify the effect. For example, *Big Anthony was curious, so _____*, or *Strega Nona needed help, so _____.*

○ Point out the Italian words in the story, such as *grazie* and *si*. Talk with the children about the meanings of the words.

Comprehension

○ Ask the children the following questions: *How would the story have been different if Anthony had known the whole spell? If you had a magic pot, what would it cook?*

Special Activities

○ Visit an inexpensive, family-style Italian restaurant. Look at the menus. Ask questions: *How much does a meal cost? How much does a bowl of pasta cost?* Look at the décor. *Does the restaurant look like any of the buildings in the story?* (Linguistic, Logical-Mathematical, Interpersonal, Intrapersonal)

○ Dance Italian dances and play Italian games. "The Tarantella" is a very famous Italian dance. Legend has it that this dance, the Tarantella, was designed to be a cure for tarantula bites. Dancers hold hands and move in a circle first in one direction and then in the other. Each time the direction is changed the speed is increased. See www.sicilianculture.com/folklore/tarantella.htm for more information. (Musical, Interpersonal)

Learning Activities

Art

(Spatial, Bodily-Kinesthetic)
Cut pieces of yellow yarn to represent pasta. Provide paper and glue. Encourage the children to make "pasta" collages.

Gross Motor

(Bodily-Kinesthetic)
Use yellow yarn to create a pasta maze. Run the yarn back and forth around and through tables and chairs. Challenge children to crawl through the maze without touching the "pasta."

Discovery

(Musical, Interpersonal)
Gather items that are representative of Italy, such as a map with Italy outlined, Italian music, Italian clothing items, Italian tiles, tableware, and so on. Encourage the children to listen to the music and explore the other items.

Math

(Logical-Mathematical, Bodily-Kinesthetic)
Provide squiggle Styrofoam packing chips (to represent pasta), three cooking pots, and a measuring cup. Place a numeral 3 by one pot, a numeral 4 by the second pot, and a numeral 5 by the last pot. Invite the children to measure the number of cups of "pasta" (squiggles) indicated by the numerals beside the pots.

Dramatic Play

(Linguistic, Musical, Interpersonal, Intrapersonal)
Encourage the children to use a large pot with a long piece of yellow yarn inside to represent pasta to chant the spell from the book or make up a new chant as they re-enact the story.

Snack

(Linguistic, Logical-Mathematical, Interpersonal, Intrapersonal)
Invite the children to help make pasta. Cook several different types of pasta. Ask children which pasta they like best.

Let's Keep Reading

The Amazing Bone by William Steig
Big Anthony and the Magic Ring by Tomie dePaola
The Talking Pot, Vol. 1: Danish Folktales by Virginia Haviland

Thinking About What We Learned

1. What do you think would have happened if Strega Nona had not returned?
2. What did Big Anthony forget to do?

Swimmy

Author and Illustrator: Leo Lionni

About the Book
A clever little fish solves a big problem. Swimmy learns how to protect himself and his friends from the bigger fish in the ocean.

Learning Literacy

Oral Language
○ Talk about problem solving with the children. *What problem do the red fish have? How does Swimmy solve the problem?*
○ Discuss words that may be new to the children, such as *school* (of fish), *swift, fierce, marvel, medusa,* and so on.

Comprehension
○ Ask the children the following questions: *What would happen to Swimmy and his friends if they didn't stick together? What would the red fish have missed if they had stayed hidden in the coral and rocks?*

Print Awareness/Phonological Awareness
○ Sing "Tiny Red Fish" to the tune of "Three Blind Mice." Challenge the children to write a second verse about Swimmy.

Tiny Red Fish
Tiny red fish, tiny red fish,
See how they swim, see how they swim.
They swim together through ocean waves,
They stick together through coral caves,
Did you ever see such a sight in your life,
As tiny red fish?

Special Activities

○ Visit an aquarium. Before leaving on the trip, discuss and make a list of the sea life the children might see. At the aquarium, see if you can find all of the fish and sea creatures on the list. After returning to the classroom, invite the children to make a graph of their favorite sea creatures. Encourage them to draw pictures depicting their favorite parts of the trip. (Linguistic, Logical-Mathematical, Spatial, Naturalist)
○ Play classical musical and encourage the children to swim like sea animals. (Bodily-Kinesthetic, Musical, Interpersonal, Intrapersonal)

Learning Activities

Art *(Spatial)*
Provide sponges, paper, and watery tempera paint. Show the children how to use the sponges to create all kinds of watery effects. Provide some sponges cut into fish shapes. Encourage the children to look at the illustrations in the book for inspiration.

Gross Motor *(Logical Mathematical, Spatial, Bodily-Kinesthetic, Interpersonal, Intrapersonal)*
Twist several different brown paper bags together so they look like coral. Place the pieces of coral in a pathway in the form of a maze. Encourage the children to crawl through the maze like lobsters, swim through the maze like fish, and slowly float through the maze like jellyfish.

Discovery *(Linguistic, Naturalist)*
Provide real-life photos of sea creatures. Encourage the children to name them. Ask the children about the animals: *Which sea creatures are large? Which ones are small? Which ones swim? Which ones do not move?*

Science *(Linguistic, Naturalist, Intrapersonal)*
Place a goldfish in the science center, and encourage the children to observe how the fish swims. Feed the fish so they can watch how it eats. Ask: *Do you think goldfish get tired of swimming around in such a small space? Do they close their eyes? How do they sleep? Do they get lonely?*

Fine Motor *(Logical-Mathematical, Bodily-Kinesthetic, Interpersonal)*
Invite the children to make collages on poster board using bright colors of tissue paper, such as orange, yellow, and red. Provide fish templates for the children to trace onto the poster board collages. Cut out the fish. Encourage the children to lay the fish together so they make one large fish shape. Provide a black fish for the eye.

Water Table *(Linguistic, Musical, Naturalist, Interpersonal)*
Put out containers of water, funnels, cups, spray bottles, plastic fish, sea creatures, and so on. Encourage the children to play with the items in the water. Ask questions: *What sounds do you make when you splash the water? What sounds to you make when you pour water into the water in the table? Are there onomatopoeic words that describe these sounds?*

Let's Keep Reading
Fish Is Fish by Leo Lionni

Thinking About What We Learned
1. What games are more fun when you play them with others?
2. What sounds did you make with the water? Do fish make any sound when they swim in the water?

Ten Black Dots

Author and Illustrator: Donald Crews

About the Book
A clever story about all the things you might make with 10 black dots.

Learning Literacy

Phonological Awareness
❍ Point out to the children the rhyming words in the story.

Comprehension
❍ Ask the children the following questions: *What would you make with 10 black dots? Which is your favorite black dot picture in the book?*

Comprehension/Print Awareness
❍ Invite the children to retell the story, using a red dot instead of a black dot. Write their story on chart paper.

Special Activities

❍ Cut black dots from construction paper and use them to tell a black dot story on the overhead projector. When the story is over, invite the children to tell stories of their own. Add music, and see if the stories change. (Linguistic, Logical-Mathematical, Spatial, Musical, Interpersonal, Intrapersonal)

❍ Play Drop the Dot as you would play Drop the Handkerchief. Cut a large dot from construction paper. Have the children form a circle. Select one child to be IT. IT walks around the circle and eventually drops the dot behind another child. The selected child chases IT around the circle and attempts to tag him before he can get back around to the child's place in the circle. (Bodily-Kinesthetic, Interpersonal)

❍ Take a walk outdoors. Encourage the children to look for things that are black and circular. (Logical-Mathematical, Naturalist)

❍ Cut large circles from construction paper and staple them to 24" pieces of yarn to make necklaces. Invite the children to put on the necklaces and pretend they are black dots. Play music and encourage the children to invent a "dance of dots." (Bodily-Kinesthetic, Musical, Intrapersonal)

Learning Activities

Construction *(Linguistic, Spatial)*
Suggest that the children use their imaginations to create pictures using crayons and black stick-on dots. When they are finished, invite them to describe their creations, and with their permission, transcribe their descriptions onto the backs of their drawings.

Gross Motor *(Spatial, Bodily-Kinesthetic, Interpersonal)*
Paint 10 6" paper plates black. Lay them on the floor, and invite the children to see what they can make with the black dots.

Fine Motor *(Logical-Mathematical, Bodily-Kinesthetic)*
Help the children use quarters to trace 10 circles onto their papers. The children can color the dots with black markers.

Math *(Logical-Mathematical)*
Paint 15 6" paper plates black, or cut 15 6" circles from black construction paper. Lay the circles on the floor. Show the children how to place them in rows, adding one dot to each row. Challenge the children to use 10 black dots to make a triangle. Start them off by placing one circle on the floor, the "top" of the triangle.

Games *(Logical-Mathematical, Naturalist, Interpersonal)*
Make a game board using stick-on black dots as the board's spaces. Intersperse four dots of another color. Provide one die, and buttons to use as markers. The children take turns rolling the die and moving the number of spaces. If they land on one of the colored dots, they must go back to start and try again. The first player to reach the end of the line of dots wins.

Music *(Musical, Interpersonal, Intrapersonal)*
Collect 10 margarine tubs. Use a lid to trace circles onto black construction paper. Cut out the circles and glue them to the tops of the tub lids. Place one jingle bell in one tub, two in the next, all the way up to 10. Put the lids on the tubs. The children use them to create a "black dot jingle band."

Let's Keep Reading
The Shape of Things by Tana Hoban
Shapes, Shapes, Shapes by Tana Hoban

Thinking About What We Learned
1. What was your favorite "black dot" activity today?
2. Would the story be different if the dots were red instead of black?

Ten, Nine, Eight

Author and Illustrator: Molly Bang

About the Book
A father and his daughter count down to bedtime.

Learning Literacy

Oral Language

❍ Invite the children to talk about the things they do before they go to bed.

❍ Ask the children to count the items on each page of the book.

❍ Encourage the children to count and discuss the buttons on their clothing. *What colors of buttons are on your clothing? Are all the buttons the same shape? Are all the buttons the same size? How many buttons were on the little girl's nightgown? Does anyone have the same number of buttons on their clothing?*

Comprehension

❍ Ask the children the following questions: *What things do you do before you go to bed? Who put the little girl to bed? Who puts you to bed?*

Special Activities

❍ Encourage the children to count their fingers. Invite them to take off their shoes and count their toes. Teach the children the fingerplays and rhymes about counting (see appendix page 233). (Linguistic, Logical-Mathematical, Bodily-Kinesthetic)

❍ Invite the children to look at magnetic numbers 1–10. Encourage them to sort the numbers based on whether they are made with straight lines, curved lines, or both straight and curved lines. (Logical-Mathematical, Naturalist)

❍ Play Who's Got the Button? Have children sit in a circle. Choose a child to be IT. Give IT a button. Have children close their eyes. Help IT choose a friend to give the button to. Invite children to open their eyes and try to guess who has the button. The child who guesses correctly becomes the next IT. (Logical-Mathematical, Interpersonal, Intrapersonal)

❍ Invite the children to act out "Ten in the Bed." (Linguistic, Logical-Mathematical, Spatial, Bodily-Kinesthetic, Musical, Interpersonal)

Ten in the Bed

There were ten in the bed (hold up 10 fingers)
And the little one said,
"Roll over! Roll over!" (roll hand over hand)
So they all rolled over
And one rolled out. (hold up one finger)
There were nine in the bed... (repeat hand motions, holding up nine fingers)

Additional verses:
Eight in the bed...
Seven in the bed...
Six in the bed...
Five in the bed...
Four in the bed...
Three in the bed...
Two in the bed...

There was one in the bed
And the little one said,
"Alone at last!" (place head on hands as if sleeping)

Learning Activities

Construction *(Logical-Mathematical Spatial, Bodily-Kinesthetic, Naturalist, Intrapersonal)*
Provide a box of shells, some sticks, and 12" pieces of string. Invite the children to pick six shells that they like. Show them how to make shell mobiles like the one in the story.

Dramatic Play *(Linguistic, Musical, Interpersonal, Intrapersonal)*
Suggest that the children use baby dolls, books, lullaby music, and toy beds and pretend to put the babies to bed, using some familiar bedtime routines and rituals. For example, they might read a book to the babies, hug and kiss the babies, rock them to sleep, and so on. Talk with the children as they put the babies to bed.

Language Language *(Linguistic, Logical-Mathematical, Spatial)*
Cut large numerals from felt and encourage the children to arrange the numbers in ascending order on a flannel board.

Math *(Logical-Mathematical, Interpersonal)*
Provide four large wiggle eyes. Invite the children to hold the eyes in their hands and then drop them onto paper plates. Ask, *How many eyes land with the eye looking up* (wakeful eyes) *and how many eyes land with the eye facing down* (sleepy eyes)? Encourage the children to count the eyes and see how many of each they have.

Music *(Musical, Interpersonal, Intrapersonal)*
Play lullaby music for the children to enjoy. Ask them to pick their favorite lullabies and recite them.

Science *(Linguistic, Naturalist)*
Provide photos of animals sleeping. Ask questions: *How are animals' sleeping habits like those of humans? How are they different?* Encourage the children to describe the sleeping habits of their pets.

Let's Keep Reading

Goodnight Moon by Margaret Wise
The Napping House by Audrey Wood

Thinking About What We Learned

1. Do you have a special stuffed animal that you sleep with? What kind of animal? What is the animal's name?
2. Which activity did you like best today?

There's a Cow in the Cabbage Patch

Author and Illustrator: Claire Beaton

About the Book
All the animals are mixed up and in the wrong places, but when dinnertime comes everyone finds their way home.

Learning Literacy

Oral Language
○ Discuss the words in the story that may be new to the children, such as *dairy*, *cabbage*, *stable*, and so on.
○ Look at the illustrations in the story. Point out that the illustrations are made of fabric, and that the illustrator often uses buttons for eyes. If possible, show other books where the illustrator has used fabrics to make the illustrations, such as *You're Wonderful* by Debbie Clement.

Phonological Awareness
○ Read the story to the children, taking time to identify the *onomatopoeic* words (words that imitate the sounds they are describing) such as *moo, quack,* and *oink*.
○ Encourage the children to name examples of *alliteration* (phrases that have several words that begin with the same consonant sound), such as *cow in the cabbage patch, dove in the dairy, and piglets pink*. Encourage the children to listen for the initial consonant sounds in the phrases. Ask them to describe the sounds they hear. It is not important that the children know which letters are making the sounds, but it is important that they are able to hear and recognize the similar sounds.

Comprehension
○ Ask the children the following questions: *Where was the cow? Where is the cow supposed to be? What makes the animals return to their right places? Have you ever lost something and just couldn't find it?*

Print Awareness
○ Make a list of all the animals in the book in one column on chart paper and the locations where the animals were found in a second column on the chart paper. List the locations in random order so that each animal and its location do not appear beside one another. Ask the children where each animal was found, then draw a line from that animal to the location the children name.

Special Activities
○ Sing farm songs, such as "The Farmer in the Dell," "Old MacDonald Had a Farm," "Bingo," and so on. (Bodily-Kinesthetic, Musical, Interpersonal)
○ Play Pin the Tail on the Donkey. (Spatial, Bodily-Kinesthetic, Interpersonal)

Learning Activities

Art *(Spatial)*
Provide scissors, glue, and scraps of fabric similar to those used in *There's a Cow in the Cabbage Patch.* Invite the children to make collages using the fabrics.

Library *(Linguistic, Interpersonal, Intrapersonal)*
Fill the library with books about farms and invite the children to explore them. Ask, *How many different types of farms are there?* Ask the children to select their favorite books and share them with friends.

Blocks *(Spatial, Naturalist, Interpersonal)*
Help the children use plastic farm animals and other farm props, such as tractors, silos, and so on, to build a farm with a dairy, stable, garden, birdhouse, and barn. Encourage the children to place the animals in the appropriate places on the farm.

Listening *(Musical)*
Make a recording of the story, inviting the children to add sound effects. Place the recording in the center with a copy of the book. Invite the children to listen to the story.

Fine Motor *(Bodily-Kinesthetic)*
Draw a simple farm image on the inside of a file folder. Make a pathway that goes through the farm, from the cabbage patch to the dairy. Draw a simple cow head on a piece of poster board. Cut it out and glue a strip of magnetic tape to the back. The children use a regular magnet on the underside of the folder to guide the cow along the pathway.

Writing *(Linguistic)*
Print the names of the animals in the story on 4" x 6" index cards. Provide magnetic letters and encourage the children to use the letters to copy the animals' names.

Let's Keep Reading
The Pig in the Pond by Martin Waddell

Thinking About What We Learned
1. How are dairy farms different from produce farms?
2. Did anyone ever say that the mice were not where they belonged?

There Was an Old Lady Who Swallowed a Fly

Traditional. Illustrator: Simms Taback

About the Book

A silly story of an old woman with an insatiable appetite.

Learning Literacy

Oral Language

○ Discuss the phrase, *I'm so hungry I could eat a horse.* Ask the children if this is an overstatement. (Explain to the children what an overstatement is.)

○ Talk with the children about exaggerated statements, such as, *she runs like the wind, he's as big as a bear, I could sleep for a week,* and so on.

Phonological Awareness

○ Invite the children to find the rhyming words on each page of the book.

Comprehension

○ Ask the children the following questions: *Is it possible to swallow all of the things the old woman swallowed? How would the story be different if the old woman had stopped eating after she swallowed the fly?*

Special Activities

○ Make a list of all the things the old lady swallowed. Take a walk around the neighborhood. See how many of the things on the list the children can find in the neighborhood. Ask, *Do you see other things the old lady might swallow?* (Linguistic, Logical-Mathematical, Naturalist)

○ Play Simon Says, using the movements of the animals in the story; for example, say *Simon says buzz like a fly, stretch like a cat, roll over like a dog, fly like a bird, snort like a hog, shake your head like a cow,* and so on. (Linguistic, Bodily-Kinesthetic, Interpersonal)

○ Invite the children to draw illustrations of their favorite moments in the story, and encourage them to wave their drawings as they sing the song, "There Was an Old Lady Who Swallowed a Fly."(Linguistic, Spatial, Musical, Interpersonal, Intrapersonal)

Learning Activities

Art
(Logical-Mathematical, Spatial, Naturalist)
Discuss things that people commonly swallow during the day, such as water, vitamins, and various foods. Set out paper, markers, and crayons, and invite the children to draw pictures of things they typically swallow during the day.

Construction
(Bodily-Kinesthetic)
Give each child four black fuzzy pipe cleaners. Show them how to twist the pipe cleaners together in the middle to create spiders. Encourage the children to shape the spider legs. Attach 24" pieces of elastic string to the center of the spiders so that the children can make their spiders wiggle and jiggle.

Discovery
(Logical-Mathematical, Naturalist)
Cut a 3" diameter hole in the plastic lid of a 5-pound coffee can. Decorate the lid to look like a face, with the hole as the mouth. Provide a box of items, such as beads, blocks, buttons, small plastic animals, balls and so on. Make sure some items are too large to fit into the hole. Ask the children to sort the items into those too large to fit and those that fit.

Dramatic Play
(Interpersonal, Intrapersonal)
Provide "old lady" dress-up clothes for the children, for example, glasses, floppy hats, shawls, purses, boots, and so on. If you have a gray wig, add it to the fun. Encourage the children to dress like the old lady.

Listening
(Linguistic, Musical, Intrapersonal)
Make a recording of the children singing the book. Place the book and the recording in the center and invite the children to listen to it.

Writing
(Linguistic)
Print *fly, spider, cat,* and *dog* on a sheet of chart paper. Set out several sets of magnetic letters and encourage the children to use the letters to copy the words.

Let's Keep Reading

Fat Cat: A Danish Folktale by Margaret Read MacDonald
Gobble, Gobble, Slip, Slop: The Tale of a Very Greedy Cat by Meilo So
Hungry Hen by Richard Waring

Thinking About What We Learned

1. Can you name all the things you have eaten today? What is the largest thing you have eaten?
2. Do you know any old ladies that look like the old lady in the story?

Tikki Tikki Tembo

Author: Arlene Mosel. Illustrator: Blair Lent

About the Book
This story is about a boy with a long name who falls down a well. Sometimes, having an honorable (but long) name is not necessarily a good thing (even if it does mean "the most wonderful thing in the whole wide world"). The story explains how this long name almost caused the boy to drown when he fell down the well.

Important note from the authors: *Please note that Tikki Tikki Tembo does not have roots in Asian folk tales as some believe and, therefore, should not be used as a representation of multicultural literature. Teachers should also be careful not to promote possible stereotypes. Discuss this with your class so that this is not an outcome of the story. Use this book on the merit that the rhythm and meter of the text is appealing to young children and that all children are fascinated with their names.*

Learning Literacy

Oral Language

❍ Discuss the children's names. Talk about full names and nicknames. If you have a nickname, share it with the children. Ask the children why their parents gave them their names. *Are you named after a family member?*

Phonological Awareness

❍ Invite the children to clap out the syllables in Tikki tikki tembo's full name. Clap his brother's name, *Chang.* Ask the children which brother has the longer name.

Comprehension

❍ Ask the children the following questions: *How did Chang get out of the well? Why did the old man pump the water out of him and push the air into him? Who went for help when Tikki tikki tembo fell into the well? Why did it take the old man so long to hear what Chang was saying about his brother?*

Special Activities

❍ Print the children's names on chart paper and count the letters and syllables in their names. Ask questions: *Who has the longest name? How many names begin with the same letter?* (Linguistic, Logical-Mathematical, Naturalist)

❍ Display a globe. Explain to the children that *Tikki Tikki Tembo* is not a Chinese folktale, however, it is story that takes place in China. Show the children where China is on the map. Discuss customs that are part of Chinese culture. Find some pictures of modern China and share them with the children. (Logical-Mathematical, Spatial, Interpersonal, Intrapersonal)

- Chinese names reverse the order of Western names, so the surname is said first, and then the given name.
- Rice or noodles are a part of virtually every meal, even breakfast. Bacon, eggs, toast, and cold cereal are not parts of the typical Chinese breakfast.
- The color red is a symbol of good luck and prosperity to the Chinese.

Learning Activities

Art *(Linguistic, Spatial)*

Print each child's name in block or bubble letters on a strip of poster board. Provide markers and invite the children to decorate the letters in their names. Older children may be able to trace magnetic letters to put their own names on the strips of poster board.

Dramatic Play *(Interpersonal)*

Provide a doll and medical props. Encourage the children to pretend that the doll is Tikki tikki tembo, and they are nursing him back to health after his fall into the well.

Blocks *(Spatial, Bodily-Kinesthetic, Interpersonal)*

Challenge the children to use the blocks to build a well. Help them create a ladder using cardboard or straws. Use scraps of blue paper to simulate water. Invite the children to retell the story using these materials.

Language *(Linguistic, Spatial)*

Help the children make name puzzles. Provide 4" x 8" strips of poster board. Help the children print their names on the poster board strips, leaving space between each letter. Cut the letters of the names apart, cutting the edges of each letter so all the letters fit together in the correct order. Invite the children to put together their name puzzles.

Discovery *(Naturalist, Intrapersonal)*

Provide pictures and other objects that relate to China, and encourage the children to explore the pictures and objects.

Music *(Logical-Mathematical, Bodily-Kinesthetic, Musical)*

Provide drums and invite the children to chant *Tikki tikki tembo-no sa rembo-chari bari ruchi-pip peri pembo* to the beat of the drums. If the children can't remember Tikki's full name, invite them to beat and chant his short name.

Let's Keep Reading

Chrysanthemum by Kevin Henkes

Rikki Tikki Tavi by Rudyard Kipling, adapted and illustrated by Jerry Pinkney

Rumplestiltskin by Hans Christian Andersen (many versions available)

Thinking About What We Learned

1. What names do you like?
2. Which name activity was your favorite today?

To Market, To Market

Author: Anne Miranda. Illustrator: Janet Stevens

About the Book
A woman's simple trip to the market soon turns into chaos.

Learning Literacy

Oral Language

○ Discuss the market with the children. Explain how a market is different from a grocery store. At markets, vendors sell such diverse items as rugs, animals, furniture, and clothing.

○ Invite the children to talk about the meaning of the phrase, *This is the last straw!*

Phonological Awareness

○ Read the book a second time, pausing to allow children to fill in the second rhyming words in rhyming pairs.

Comprehension

○ Ask the children the following questions: *What was the first thing the lady went to the market to buy? Why did the lady decide to make soup? How would the story have been different if the lady had put the animals she brought home in cages? Why was the lady cranky? Do you ever get cranky? What causes you to be cranky? What helps you feel better?*

Print Awareness/Oral Language

○ Make a list on chart paper of all the animals the lady brought home from the market, including the adjectives that describe them (*fat* pig, *red* hen, *plump* goose, and so on). Underline and talk about the meaning of each adjective. Explain that adjectives make information more clear.

Special Activities

○ Take the children to a market, if possible. If not, take a trip to the grocery store. Make a list of all the things the lady used to make her soup. Purchase the ingredients. Make sure the children help locate the items in the store, weigh the vegetables, and so on. Talk about the location of the items that are on the list. Point out that the spices are grouped together, and that the vegetables are grouped together, and that foods are grouped in other ways, such as *dairy, meat, frozen foods,* and so on. After returning to the classroom, invite the children to help you make a pot of soup. (Linguistic, Logical-Mathematical, Naturalist, Interpersonal)

○ Compare the illustrations in *To Market, To Market* and in *Epossumondas* by Coleen Salley. Ask, *Do Auntie's and Mama's clothes look like the clothes of the leading character in this story?* (Linguistic, Spatial)

Learning Activities

Art

(Linguistic, Spatial, Intrapersonal)
Invite the children to use paper, crayons, and markers to draw pictures of what they look like when they are feeling cranky. Encourage the children to tell you what makes them feel cranky. With permission, write their reasons for feeling cranky on the backs of their pictures.

Language

(Linguistic, Interpersonal)
Suggest that the children use plastic animals (a pig, hen, goose, lamb, goat, cow, and duck) to retell the story. Challenge the children to remember the adjectives that described each animal.

Cooking

(Linguistic, Logical-Mathematical, Naturalist, Interpersonal, Intrapersonal)
Invite the children to help clean and prepare vegetables and the other ingredients for soup. Encourage them to discuss the texture and colors of the vegetables, and to smell the spices and describe their aromas.

Listening

(Linguistic, Musical, Interpersonal)
Ask the children to imagine what it sounded like in the lady's house when all the animals were running loose. Invite the children to think of the animals in the story and the sounds they make. Challenge them to recreate the sounds appropriate for each animal and record the chaos.

Dramatic Play

(Linguistic, Logical-Mathematical, Spatial, Naturalist, Interpersonal)
Provide grocery store props, such as empty food containers, plastic fruits and vegetables, bags, boxes, aprons, play money, and a cash register. Encourage the children to make signs for the market and to arrange the items in the market in a logical order. Suggest that they decorate the market and add illustrations to their signs.

Writing

(Linguistic, Naturalist)
Open the book to the page of soup ingredients that begins with cabbage. Provide paper, magnetic letters, and pencils. Encourage the children to create a grocery list using either the magnetic letters or their pencils.

Let's Keep Reading

Catch That Goat by Polly Alakija

Thinking About What We Learned

1. What did you learn about cooking today?
2. What did you learn about being cranky today?

The Tortilla Factory

Author: Gary Paulsen. Illustrator: Ruth Wright Paulsen

About the Book
Simple text describes how corn is harvested and made into tortillas. The story covers all the seasons and is beautifully illustrated in warm-toned paintings.

Learning Literacy

Oral Language
○ Place question marks on the outside of a box, and decorate it to look intriguing. Place a few corn tortillas inside. Give the children clues as to what is inside the box, so that they eventually guess there are tortillas in it. After they guess there are tortillas inside, take them out and offer bites to the children.

Comprehension
○ Ask the children the following questions: *What kind of seed was planted? What color were the seeds? Have you ever eaten corn tortillas? When?*

Print Awareness/Oral Language
○ Make a list of the colors mentioned in the story. Invite the children to try to remember the colors of the objects in the story.

Print Awareness
○ Invite the children to brainstorm a list of ways we eat corn; for example, popcorn, corn on the cob, creamed corn, cornbread, and tortillas. List their ideas on chart paper.

Special Activities

○ Plant a garden. Encourage the children to help find a location, decide what vegetable to plant, plant the seeds, and care for them as they grow into vegetables. (Linguistic, Logical-Mathematical, Naturalist, Interpersonal)
○ If you know someone who knows how to make tortillas, invite them to class to demonstrate. (Linguistic, Interpersonal)
○ Encourage the children to participate in the action story, "Let's Make Tortillas" (see appendix page 231). Encourage the children to copy your actions. (Linguistic, Logical-Mathematical, Bodily-Kinesthetic)

○ Pop popcorn. Encourage the children to talk about the sounds and smells of the corn cooking. (Linguistic, Interpersonal)
○ Invite one child at a time to look through *The Tortilla Factory*. Encourage them to look carefully at the paintings that show the land, and challenge them to determine what time of the year they think might be represented in the illustrations. (Spatial, Intrapersonal)

Starting With Stories

Learning Activities

Art

(Spatial, Naturalist)
Give the children paper, brushes, and earth-tone paints to paint a picture of a field. Suggest that they either paint the field when the corn is being planted or paint the crop as it grows.

Library

(Intrapersonal)
Fill the library with books about people who work in the fields and crops that come from the fields, such as *Oh Lord, I Wish I Was a Buzzard* by Polly Greenberg and *My Mother Picks Strawberries* by Alma Flor Ada.

Dramatic Play

(Linguistic, Bodily-Kinesthetic, Interpersonal)
Help the children use a mortar and pestle to grind seeds into flour. Talk with the children as they work. Ask questions: *Why does the corn need to be ground? What would happen if you tried to make tortillas without grinding the corn?*

Math

(Logical-Mathematical, Bodily-Kinesthetic)
Provide five margarine tubs with the numerals 1–5 written on the lids. Cut a small hole in each lid. Provide corn and child-safe tweezers. Challenge the children to pick up the corn one piece at a time with the tweezers and place the correct number of kernels into each tub.

Fine Motor

(Linguistic, Bodily-Kinesthetic)
Give the children golden playdough to push, squeeze, and flatten into tortilla-shaped disks. Provide a rolling pin for flattening.

Music

(Musical, Intrapersonal)
Play several examples of Mexican music. Encourage the children to listen to the music and select a favorite piece.

Let's Keep Reading

Everybody Bakes Bread by Norah Dooley
Oh, Lord, I Wish I Was a Buzzard by Polly Greenberg

Thinking About What We Learned

1. What did you learn about tortillas today?
2. What was your favorite activity today?

Tricky Tortoise

Author: Mwenye Hadithi. Illustrator: Adrienne Kennaway

About the Book
A clever tortoise is fed-up with a know-it-all elephant and decides it is time to teach him a lesson.

Learning Literacy

Oral Language
- ❍ Discuss words in the story that may be new to the children, such as *trod, cross, clever,* and *foolish.*
- ❍ Talk about phrases and words such as *big-headed, self-important,* and *coat of patches.* Ask the children what they think these words and phrases mean.

Comprehension
- ❍ Ask the children the following question: *Why couldn't the elephant see his head?*
- ❍ Invite the children to act out the story.

Letter Knowledge
- ❍ Print *tricky* and *tortoise* on a piece of chart paper. Encourage the children to identify the letters in the words. *Do the words start with the same letter? Which word has the letter "e" in it?*

Special Activities

- ❍ Visit a pond or zoo to see tortoises Ask questions: *How big are the tortoises? How do they move? What do they eat?* (Linguistic, Naturalist, Interpersonal)
- ❍ Play Tortoise Says as you would play Simon Says. (Linguistic, Bodily-Kinesthetic)
- ❍ Make a maze. Encourage the children to crawl through the maze like tortoises. Ask the children if they think the tortoise would move slowly if he were sad. (Spatial, Bodily-Kinesthetic, Interpersonal, Intrapersonal)
- ❍ Sing "Two Tricky Turtles" to the tune of "Three Blind Mice" with the children. Encourage the children to rewrite the song if they are interested. (Linguistic, Musical)

Two Tricky Turtles
by Pam Schiller
Two tricky turtles, two tricky turtles,
See how they jump. Did they really jump?
They told the elephant his head was small
And pretended to jump like a bouncing ball.
"Weyo weeyo wee...yo...HUP we go!"
"Weyo weeyo wee...yo...HUP we go!"
Two tricky turtles. Two tricky turtles.

Learning Activities

Art

(Spatial)
Gather pieces of rubber tiles that resemble tortoise shells. Give the children oval sheets of paper and encourage them to lay the paper over the tiles and rub them with crayons to create tortoise shell designs.

Music

(Musical, Interpersonal, Intrapersonal)
Make tortoise shell drums. Turn several plastic bowls upside down on the floor. Cover the tops with tortoise shell paper designs. Provide coat hanger tubes or short pieces of wooden dowels for drumsticks, and invite the children to play the tortoise shell drums.

Games

(Logical-Mathematical, Interpersonal)
Provide three halved walnut shells (or three paper bowls if walnuts are not available). Hide a small button under one of the shells. Move the shells around and challenge the children to guess which shell is hiding the button. Play the game repeatedly as long as the children are interested.

Sand Table

(Naturalist, Interpersonal)
Place plastic turtles and several rocks in the sand table. Ask, *When the rocks are buried, do they look like tortoise shells?* Talk with the children about how tortoises burrow in the sand to keep cool. Point out that the tortoise lays its eggs in the sand.

Gross Motor

(Linguistic, Logical-Mathematical, Bodily-Kinesthetic, Interpersonal, Intrapersonal)
Challenge the children to crawl on all fours like tortoises. Remind them that tortoises move slowly. Invite the children to pull their feet and arms in, pretending to be tortoises inside their shells. Help the children roll onto their back with their arms and legs still pulled in. Ask, *What happens when you try to turn over?*

Science

(Naturalist)
Fill the center with photos of tortoises and sea turtles. If a real tortoise is available, put it on display. Encourage the children to examine the tortoise's feet, shell, and head, and then invite them to look at the feet, shells, and heads of the sea turtles. Ask questions: *How are tortoises different from sea turtles? Why does a sea turtle have fin-like feet?*

Let's Keep Reading

Anansi and the Talking Melon retold by Eric A. Kimmel
The Tortoise and the Hare by Aesop

Thinking About What We Learned

1. Has anyone ever played a trick on you? What did they do?
2. How do you think the tortoises felt about tricking the elephant? Do you think they ever thought they had done something that wasn't nice?

Tuesday

Author and Illustrator: David Wiesner

About the Book
A group of frogs suddenly find themselves elevated on lily pads and on a flying adventure. With few words, this book tells a dramatic and humorous story.

Learning Literacy

Oral Language
❍ Look through the pages slowly. Ask for volunteers to describe what they see on each page. Ask, *Which page is the funniest? Which page is the most frightening?*
❍ Talk with the children about other books that rely mostly on pictures to tell the story, for example, *Pancakes for Breakfast* and *Good Dog, Carl.*

Comprehension
❍ Ask the children questions: *How do you think the frogs ended up on flying lily pads? Are the lily pads or frogs magical? Were the frogs having fun? How do you know? How would the story be different if it happened during the day instead of during the night?*
❍ Find some interesting music, such as "Ride of the Valkyries" by Wagner, to play in the background while you look through the pages of the story again. Ask the children if the music adds to the drama of the story

Special Activities

❍ Challenge children to help rewrite the words to "Row, Row, Row Your Boat" to tell the story of frogs flying on lily pads. Set out paper, crayons, and markers, and invite the children to make illustrations of their song. (Linguistic, Spatial, Musical)
❍ Teach the children how to do frog jumps. Place a strip of masking tape on the floor to represent a starting line, and invite the children to take turns jumping like frogs from the starting line. Ask, *Which "frog" can jump the greatest distance?* (Logical-Mathematical, Bodily-Kinesthetic, Interpersonal)
❍ Visit an arboretum, nature center, or a pond. Ask questions: *Can you find the frogs? What color are the frogs? Are there any lily pads? How do you think the frogs like their pond? Is it possible to know whether a frog is happy?* After returning to the classroom, encourage the children to draw a picture of their favorite frogs. (Spatial, Naturalist, Intrapersonal)

Learning Activities

Dramatic Play

(Bodily-Kinesthetic, Interpersonal, Intrapersonal)
Cut large green lily pads (2' x 3') out of butcher paper or vinyl fabric. Place the lily pads on the floor and encourage the "little frogs" to pretend to fly on them.

Listening

(Musical, Interpersonal, Intrapersonal)
Invite the children to listen to "Hear the Lively Song" (see page 114 in *Jump, Frog, Jump,* for one example). Ask, *Do the frogs in this song sound like the frogs in the story?*

Games

(Spatial, Bodily-Kinesthetic, Interpersonal)
Away from the children, spray paint a meatball press with green enamel paint. Glue "wiggle eyes" on the top of the press. It will look surprisingly like a frog. Show the children how to use the press to gobble (pick up) bugs (pompoms) from a bowl and place them into a second bowl. and lay the "bugs" in a straight row.

Science

(Naturalist)
Provide pictures of frogs, or, if possible, real frogs. Encourage the children to observe the frogs. A magnifying glass will make close observation more interesting. Invite the children to discuss what they see.

Gross Motor

(Bodily-Kinesthetic, Interpersonal, Intrapersonal)
Cut large green lily pads (2' x 3') out of butcher paper or vinyl fabric (use lily pads made in Dramatic Play activity above). Place the lily pads on the floor in a pathway and encourage "little frogs" to jump from pad to pad.

Writing

(Linguistic, Spatial, Naturalist)
Use a black pen to print the days of the week, except for *Tuesday,* onto index cards. Use a red pen to print *Tuesday.* Encourage the children to use crayons and tracing paper to trace over the words on the cards. Ask questions: *How many of the days of the week start with the same letter?*

Let's Keep Reading

Hop, Jump by Ellen Stoll Walsh
Jump, Frog, Jump by Robert Kalan
The Polar Express by Chris Van Allsburg

Thinking About What We Learned

1. What would Santa have seen if the story had happened on Christmas Eve?
2. Where do you think the pigs will fly?

The Very Hungry Caterpillar

Author and Illustrator: Eric Carle

About the Book

A very hungry caterpillar hatches from his egg, eats voraciously for a week, spins a cocoon, and emerges as a butterfly. This book contains colorful pictures that appeal to all children. The days of the week provide a predictable format for the story sequence.

Learning Literacy

Oral Language

❍ Talk with the children about the meaning of *metamorphosis*. Have them act out the following "Metamorphosis" rhyme.

Metamorphosis

I'm an egg. (curl up in fetal position)
I'm an egg.
I'm an egg, egg, egg!
I'm a worm. (open up and wiggle on
   the ground)
I'm a worm.
I'm a wiggly, humpty worm!
I'm a cocoon. (curl up in a fetal position
   with hands over the face)
I'm a cocoon.
I'm a round and silky cocoon!
I'm a butterfly. (stand and fly around
   using arms for wings)
I'm a butterfly.
I'm a grand and glorious butterfly.

Book Knowledge and Appreciation

❍ Point out how the story follows a predictable sequence using the days of the week as its structure.

Comprehension

❍ Ask the children the following questions: *Which parts of the story could really happen? Which parts are made up? Why did the caterpillar finally stop eating?*

Special Activities

❍ Invite the children to participate in the action rhyme, "Caterpillar" (see appendix page 231). (Linguistic, Bodily-Kinesthetic, Intra-Personal)

❍ Take a spring walk. Invite the children to look for caterpillars and cocoons. Be sure to warn the children not to touch caterpillars because some caterpillars sting. (Naturalist)

❍ Visit an arboretum or nature center to see butterflies. Ask, *Can you find a cocoon?* (Logical-Mathematical, Naturalist)

❍ Take a trip to the library. Read to the children about the dietary habits of real caterpillars. Encourage them to make drawings to represent each stage of metamorphosis. (Linguistic, Spatial, Naturalist)

Learning Activities

Art

(Linguistic, Spatial, Intrapersonal) Invite the children to pick their favorite foods from the items the caterpillar ate. Have them draw pictures of their favorite foods, and then dictate a sentence explaining why they like those items. With the children's permission, transcribe their words onto the backs of their drawings.

Language

(Linguistic, Interpersonal) Give each child a 3" strip of green ribbon with a small bead tied to one end, to represent a caterpillar. Cut out butterfly shapes from construction paper and foods from magazines. Mount them on poster board, cut holes in them, and laminate. The children retell the story using story props.

Discovery

(Logical-Mathematical, Naturalist) Provide a variety of photos of foods, some healthy and some unhealthy. Invite the children to sort the pictures into two categories: *healthy food* and *junk food*. As the children work, point out which foods make up a balanced diet, and in which food groups they belong.

Math

(Logical-Mathematical, Naturalist) Explain to the children that a typical caterpillar is about the same size as a large paper clip. Give the children paper clips and invite them to find things in the room that are the same size as a caterpillar.

Games

(Linguistic, Spatial, Interpersonal) Away from the children, spray paint 26 paper plates green. Write one letter of the alphabet on each plate. Paint another paper plate red, glue large wiggle eyes on it, and attach pipe cleaner antennae to it. Invite the children to put the caterpillar together, starting with its red head, and place the green plates in alphabetical order.

Music

(Bodily-Kinesthetic, Intrapersonal) Play classical music, give the children colorful crepe paper streamers attached to plastic plates, and suggest that they dance like butterflies. Before they start, ask them to close their eyes and imagine the ways butterflies move. Visualizing butterfly movements will help the children move more creatively.

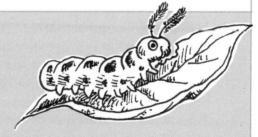

Let's Keep Reading

Charlie the Caterpillar by Dom DeLuise
Clara the Caterpillar by Pamela Duncan Edwards

Thinking About What We Learned

1. How are caterpillars and worms alike? How are they different?
2. What do caterpillars eat?

The Very Quiet Cricket

Author and Illustrator: Eric Carle

About the Book

A little cricket is born. He wants to sing but he can't. He is greeted by a host of insect friends, but each time he tries to respond, nothing happens until, finally, the little cricket finds his voice.

Learning Literacy

Oral Language

❍ Ask the children what they know about crickets. *Have you ever seen a cricket? What sounds do crickets make? Where do they live?* Here is some information about crickets.

- Adult crickets are about 1" long.
- Crickets are popular pets in China and Japan.
- Many people enjoy hearing a cricket sing.
- Crickets chirp by rubbing their wings together. They have small teeth on their wings. The small teeth produce a chirping sound when rubbed together.
- Crickets have ears in their knees.
- Crickets eat other small bugs.
- Crickets can jump 30–40 times their body length, which is about 3'. They jump from a standing position without a running start.

Oral Language/Comprehension

❍ Create a KWL chart (see appendix page 228). Draw a chart with three columns on a piece of chart paper or bulletin board paper. Label the first column *What We Know*, the second column *What We Want to Know*, and the third column *What We Learned*. Discuss crickets with the children, and then fill in the first and second columns on the chart. At the end of the period you spend studying crickets, fill in the last column.

Comprehension

❍ Ask the children the following questions: *Why was the little cricket unable to speak? Have you ever wanted to say something but just couldn't get the words out?*

Special Activities

❍ Make a maze with small boxes. Challenge the children to get through the maze by jumping over the boxes like crickets. Ask the children if they would like to be able to jump every place they needed to go. *What would it be like to jump to the bathroom in the morning? What would it be like to jump all the way to school?* (Spatial, Bodily-Kinesthetic, Interpersonal, Intrapersonal)

Learning Activities

Discovery

(Musical)
Give the children plastic combs. Encourage them to rub the teeth of their combs with their thumbs. Ask, *Does it sound like a cricket chirping?* Encourage them to rub two combs together or try rubbing the teeth with a craft stick. Ask, *Does it sound like a cricket?*

Math

(Logical-Mathematical, Interpersonal)
An adult cricket is 1" in length. Cut several 1" pieces of yarn. Challenge the children to find things in the room that are the same length as a cricket.

Gross Motor

(Bodily-Kinesthetic, Interpersonal)
Use masking tape to make a start line on the floor. Place a second masking tape line on the floor 3' from the start line. Challenge children to stand on the start line and jump to the second line. Ask, *Can you jump as far as a cricket?*

Science

(Naturalist)
Place a live cricket or photos of crickets in the center. Encourage the children to count the legs, body parts, antennae, and wings of the cricket.

Listening

(Linguistic, Musical, Naturalist)
Make a recording of the story. Leave a space on the tape after each insect speaks to the cricket so the children can make sound effects for the bugs. Encourage the children to listen to the recording, look at the book, and add sound effects for each bug the little cricket encounters.

Writing

(Linguistic, Bodily-Kinesthetic)
Print *cricket* on an index card. Give the children crayons and paper and encourage them to copy the word onto their own sheets of paper.

Let's Keep Reading
The Grouchy Ladybug by Eric Carle
The Very Hungry Caterpillar by Eric Carle

Thinking About What We Learned
1. How do you think it would feel to have no voice?
2. What did you learn about crickets today?

The Wheels on the Bus

Author: Raffi. Illustrator: Silvie Kantorovitz Wickstrom

About the Book
A rickety old bus travels through a quaint town picking up an assortment of passengers including a puppy and a duck. The book is Raffi's rendition of the traditional song, "The Wheels on the Bus." The illustrations are whimsical and delightful.

Learning Literacy

Oral Language
- Ask the children if they have ever ridden on a bus. Ask those who have to describe their experiences.

Phonological Awareness/Print Awareness
- Make a list of the *onomatopoeic* words (words whose sounds imitate their meanings) in the story, such as *beep*, *swish*, and *clink*.

Comprehension
- Ask the children the following questions: *Which of the passengers is the funniest passenger the driver picked up? Would you like to be a passenger on this bus? Why? Do you think the driver could fit more passengers on the bus? How? How would the story be different if the vehicle was a boat instead of a bus?*

Print Awareness
- Change the title to another mode of transportation and write a class song. For example, *the tires on the car, the wings on the plane,* or *sails on the boat*.
- Encourage the children to brainstorm a list of the many different ways people travel. Write their ideas on chart paper.

Special Activities

- Take a ride on a bus and sing "The Wheels on the Bus." (Linguistic, Bodily-Kinesthetic, Musical)
- During outdoor play, turn tricycles upside down and invite the children to explore turning the wheels. Identify the parts of the wheels (rim, tire, spoke). Ask questions: *What shape are the wheels? How fast can you make the wheels spin?* (Linguistic, Logical-Mathematical, Bodily-Kinesthetic)
- Make a class graph showing the ways that children travel to school. Ask the children how many of them ride the bus and how many come to school a different way. (Linguistic, Logical-Mathematical, Naturalist, Interpersonal)

- Fill the library with books about transportation. Suggest that the children look for buses in the books. (Linguistic, Spatial, Intrapersonal)

Learning Activities

Art *(Spatial)*
Provide empty spools, drawing paper, and tempera paint. Invite the children to dip the spools in paint and stamp them on paper to make wheel designs.

Dramatic Play *(Linguistic, Interpersonal)*
Provide props for a bus station, such as bus tickets, travel schedules, bus driver hat, play money, and so on. Set up the chairs in pairs to represent the seats on a bus. Invite the children to run the bus station: sell tickets, print schedules, and take trips. Add a stuffed duck and puppy for passengers.

Blocks *(Spatial, Bodily-Kinesthetic)*
Set out blocks and challenge the children to build a town. Provide buses for them to drive "all around the town." Provide plastic people and animals as passengers.

Listening *(Linguistic, Musical, Interpersonal)*
Re-create the sounds heard on the bus: money to clink into tin cans, a squeegee to rub across a flat surface (cookie sheet) to represent wipers, horns to beep, baby dolls that cry, and so on. Encourage the children to sing the song and insert the sound effects, including sound effects for the puppy and the duck.

Discovery *(Logical-Mathematical, Naturalist)*
Provide a variety of items, including some that will roll, such as buttons, beads, and crayons, and some that will not roll, such as blocks, books, Legos, and puzzle pieces. Challenge the children to test each item to determine which ones will roll and which ones will not roll. Ask, *Why do some roll while others do not?*

Writing *(Linguistic, Spatial, Intrapersonal)*
Encourage the children to think of a place they would like to go on a bus. Have them describe the trip they would take. Write their ideas down on drawing paper, and invite them to illustrate the places they describe.

Let's Keep Reading

Don't Let the Pigeon Drive the Bus! by Mo Willems
School Bus by Donald Crews
The Wheels on the Bus by Paul O. Zelinsky

Thinking About What We Learned

1. Do you think the bus driver enjoyed people singing on his bus? How do you know?
2. Which verse of the song do you like best?

Who Is the Beast?

Author and Illustrator: Keith Baker

About the Book

As a tiger walks through the jungle, he notices that all the animals seem to be afraid of something they are calling a beast. He soon figures out that he may be the cause of their fear. He retraces his steps to find out who is the beast.

Learning Literacy

Oral Language

○ Talk with the children about the meaning of *beast*.

Comprehension

○ Ask the children the following questions: *How does the tiger feel when he thinks that everyone is afraid of him? Can you think of other animals that have stripes?*

○ Invite the children to look at the face and body language of the tiger on the cover of the book. *Can you tell by his face how he is feeling? Is he confused? Is he sad? Is he frightened?*

Special Activities

○ Take a trip to the zoo. Challenge the children to find examples of the animals that are in the story. Look at each animal for the body parts they share with the tiger. Ask, *Does the catfish really have white whiskers?* (Linguistic, Logical-Mathematical, Spatial, Naturalist, Interpersonal)

○ Encourage the children to move like tigers, monkeys, frogs, snakes, and fish. Ask questions, *Which animal moves the fastest? Which animal moves the slowest?* (Bodily-Kinesthetic, Naturalist, Interpersonal, Intrapersonal)

○ Cut tiger paw prints from construction paper. Place them on the floor in a trail. Place a stuffed tiger at the end of the trail, and encourage the children to track the tiger. (Naturalist, Interpersonal)

Learning Activities

Art

(Spatial, Naturalist)
Give the children orange and black paint and paper and encourage them to paint tiger-striped pictures.

Language

(Linguistic, Intrapersonal)
Cut four circular faces and draw features on each face: one to look happy, one to look sad, one surprised, and one angry. Lay the cards facedown on the floor. Provide an unbreakable mirror and encourage the children to take turns turning over the card and imitating in the mirror the faces on the cards.

Blocks

(Linguistic, Spatial, Naturalist, Interpersonal)
Make a jungle floor by spray painting an old bed sheet (adults only) with green, gray, brown, and black spray paint. Cut a river or lake from blue bulletin board paper and attach it to the sheet. Provide plastic animals and additional props to create a jungle, and encourage the children to recreate the story.

Listening

(Musical)
Encourage the children to record themselves making tiger growls and roars. Challenge them to record growls and roars to a familiar tune.

Gross Motor

(Bodily-Kinesthetic)
Teach the children how to do frog jumps. Use masking tape to make a starting line on the floor. Use beanbags to mark the distances the children jump. Remind them of the part of the book where a frog's legs are compared to the tiger's legs. Ask, *Do both the tiger and the frog have strong legs?*

Math

(Logical-Mathematical)
Cut circles, squares, and triangles from construction paper.
Encourage the children to sort through the shapes to find the ones that are green and round. Remind them about the part of the story where the round green eyes of the snake are compared to the eyes of the tiger.

Let's Keep Reading

Hug by Jez Alborough
Sam and the Tigers by Julius Lester

Thinking About What We Learned

1. What parts of our bodies can we compare to the tiger's?
2. Why were the animals in the story afraid of the tiger?

Who Took the Cookies From the Cookie Jar?

Author: Bonnie Lass and Philemon Sturges
Illustrator: Ashley Wolff

About the Book
A story based on the traditional children's chant/game with animal characters adding to the storyline and to the fun.

Learning Literacy

Oral Language

❍ Encourage the children to describe their favorite kinds of cookies. Help the children add information to give better descriptions by asking, *Is your favorite cookie round? Is it square? Is it soft? Is it chewy? Is it crunchy? Is it crumbly? Is it chocolate? Is it a sandwich cookie?* Help the children understand that the better they are able to describe something, the better others will understand what they are trying to communicate.

Phonological Awareness

❍ Ask the children to help make a list of the rhyming words used by the animals in the story, such as *oh/know, please/cheese, squirm/worm, munch/lunch, hop/stop, know/slow, crazy/lazy, speak/week, snack/stack,* and *true/you.*

Comprehension

❍ Ask the children the following questions: *Have you ever recited the chant "Who Took the Cookie From the Cookie Jar?" How is this story like the chant you know? How is it different? What kind of cookies are in the story? Do you have a cookie jar at home?*

Special Activities

❍ Visit a bakery. Make a list of all the types of cookies that are available. Talk with the bakers about how they make the cookies. Ask the children which cookies they like the most. Talk about the shapes and sizes of the cookies. (Linguistic, Logical-Mathematical, Spatial, Naturalist)

❍ Fill the library with books about cookies. (Linguistic, Intrapersonal)

❍ Recite "Who Took the Cookies From the Cookie Jar?" with the children. Add a clapping pattern to the chant; for example, as they sing, encourage the children to slap their thighs twice, clap twice, slap their thighs twice, clap twice, and so on. (Linguistic, Bodily-Kinesthetic, Interpersonal)

Who Took the Cookies From the Cookie Jar?

Who took the cookies from the cookie jar?
(child's name) took the cookies from the cookie jar.
Who me?
Yes, you.
Not me.
Then who?
(another child's name) took the cookies from the cookie jar.
(continue until all children have had a turn)

Learning Activities

Dramatic Play *(Linguistic, Bodily-Kinesthetic, Intrapersonal)*
Provide playdough, rolling pins, cookie cutters, decorations (beads, sequins, buttons, and so on), and cookie trays. Encourage the children to bake pretend cookies. Ask them how long they will need to cook the cookies.

Language *(Linguistic, Spatial)*
Invite the children to make up recipes for imaginary cookies. Print their directions on paper, then invite them to decorate their recipes.

Games *(Logical-Mathematical, Interpersonal)*
Cut cookies from construction paper and hide them around the classroom. Invite the children to look for the lost cookies. If they have trouble finding the cookies, give them clues.

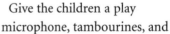

Math *(Logical-Mathematical, Intrapersonal)*
Serve two or three different kinds of cookies for snack. After the children eat their snack, ask them to vote for their favorite cookie. Create a graph to determine which cookies are the most and least popular. Discuss the results with the children.

Gross Motor *(Bodily-Kinesthetic, Interpersonal)*
From construction paper cut cookies and a large cookie jar shape. With masking tape, create a line on the floor. Place the cookie jar on the floor at an appropriate distance away from the masking tape line. Encourage the children to stand at the line and attempt to toss the cookies in the cookie.

Music *(Linguistic, Musical)*
Give the children a play microphone, tambourines, and drums. Encourage the children to make up songs and raps about cookies. Suggest some possible rhythms and tunes.

Let's Keep Reading

The Doorbell Rang by Pat Hutchins
If You Give a Mouse a Cookie by Laura Joffe Numeroff

Thinking About What We Learned

1. Which cookie activity did you like best today?
2. What did you learn about cookies today?

Why Mosquitoes Buzz in People's Ears

Author: Verna Aardema. Illustrator: Leo and Diane Dillon

About the Book

A mosquito says something foolish to an iguana. He promptly pokes a pair of sticks in his ears so he can't hear the mosquito anymore. This simple act causes a chain reaction that is all blamed on the mosquito. The buzz you hear in your ear when a mosquito is near is the mosquito asking if you are still angry with him.

Learning Literacy

Oral Language/Phonological Awareness

❍ Some of the words in the story, *mek, wasawusu, krik, purup*, and so on, are from African languages. Make a list of the words and try to figure out their meaning. Talk with the children about how *onomatopoeia* occurs in all languages.

❍ Discuss words that might be new for the children, such as *yam, reeds, mischief, burrow, prowling, fetch, alarm*, and *council*.

Book Knowledge and Appreciation

❍ Point out that stories like this, which try to explain why something happens, are called *pourquoi* (pronounced *poor-KWAH*, which means *why* in French) stories. Show the children other examples of this type of story, such as *Grandfather Twilight* by Barbara Berger and *Why the Sun and the Moon Live in the Sky* by Elphinstone Dayrell.

Comprehension

❍ Ask the children the following questions: *How would the story be different if the mosquito had not said something foolish to the iguana? What would have happened if the animals had talked to one another instead of running?*

Special Activities

❍ Take a trip to the zoo. Try to find all the animals mentioned in the story. Encourage the children to use the zoo's maps to find the animals. (Logical-Mathematical, Spatial, Naturalist, Interpersonal)

❍ Invite the children to act out the story, labeling each of them with signs that say which creatures from the book they are. Encourage the children to move and make sounds like the animals they represent. (Linguistic, Bodily-Kinesthetic, Musical, Naturalist, Interpersonal, Intrapersonal)

❍ Sing "Mosquitoes" to the tune of "Mary Had a Little Lamb." Invite some of the children to play kazoos as others sing the song. (Linguistic, Musical)

Mosquitoes
by Pam Schiller

Mosquitoes like it wet and damp,
Wet and damp, wet and damp.
Mosquitoes like it wet and damp.
They hang out where you camp.

Mosquitoes like to buzz and buzz,
Buzz and buzz, buzz and buzz.
Mosquitoes like to buzz and buzz.
That's what a mosquito does.

Learning Activities

Construction *(Spatial, Bodily-Kinesthetic)*
Draw a snake on posterboard. Cut the snake out, then cut it into puzzle pieces. Number the pieces so you will have an easy way to check how the pieces fit back together. Give each child one piece and challenge them to make their parts of the snake puzzle colorful and fun. Help the children put the snake back together.

Math *(Logical-Mathematical)*
Give the children photos or plastic animals to represent each animal in the story. Challenge them to put the animals in the order in which they appear in the book, then order them based on size, then based on the number of legs on each animal.

Library *(Linguistic, Naturalist)*
Place *Why Mosquitoes Buzz in People's Ears* in the center along with several other books, some of which are about Africa, such as *Count Your Way Through Africa* by James Haskins or *Ashanti to Zulu: African Traditions* by Margaret Musgrove. Ask the children how they are able to identify the African books. Ask the children to find illustrations similar to those in *Why Mosquitoes Buzz in People's Ears.*

Science *(Logical-Mathematical, Naturalist)*
Place photos of the animals that appear in the book in the science center, and invite the children to order based on the type of covering each animal has, for instance, fur, scales, and so on.

Listening *(Musical)*
Help the children make kazoos. Use a rubber band to secure a piece of wax paper over one end of an empty toilet paper tube. Encourage the children to use their kazoos to imitate the buzz of a mosquito.

Writing *(Linguistic)*
Print some animal sound words, such as *buzz* and *kaa*, on a piece of chart paper. Encourage the children to use magnetic letters to copy the words.

Let's Keep Reading

A Fly Went By by Mike McClintock
Henny Penny by Paul Galdone

Thinking About What We Learned

1. Have you ever been blamed for something you didn't do? How did you feel?
2. Which character in the story is your favorite?

Starting With Stories

Appendix

Open House Suggestions for Teachers

Family Letters

Using Children's Books and Multiple Intelligences as a Springboard to Learning
Determining Your Child's Multiple Intelligences
A List of 100 Children's Books
Sample Letters to Accompany Books
The Very Hungry Caterpillar
Little Red Hen
Who Took the Cookies From the Cookie Jar?

Patterns

Venn Diagram
KWL Chart
Story Pyramid
Word Web

Action Story, Action Rhymes, Rhyme, Fingerplays, and Recipe

Interactive Story Time Strategies

American Sign Language Signs

Thematic Assignment of Literature

Literacy Checklist

The letters in this appendix are examples of the type of letters you can send home to families each time you read a new book to children. If necessary, adapt the extension activities provided for each book in *Starting With Stories* to help families extend their child's learning in the home environment. This way, families can help learn and expand their understanding of the concepts and skills you are teaching.

Open House Suggestions for Teachers

An ideal way to introduce families to *Starting With Stories*, which is a curriculum based on children's books that supports the multiple intelligences, is to have a "Storybook" Open House. For the open house, arrange your room so that each learning center focuses on a particular book. For example, if you currently have space for six learning centers in your classroom, select six books and in each area set up multiple intelligences activities related to that particular book. The activities you plan should be ones family members can do.

Display the books prominently so that families can read them. The activities, with all the necessary materials and equipment, should be described and labeled so that all can participate. The children, you, and other adults in your program can help facilitate the activities in each area.

If classroom space is an issue, highlight only one or two books and use the entire classroom or half of the classroom for the related activities. Another idea is to have the entire program or school participate and each classroom would use a different book for its focus.

Once you decide which type of room arrangement will work best for you, decide how many books you will need and make your selections. A great way to decide which books to choose is to let the children vote for their favorites.

After selecting the books, the rest is easy. Just turn to those pages in *Starting With Stories* that focus on the books you've selected and review the extension activities. While these activities will work just as well with families as they do with the children in your class, feel free to adapt the activities or create your own activities that might be more relevant to the children and families in your classroom and program.

Lastly, what is an open house without refreshments? You can either have refreshments in a central location or disbursed throughout the book areas. Consider including a snack or drink that relates to each particular book. For example, if you chose *Anansi and the Talking Melon* as one of your books, then provide melon slices (cantaloupes) in that book area. Other examples include:

- Gingerbread—*The Gingerbread Baby*
- Cookies—*The Doorbell Rang*
- Apple slices—*Apples Here!*
- Blueberries—*Blueberries for Sal*
- Gelatin, meatballs, and a variety of other foods—*Cloudy With a Chance of Meatballs*
- A variety of fruit—*The Very Hungry Caterpillar*
- Cake slices—*Alicia's Happy Day*

Family Letters

Dear Family,

As you know, nothing delights children more than having wonderful books read to them. Looking at, reading, and sharing books with children provides a great foundation for expanding children's learning across the curriculum. Because children learn in many different ways, the learning opportunities need to be varied.

Dr. Howard Gardner, a prominent psychologist at Harvard University, developed a theory called *The Multiple Intelligences*. In this theory, Dr. Gardner identified eight different intelligences, or eight ways in which learning occurs. We like to call it the eight ways of being smart. Your child possesses each intelligence, but the strength of each one varies. For example, your child might be very strong or talented in two or three areas and not as strong in others.

Dr. Gardner identified the following intelligences:

Linguistic (word smart)   Musical (music smart)
Logical-Mathematical (number smart)   Naturalist (nature smart)
Spatial (picture smart)   Interpersonal (people smart)
Bodily-Kinesthetic (body smart)   Intrapersonal (self-smart)

By using children's books as a gateway to your child's intelligences, you will enhance his or her learning through reading, writing, math, music, art, building, moving, outdoor experiences, interactions with others, thinking, and reflecting.

Starting With Stories, which is used in the classroom with your children, is a literature-based curriculum that supports the multiple intelligences. As we move throughout the school year, I will send you more information on things you can do at home to expand on our classroom activities and how you can become more involved here in the classroom, so you will be an active participant in your child's learning.

Sincerely,

Dear Family,

In an earlier letter to you, I explained how we plan to use children's books as a way to teach your child by multiple intelligences (the many ways in which each child is smart). Below is a chart with ideas that you can do at home to support the concepts and skills your child is learning in the classroom. This chart identifies each of the eight multiple intelligences, lists some of the things children who excel in those areas like to do, and provides some ideas of what you can do to at home to help foster your child's intelligences.

If you are wondering about which areas your child is stronger in, just observe him or her in play situations. The types of play he or she enjoys and the type of toys he or she likes best will help you pinpoint those intelligences. While it is good to encourage your child to continue to develop those intelligences in which he or she is strong, it is best to encourage your child to enjoy activities that are also outside his or her areas of strength.

Intelligence	What Children Like to Do	What Families Can Do
Linguistic	Read, write, and listen; tell stories, rhymes, riddles, and tongue twisters; play verbal memory and word games; create jingles, raps, and creative drama scenes	• Read to your child. Let your child read to you. • Provide a special place for books. • Provide a variety of writing materials for your child. • Discuss favorite authors and/or illustrators with your child. • Talk to your child. Listen to what he or she has to say. • Visit libraries, bookstores, and other places that can be talked or written about. • Encourage your child to keep a journal of significant events. • Encourage your child to write stories, poems, and books. • When reading new books, let your child predict the endings. • Encourage your child to summarize and retell a story. • Ask your child about his or her favorite activity of the day.
Logical-Mathematical	Ask questions; explore patterns and relationships; do experiments, figure things out, and solve problems; play checkers, board games, and other strategy games; engage in classification activities, counting and number games	• Play logic, card, and board games with your child (for example, Dominoes, Concentration, Go Fish, War, Crazy Eights, and Old Maid). • Encourage your child to think about and see patterns in his or her daily activities. • Visit science museums, electronic exhibits, children's museums, hobby stores, and so on. • Allow time for your child to think in game situations. • Encourage your child to make up games. • Count and sort objects around the house.

Intelligence	What Children Like to Do	What Families Can Do
Spatial	Put things together, take things apart, and do woodwork activities; make collages, sculptures, and constructions; draw, paint, and do other art projects; design and build things with Legos and other types of blocks; look at pictures; daydream and visualize	• Have a variety of art and craft materials available. • Provide maps, charts, and cameras. • Provide puzzles, mazes, and blocks. • Provide an area where your child can design and construct creations. • Visit art museums, hands-on children's museums, and natural history museums. • Look at the ways houses and buildings are designed and constructed. • Play with puzzles, mazes, and tangrams. • Go for walks and then ask your child to draw a map or paint a mural of the walk. • Encourage your child to build, build, build with blocks, clay, sand, and other media.
Bodily-Kinesthetic	Participate in hands-on active learning activities; engage in gross and fine motor activities; move around the classroom, touch and explore objects; dance, do creative dramatics and role playing; use body language, gesture, and touch people while talking to them; hear or read action-packed stories; participate in sports and games; move, twitch, tap, or fidget while sitting; fix things and build models	• Provide opportunities for physical activity both inside and outside the home. • Provide balls, jump ropes, scarves, and so on. • Provide clay, paint, paper, and other craft materials. • Provide areas indoors and outdoors in which your child can play. • Go to sporting events, to ballets, and to arts and crafts shows. • Go on camping trips. • Encourage your child to make up different types of dances. • Play physically active games with rules. • Provide old unusable mechanical objects for your child to figure out or to reassemble.
Musical	Sing, hum, and/or whistle tunes; play musical instruments; listen to and respond to music; make up lyrics; listen to music while engaged in classroom activities; use movement, tapping, humming, or singing to convey information	• Provide a tape recorder/record player/CD player. • Provide a variety of musical instruments. • Play a variety of music on the radio. • Have a variety of records/tapes/CDs. • Play music while riding in the car. • Take your child to children's performances, classical and jazz concerts, operas, ballets, musical productions, and other musical events. • Attend and watch parades. • Encourage your child to make up songs. • Encourage your child to change the words of songs to create new songs. • Make homemade rhythm instruments. • Create and sing raps and chants. • Dramatize and sing nursery rhymes or stories.

Intelligence	What Children Like to Do	What Families Can Do
Naturalist	Experience nature or the natural surroundings; take walks and collect samples of rocks, soil; classifying insects, birds, rock; care for plants and animals; spend time outdoors; go on field trips, do science projects; work on projects that protect the environment	• Go on nature walks with your child. • Plant a small garden outdoors with your child or indoors in pots. • Set up outdoor scavenger hunts for your child to find a variety of items. • Plan a variety of outdoor activities. • Go on a picnic. • Engage in recycling activities with your child. • Visit all types of nature centers and museums. • Help your child create nature collages and collections. • Go with your child on a bird watch. • Let your child take responsibility for a pet. • Go on camping trips. • Visit a farm. • Take walks around the neighborhood. • Lie down in the backyard or in a park and let your child describe the clouds.
Interpersonal	Socialize with peers; talk to people; have lots of friends; to be selected by others to help; mediate conflicts and organize activities; organize, communicate, and sometimes manipulate others; work on cooperative projects	• Let your child work in groups around the home and neighborhood. • Encourage the use of leadership skills. • Help your child develop communication skills. • Provide group games for your child to play. • Provide areas for dramatic play, both indoors and outdoors. • Encourage your child to express his or her feelings. • Go to cultural and social events. • Participate in clubs and group activities. • Encourage your child to create games and rules. • Encourage your child to think about what the fair and just thing is to do.
Intrapersonal	Work alone and pursue personal interests—projects and hobbies; follow own instincts; be original; engage in self-paced, self-selected, and individualized projects and activities; express self in own unique style of dress, behavior, and general attitude; reflect on activities	• Provide your child with a special place to pursue hobbies or interests. • Provide supplies and materials for those interests. • Listen to your child's expression of feelings. • Allow your child to have his or her dreams. • Take vacations in tranquil settings. • Visit hobby shops, museums, and art stores. • Let your child plant a garden. • Encourage your child to use his or her imagination and take imaginary "trips." • Help your child build a tree house.

Dear Family,

Below is a list of 100 children books I plan to share with the class this year. As your child hears these stories and engages in the activities related to each book, I am quite sure he or she will have some favorites. These books are available at libraries and stores. I encourage you to read them with your child. It is very important that you read at least one book with your child every day.

Throughout the year, I will send you examples of familiar children's books with related activities that you can do at home. Involving your child in a variety of activities is a great way to enhance his or her multiple intelligences.

Abiyoyo by Pete Seeger, illustrated by Michael Hayes
Alicia's Happy Day by Meg Starr, illustrated by Ying-Hwa Hu and Cornelius Van Wright
Alphabet Soup: A Feast of Letters written and illustrated by Scott Gustafson
Amazing Grace by Mary Hoffman, illustrated by Caroline Binch
Anansi and the Talking Melon Retold by Eric A. Kimmel, illustrated by Janet Stevens
Animal Orchestra: A Counting Book written and illustrated by Scott Gustafson
Apples Here! written and illustrated by Will Hubbell
Barnyard Banter written and illustrated by Denise Fleming
Beatrice's Goat by Page McBrier, illustrated by Lori Lohstoeter
Be Brown! by Barbara Bottner, illustrated by Barry Gott
Blueberries for Sal written and illustrated by Robert McCloskey
Bob written and illustrated by Tracey Campbell Pearson
Brown Bear, Brown Bear, What Do You See? by Bill Martin, Jr., illustrated by Eric Carle
The Bug Cemetery by Frances Hill, illustrated by Vera Rosenberry
Busy Fingers by C.W. Bowie, illustrated by Fred Willingham
Can I Keep Him? written and illustrated by Steven Kellogg
Caps for Sale written and illustrated by Esphyr Slobodkina
Catch That Goat written and illustrated by Polly Alakija
Chicka Chicka Boom Boom by Bill Martin, Jr. and John Archambault, illustrated by
     Lois Ehlert
Cloudy With a Chance of Meatballs by Judi Barrett, illustrated by Ron Barrett
A Cool Drink of Water written and photographed by Barbara Kerley
Dance by Bill T. Jones, illustrated by Susan Kuklin
Dinosaurumpus! by Tony Mitton, illustrated by Guy Parker-Rees
Do Your Ears Hang Low? written and illustrated by Caroline Church
Don't Let the Pigeon Drive the Bus! written and illustrated by Mo Willems
The Doorbell Rang written and illustrated by Pat Hutchins
The Dot written and illustrated by Peter H. Reynolds
Dream Carver by Diana Cohn, illustrated by Amy Cordova
Edward the Emu by Sheena Knowles, illustrated by Rod Clement
Eight Animals Bake a Cake by Susan Middleton Elya, illustrated by Lee Chapman
Epossumondas by Coleen Salley, illustrated by Janet Stevens
Exactly the Opposite written and illustrated by Tana Hoban
A Family Like Yours by Rebecca Kai Dotlich, illustrated by Tammie Lyon
Fancy Nancy by Jane O'Connor, illustrated by Robin Preiss Glasser

"Fire! Fire!" Said Mrs. McGuire by Bill Martin, Jr., illustrated by Richard Egielski

Fish Wish written and illustrated by Bob Barner

Flower Garden by Eve Bunting, illustrated by Kathryn Hewitt

Freight Train written and illustrated by Donald Crews

Gingerbread Baby written and illustrated by Jan Brett

Guess Who? written and illustrated by Margaret Miller

Hello, Hello by Miriam Schlein, illustrated by Daniel Kirk

Henny Penny written and illustrated by Paul Galdone

A House for Hermit Crab written and illustrated by Eric Carle

Hungry Hen by Richard Waring, illustrated by Caroline Jayne Church

Hurray for Pre-K written and illustrated by Ellen B Senisi

If You Give a Mouse a Cookie by Laura Joffe Numeroff, illustrated by Felicia Bond

Imogene's Antlers written and illustrated by David Small

In the Tall, Tall Grass written and illustrated by Denise Fleming

It Looked Like Spilt Milk written and illustrated by Charles Shaw

The Itsy Bitsy Spider written and illustrated by Iza Trapani

Jump, Frog, Jump by Robert Kalan, illustrated by Byron Barton

Koala Lou by Mem Fox, illustrated by Pamela Lofts

Listen to the Rain by Bill Martin, Jr. and John Archambault, illustrated by James Endicott

The Little Engine That Could by Watty Piper, illustrated by George and Doris Hauman

The Little Red Hen written and illustrated by Paul Galdone

Make Way for Ducklings written and illustrated by Robert McCloskey

Matthew and Tilly by Rebecca C. Jones, illustrated by Beth Peck

Max Found Two Sticks written and illustrated by Brian Pinkney

Miss Polly Has a Dolly Retold by Pamela Duncan Edwards, illustrated by Elicia Castaldi

Miss Tizzy by Libba Moore Gray, illustrated by Jada Rowland

The Mitten written and illustrated by Jan Brett

Mouse Paint written and illustrated by Ellen Stoll Walsh

Mr. Gumpy's Outing written and illustrated by John Burningham

Mrs. Goose's Baby written and illustrated by Charlotte Voake

The Napping House by Audrey Wood, illustrated by Don Wood

Noisy Nora written and illustrated by Rosemary Wells

Nonsense written and illustrated by Sally Kahler Phillips

Oh Lord, I Wish I Was a Buzzard by Polly Greenberg, illustrated by Aliki

The Old Man and His Door by Gary Soto, illustrated by Joe Cepeda

On the Go by Ann Morris, illustrated by Ken Heyman

Once Upon MacDonald's Farm written and illustrated by Stephen Gammell

One Cow Moo Moo by David Bennett, illustrated by Andy Cooke

Over in the Meadow Traditional, illustrated by Ezra Jack Keats

Owl Babies by Martin Waddell, illustrated by Patrick Benson

Owl Moon by Jane Yolen, illustrated by John Schoenherr

Peter's Chair written and illustrated by Ezra Jack Keats

The Pig in the Pond by Martin Waddell, illustrated by Jill Barton

The Pigeon Finds a Hot Dog! written and illustrated by Mo Willems

Right Outside My Window by Mary Ann Hoberman, illustrated by Nicholas Wilton

Rosie's Walk written and illustrated by Pat Hutchins

Silly Sally written and illustrated by Audrey Wood

"Stand Back," Said the Elephant, "I'm Going to Sneeze!" by Patricia Thomas, illustrated by Wallace Tripp

Stone Soup written and Illustrated by Marcia Brown

Strega Nona written and illustrated by Tomi dePaola

Swimmy written and illustrated by Leo Lionni

Ten Black Dots written and illustrated by Donald Crews

Ten, Nine, Eight written and illustrated by Molly Bang

There's a Cow in the Cabbage Patch written and illustrated by Clare Beaton

There Was an Old Lady Who Swallowed a Fly Traditional, illustrated by Simms Taback

Tikki Tikki Tembo by Arlene Mosel, illustrated by Blair Lent

To Market, To Market by Anne Miranda, illustrated by Janet Stevens

The Tortilla Factory by Gary Paulsen, illustrated by Ruth Wright Paulsen

Tricky Tortoise by Mwenye Hadithi, illustrated by Adrienne Kennaway

Tuesday written and illustrated by David Wiesner

The Very Hungry Caterpillar written and illustrated by Eric Carle

The Very Quiet Cricket written and illustrated by Eric Carle

The Wheels on the Bus by Raffi, illustrated by Silvie Wickstrom

Who Is the Beast? written and illustrated by Keith Baker

Who Took the Cookies From the Cookie Jar? by Bonnie Lass & Philemon Sturges, illustrated by Ashley Wolff

Why Mosquitoes Buzz in People's Ears by Verna Aardema, illustrated by Leo and Diane Dillon

Sincerely,

Dear Family,

Next week I will be reading *The Very Hungry Caterpillar* by Eric Carle to the children. We will also do a number of activities related to the book. Below are some things you can do at home to help develop your child's multiple intelligences as well as extend the concepts and skills your child is learning as we enjoy this wonderful book.

Home Extension Activities

○ Obtain a copy of the book to read to your child. Encourage your child to read along with you. Later ask him or her to write or draw his or her favorite part of the story. (Linguistic Intelligence)

○ Encourage your child to draw and color the different stages of the caterpillar: egg, worm, cocoon, butterfly. (Spatial Intelligence)

○ Play music without any lyrics (such as jazz, classical, and so on) and ask your child to dance to the music in ways that portray each stage of the caterpillar's life. Be sure to join in the fun, too. (Musical, Bodily-Kinesthetic, Interpersonal Intelligences)

○ Go outside on several days with your child and count all the worms and butterflies you see. Tally the count each day. At the end of the week, help your child graph the numbers you found on each day. Also, discuss what you found most or least on the various days. Help child summarize your findings. (Linguistic, Logical-Mathematical, Naturalist, Intelligences)

Have fun exploring and experiencing this wonderful book.

Sincerely,

Dear Family,

Next week I will be reading *The Little Red Hen* by Paul Galdone or versions by other authors to the children. We will also do a number of activities related to the book. Below are some things you can do at home to help develop your child's multiple intelligences as well as extend the concepts and skills your child is learning as we enjoy this wonderful book.

Home Extension Activities

○ Obtain a copy of the book to read to your child. Encourage your child to read along with you. Discuss the similarities between the little red hen's friends not wanting to help and how your child can help with chores around the house. Ask your child how he or she can help with chores around the house. If your child needs help, you can say a chore and ask if this is something he or she can do. (Linguistic Intelligence) For example:

Chore	Possible Response
Set the table	Yes
Put toys away	Yes
Wash the clothes	No
Help fold the clothes	Yes
Mow the yard	No
Clean the gutters	No

○ Invite your child to make a book (one page for each chore) by drawing and coloring those things he or she can and cannot do. (Spatial, Intrapersonal Intelligences)

○ Go to a grocery store and let your child help select items needed to bake bread or cookies. Then go home and let your child help with the baking. (Logical-Mathematical, Naturalist Intelligences)

○ Invite siblings and/or other children from the neighborhood to come over and listen to/read the story, and then make up dances that could relate to the story, such as the Chicken Dance, Pig Jig, Cat Stalk, Dog Roll, and Mouse Scurry. (Bodily-Kinesthetic, Musical, Interpersonal Intelligences)

Have fun exploring and experiencing this wonderful book.

Sincerely,

Dear Family,

Next week I will be reading *Who Took the Cookies From the Cookie Jar?* by Bonnie Lass & Philemon Sturges to the children. We will also do a number of activities related to the book. Below are some things you can do at home to help develop your child's multiple intelligences as well as extend the concepts and skills your child is learning as we enjoy this wonderful book.

Home Extension Activities

○ Obtain a copy of the book to read to your child. After reading the book, invite your child to discuss who he or she thought had taken the cookies from the cookie jar and why. (Linguistic Intelligence)

○ The inside cover of the book has a rhythmic clapping chant for the story. Perform the chant, with you and your child alternating as the animal suspected of taking the cookies. At the end, let your child be the ants and confess to taking the cookies. As an alternative activity, you, your child, other siblings, and friends can march around the yard or around a room in the house, singing the song, inserting the names of possible suspects. (Linguistic, Bodily-Kinesthetic, Musical, Interpersonal Intelligences)

○ Ask your child how he or she would solve the mystery if the cookies were missing from your home's cookie jar? Be sure to bake cookies with your child. (Logical-Mathematical Intelligence)

○ Hide a cookie in the house and invite your child to find it by following the visual clues you have left, such as a trail of small bits of paper. (Cut small round pieces from a brown paper sack and use a black marker to make the piece of paper look like a chocolate chip cookie.) Each time you play this game and your child successfully finds the cookie, you can make the game more difficult by including false trails with your cookie clues. When your child finds the cookie, reward him or her by sharing the cookie together. (Spatial, Bodily-Kinesthetic Intelligences)

○ Help your child write a short poem about his or her favorite type of cookie. (Linguistic, Intrapersonal Intelligences)

○ Take your child on a trip to the zoo and every time your child sees an animal that was in the story, shout "Who took the cookies from the cookie jar?" If you can't go to the zoo, gather an assortment of animal pictures (cut out from magazines) and invite your child to sort the ones that represent animals in the story. (Logical-Mathematical, Naturalist, Intelligences)

Have fun exploring and experiencing this wonderful book.

Sincerely,

Venn Diagram

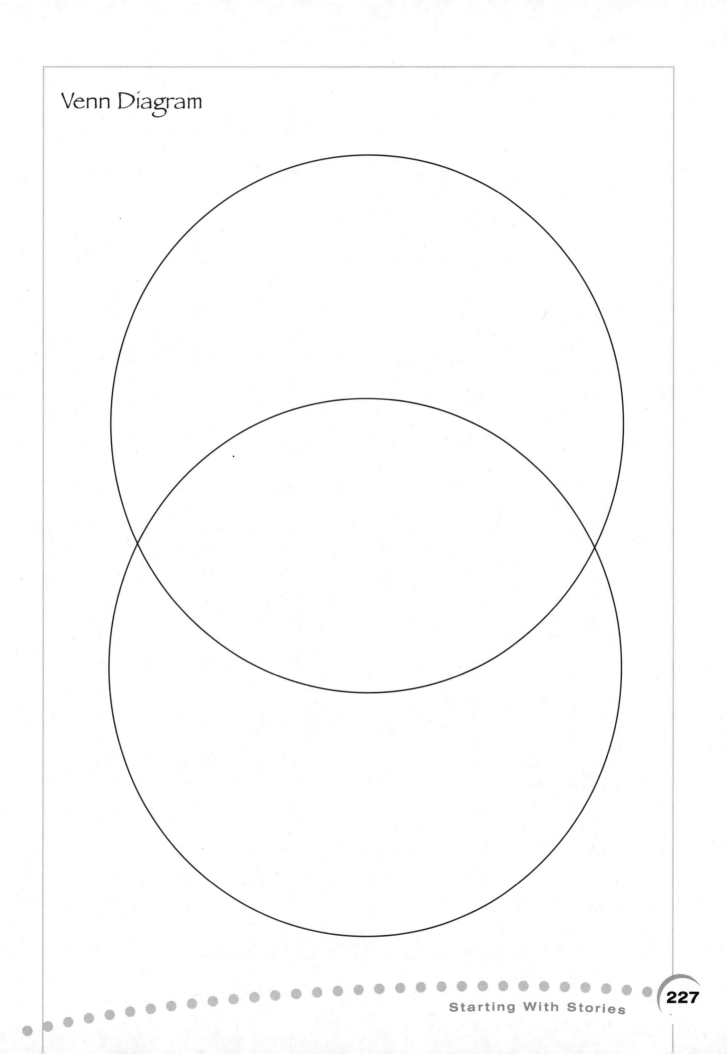

KWL Chart

KWL Chart

What We Know	What We Want to Know	What We Learned

Story Pyramid

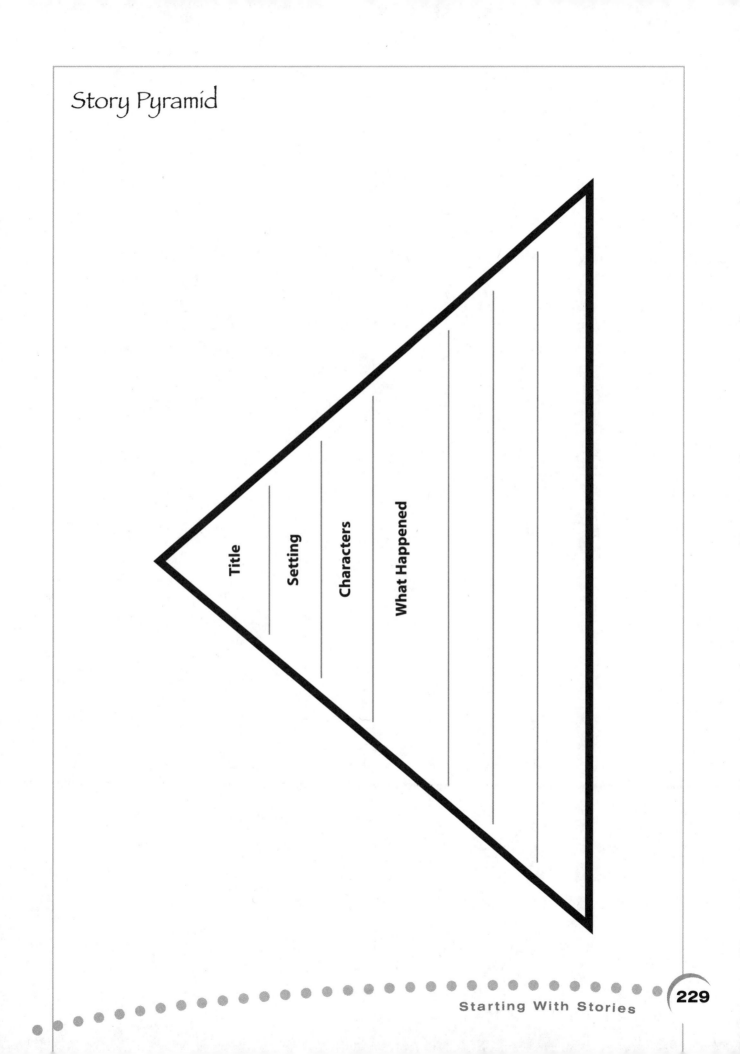

Title

Setting

Characters

What Happened

Word Web

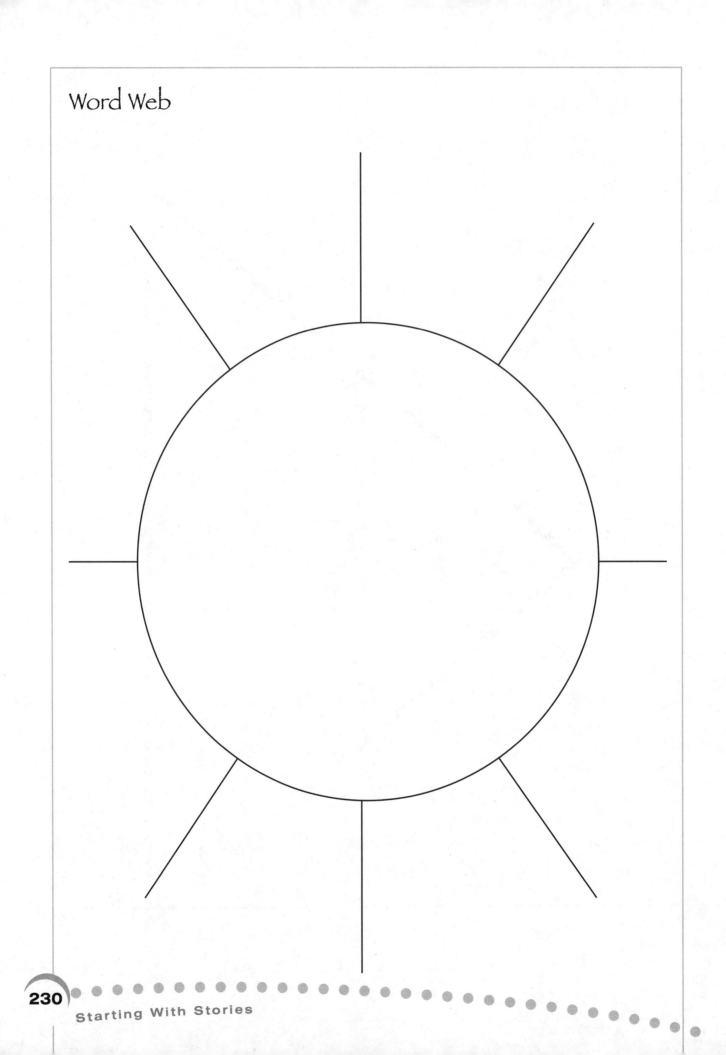

Action Story

Let's Make Tortillas

(Use pretend equipment and ingredients. Encourage the children to copy your motions as you pretend to make tortillas as described in the story.)

Who wants to make tortillas? I need all of the workers to sit with me. Let's see. We need a mixing bowl, a measuring cup, a tortilla press, a piece of plastic, and water. (Pretend to take items out of shelves and drawers.) *Now I think we are ready.*

First we put the flour in the mixing bowl. We add the water from the measuring cup. Now we knead the flour with our hands.

Now the dough is starting to look good. It looks smooth and bright. Next we need to make little balls of dough to put in the tortilla press.

How nice and round the dough balls are. Now we will place them in the tortilla press, one by one. Open the tortilla press and put the sheet of plastic inside.

Place a dough ball on top of the plastic. Now close the tortilla press and press it with the handle of the press. Don't press it too strongly.

Open the tortilla press and the plastic, and carefully remove the tortilla.

Now we are ready to cook, so I'll place it carefully on the hot skillet. Mmmm, the tortillas smell good. Flip the tortilla to make sure it is firm. It is ready to eat. Who would like to eat the tortilla?

Action Rhymes

Caterpillar

A caterpillar crawled to the top of the tree. *(creep fingers up one arm)*
 "I think I'll take a nap," said he. *(place one hand over opposite fist)*
So under a leaf he began to creep
To spin his cocoon,
And he fell asleep.

All winter long he slept in his bed,
'Til spring came along one day and said,
"Wake up, wake up, little sleepyhead, *(shake fist with other hand)*
Wake up, it's time to get out of bed."
So he opened his eyes that sunshiny day. *(spread fingers, hook thumbs)*
Lo! He was a butterfly, and flew away. *(flap hands as wings and fly away)*

Monkey See, Monkey Do
by Pam Schiller
(*The teacher is the storyteller and the children are the monkeys. Suit your actions to words.*)

When my friends and I go to the zoo, our favorite spot is the monkey house. We love to watch the funny things the monkeys do. I think perhaps the monkeys like to watch us too. I wonder if they think we are as funny as we think they are. I am never really sure exactly who is watching whom.

Hey, I have an idea. You pretend to be the monkeys, and I'll be me. I'll show you what happens at the zoo. Listen carefully, because sometimes you will be leading. Remember, you are the monkeys.

When we run up to the monkey cages, we clap our hands with glee. In no time at all, the monkeys are clapping their hands too. They jump up and down, and so do we.

We make funny faces, and so do they. They turn in circles, and so do we.

We swing our arms monkey-style (*randomly all around*), and they do the same.

They lift their legs up monkey-style (*out to the side and up and down*), and we do the same.

We scratch our heads, and they scratch their heads. They scratch under their arms, and we scratch under our arms. We pull our ears, and they pull theirs. We sit on the ground and count their toes. They pretend to do the same. Then we laugh tee-hee-hee, tee-hee-hee. That makes us roll on the ground with laughter. Guess what the monkeys do then? You got it! They roll on the ground with laughter.

Have you ever seen the monkeys at the zoo? You really must go to see them.

When you get there, be sure to play our funny game of Monkey See, Monkey Do.

Rhyme

Apples and Bananas
I like to eat, eat, eat apples and bananas.
I like to eat, eat, eat apples and bananas.

I like to ate, ate, ate, aypuls and baynaynays.
I like to ate, ate, ate, aypuls and baynaynays.

I like to eet, eet, eet eeples and beeneenees.
I like to eet, eet, eet eeples and beeneenees.

I like to iit, iit, iit, ipples and biiniiniis.
I like to iit, iit, iit, ipples and biiniiniis.

I like to ote, ote, ote opples and bononos.
I like to ote, ote, ote opples and bononos.

I like to ute, ute, ute upples and bununus.
I like to ute, ute, ute upples and bununus.

Starting With Stories

Fingerplays

Birthday Candles

Birthday candles, one, two three. (hold up finger as
    each number is counted)
Birthday candles just for me! (point to self)
Last year two, next year four.(hold two fingers on left
    hand and four on right)
Birthday candles, I want more! (hold up 10 fingers)

Five Little Fingers

One little finger standing on its own. (hold up index
    finger)
Two little fingers, now they're not alone. (add middle
    finger)
Three little fingers happy as can be. (add ring finger)
Four little fingers go walking down the street. (add
    pinky)
Five little fingers. This one's a thumb. (add thumb)
Wave bye-bye, 'cause now we're done. (wave goodbye)

Jack-in-the-Box

Jack-in-the-box, (tuck thumb into fist)
Oh, so still.
Won't you come out? (raise hand slightly)
Yes, I will. (pop thumb out of fist)

Slowly, Slowly

Slowly, slowly, very slowly (walk finger slowly up arm)
Creeps the garden snail.
Slowly, slowly, very slowly
Up the wooden rail.

Quickly, quickly, very quickly (quickly run fingers
    up arm)
Runs the little mouse.
Quickly, quickly, very quickly
Round about the house.

Ten Little Fingers

I have ten little fingers, (hold up ten fingers)
And they all belong to me. (point to self)
I can make them do things. (wiggle fingers)
Do you want to see? (tilt head)

I can make them point. (point)
I can make them hold. (hold fingertips together)
I can make them dance. (dance fingers on arm)
And then I make them fold. (fold hands in lap)

Recipe

Banana Quick Bread Recipe

1 cup sugar
½ cup shortening
2 eggs
2 cups flour
1 teaspoon baking soda
3 soft, ripe bananas, mashed

Place sugar and shortening in a large bowl, cream
thoroughly. Add eggs, flour, baking soda, and
bananas. Pour banana bread batter into a greased
and floured loaf pan; bake at 325° for about 1 hour
and 15 minutes, or until a toothpick inserted in the
center comes out clean. This recipe makes one loaf.

Interactive Story Time Strategies

1. Conduct interactive story times with small groups of children and encourage additional book reading.
2. Select books for interactive story time experiences that have:
   - clear story lines
   - clear illustration contexts
   - age-appropriate themes or topics
   - rhythmic language
   - interesting vocabulary
   - sensitivity to diversity
   - themes or objectives related to current study
3. Familiarize yourself with the book and create a plan for learner outcomes, such as identifying concepts to develop, vocabulary to discuss, and questions to ask.
4. Print vocabulary on sentence strips in lowercase letters with appropriate illustrations (if possible). If you are using a pocket chart, display it at the children's eye level.
5. Before reading the book:
   - Encourage children to look at the book cover, describe what they see, and predict what the story is going to be about.
   - Discuss the role of the author (writes the words) and illustrator (draws the pictures).
   - Make the connection that children are also authors and illustrators.
   - Point out the spine, front, and back of the book.
   - Introduce and discuss new vocabulary (you might thumb through pictures and text).
   - Connect with prior knowledge and create a personal connection.
6. During reading:
   - Track print with your finger or a pointer (large print for group).
   - Involve children by asking questions, pausing, and reflecting (no more than two times in one reading).
   - Create mental images as appropriate; for example, consider sights, sounds, smells, tastes, and physical sensations related to the story.
   - Reinforce vocabulary.
   - Use facial expressions and voice variations to add excitement to the story.
   - Pace the story to fit the type of book and to invite children to participate.
7. After reading the book:
   - Review the story plot and help the children summarize the story and make personal connections.
   - Ask questions to encourage reflection.
8. Extend the story time with follow-up activities, such as using story maps, word webs, sequencing activities, role-play, or story retelling with props or flannel board characters.

Reminders

- ○ Take care not to destroy the joy of the story line by dissecting it with too many interactive strategies. Preschool children have an attention span that ranges from 10 to 12 minutes. Once it is exhausted, learning is no longer fun.
- ○ Not every activity needs to be addressed in every reading. Interactive strategies are designed to develop book concepts and print awareness. Vary the strategies from book to book and from reading to reading. It usually works best to use a book that the children have read once before for interactive reading.

American Sign Language Signs

Bear

Bird

Cat

Dog

Duck

Fish

Frog

American Sign Language Signs

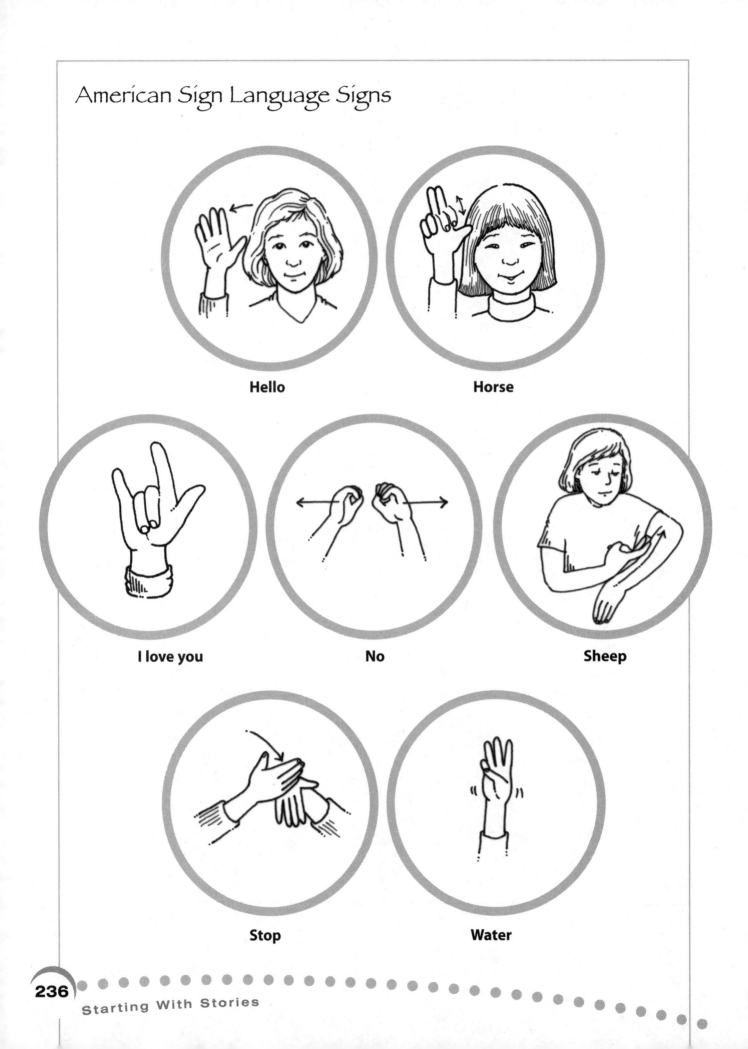

Hello

Horse

I love you

No

Sheep

Stop

Water

Thematic Assignment of Literature

Theme	Title	
All About Me	*Alicia's Happy Day*	*Dream Carver*
	Amazing Grace	*Hurray for Pre-K*
	Busy Fingers	*The Little Engine That Could*
	Dance	*Koala Lou*
	The Dot	*Ten, Nine, Eight*
Family	*Amazing Grace*	*Koala Lou*
	Blueberries for Sal	*Imogene's Antlers*
	Can I Keep Him?	*The Mitten*
	Catch That Goat	*Mrs. Goose's Baby*
	Chicka Chicka Boom Boom	*Noisy Nora*
	Dream Carver	*Over in the Meadow*
	Epossumondas	*Owl Moon*
	A Family Like Yours	*Ten, Nine, Eight*
	Flower Garden	*Tikki Tikki Tembo*
Friends	*The Bug Cemetery*	*Hurray for Pre-K*
	A Cool Drink of Water	*Matthew and Tilly*
	The Doorbell Rang	*Miss Tizzy*
	Do Your Ears Hang Low?	*The Old Man and His Door*
	Eight Animals Bake a Cake	*Pigeon Finds a Hot Dog!*
Color, Shape and Size	*Anansi and the Talking Melon*	*Freight Train*
	Be Brown	*It Looked Like Spilt Milk*
	Blueberries for Sal	*Mouse Paint*
	Brown Bear, Brown Bear, What Do You See?	*The Tortilla Factory*
Opposites	*Exactly the Opposite*	*Tikki Tikki Tembo*
	The Itsy Bitsy Spider	
Food	*Alphabet Soup: A Feast of Letters*	*If You Give a Mouse a Cookie*
	Apples Here	*The Pigeon Finds a Hot Dog!*
	Blueberries for Sal	*To Market, To Market*
	The Doorbell Rang	*The Tortilla Factory*
	A Cool Drink of Water	*Strega Nona*
	Eight Animals Bake a Cake	*Who Took the Cookies From the Cookie Jar?*
	The Gingerbread Baby	

Theme	Title	
Growing Things	Apples Here	Oh, Lord, I Wish I Was a Buzzard
	Blueberries for Sal	The Tortilla Factory
	Flower Garden	
Travel and Transportation	Don't Let the Pigeon Drive the Bus!	On the Go
	Freight Train	Silly Sally
	The Little Engine That Could	The Wheels on the Bus
	One Cow Moo Moo	
Workers	Amazing Grace	Guess Who?
	Caps for Sale	Miss Polly Had a Dolly
	Catch That Goat!	Oh, Lord, I Wish I Was a Buzzard
	Don't Let the Pigeon Drive the Bus!	The Tortilla Factory
	Dream Carver	The Wheels on the Bus
	"Fire! Fire!" Said Mrs. McGuire	
Traditional Tales	Epossumondas	Little Red Hen
	The Gingerbread Baby	Over in the Meadow
	Henny Penny	Tikki Tikki Tembo
Nursery Rhymes	The Itsy Bitsy Spider	Miss Polly Had a Dolly
	To Market, To Market	Over in the Meadow
Weather	Cloudy With a Chance of Meatballs	Owl Moon
	The Itsy Bitsy Spider	The Pig in the Pond
	Listen to the Rain	Right Outside My Window
Seasons	Anansi and the Talking Melon	Right Outside My Window
	Apples Here	The Tortilla Factory
	The Mitten	
Insects and Bugs	Anansi and the Talking Melon	There Was an Old Lady Who Swallowed a Fly
	The Bug Cemetery	The Very Hungry Caterpillar
	The Itsy Bitsy Spider	The Very Quiet Cricket
	Jump, Frog, Jump	Why Mosquitoes Buzz in People's Ears

Theme	Title	
Frogs and Turtles	*In the Tall, Tall Grass*	*Tricky Tortoise*
	Jump, Frog, Jump	*Tuesday*
	Over in the Meadow	
Animals	*Alphabet Soup*	*Jump, Frog, Jump*
	Animal Orchestra	*Koala Lou*
	Be Brown	*The Mitten*
	Bug Cemetery	*Mr. Gumpy's Outing*
	Bob	*Mrs. Goose's Baby*
	Brown Bear, Brown Bear, What Do You See?	*Once Upon MacDonald's Farm*
		One Cow Moo Moo
	Catch That Goat!	*Over in the Meadow*
	Don't Let the Pigeon Drive the Bus	*Rosie's Walk*
	Do Your Ears Hang Low?	*"Stand Back," Said the Elephant, "I'm Going to Sneeze."*
	Dream Carver	
	Epossumondas	*There's a Cow in the Cabbage Patch*
	Fish Wish	*There Was an Old Lady Who Swallowed a Fly*
	Hungry Hen	*Tricky Tortoise*
	If You Give a Mouse a Cookie	*Who Took the Cookies From the Cookie Jar?*
	In the Tall, Tall Grass	

Literacy Checklist

Child's Name: _____ Classroom: _____

Date of Birth: _____ School _____

Observation Dates

1. _____ to _____

2. _____ to _____

3. _____ to _____

Key

N: Not performing

O: Occasionally performing

C: Consistently performing

Objectives	Head Start Outcomes	Recording Periods 1 2 3 4
Listening 1. Listens with increasing attention 2. Listens for different purposes 3. Responds accurately to questions following a story	Demonstrates increasing ability to attend to and understand conversations, stories, songs, and poems	1. ○ ○ ○ ○ 2. ○ ○ ○ ○ 3. ○ ○ ○ ○
4. Follows simple oral directions	Shows progress in understanding and following simple and multiple-step directions	4. ○ ○ ○ ○
Oral Language/Speaking and Communicating 5. Engages in conversation 6. Experiments with the sounds of language 7. Shows a steady increase in listening and speaking vocabulary	Understands an increasingly complex and varied vocabulary	5. ○ ○ ○ ○ 6. ○ ○ ○ ○ 7. ○ ○ ○ ○
8. Refines and extends understanding of known words 9. Attempts to use communicate beyond current vocabulary 10. Uses new vocabulary when appropriately introduced	Uses an increasingly complex and varied spoken vocabulary	8. ○ ○ ○ ○ 9. ○ ○ ○ ○ 10. ○ ○ ○ ○
11. Uses language for a variety of purposes	Develops increasing abilities to understand and use language to communicate information, experiences, ideas, feelings, opinions, needs, questions and for other varied purposes	11. ○ ○ ○ ○

Objectives	Head Start Outcomes	Recording Periods			
		1	2	3	4
Oral Language/Speaking and Communicating (continued)					
12. Uses sentences of increasing length	Progresses in clarity of pronunciation and towards speaking in sentences of increasing length and grammatical complexity	12. ○	○	○	○
13. Tells a simple personal narrative		13. ○	○	○	○
14. Uses language for familiar routines		14. ○	○	○	○
15. Asks questions and makes comments during class discussions	Progresses in abilities to initiate and respond appropriately to conversation and discussion with peers and adults	15. ○	○	○	○
16. Engages in conversation following conversational rules		16. ○	○	○	○
17. Retells the sequence of a story		17. ○	○	○	○
Segmentation					
18. Breaks sentences into words using claps, taps, and snaps		18. ○	○	○	○
19. Breaks words into syllables; claps, taps, snaps syllable breaks	Shows growing ability to hear and discriminate separate syllables in word	19. ○	○	○	○
Phonological Awareness					
20. Recognizes differences between similar sounding words	Progresses in recognizing matching sounds and rhymes in familiar words, games, songs, stories, and poems	20. ○	○	○	○
21. Shows sensitivity to the sounds of spoken words	Shows increasing ability to discriminate and identify sounds in spoken language	21. ○	○	○	○
22. Recognizes and uses onomatopoeic words		22. ○	○	○	○
23. Begins to identify rhymes and rhyming words		23. ○	○	○	○
24. Begins to attend to beginning sounds of familiar words, for example, alliteration and onset rhyme	Associates sounds with written words, such as awareness that different words begin with the same sound	24. ○	○	○	○
Book Knowledge and Appreciation	Shows growing interest and involvement in listening to and discussing a variety of fiction and non-fiction books and poetry				
25. Understands that reading and writing are ways to obtain and communicate thoughts		25. ○	○	○	○

Objectives	Head Start Outcomes	Recording Periods
		1 2 3 4

Book Knowledge and Appreciation (continued)

Objectives	Head Start Outcomes	1	2	3	4
26. Demonstrates an interest in books; asks to have a favorite book re-read; engages in pretend reading; demonstrates delight in story time; imitates the special language of books.	Shows growing interest in reading-related activities, such as asking to have a favorite book read, choosing to look at books, drawing pictures based on stories, asking to take books home, going to the library, and engaging in pretend reading with other children	26. ○	○	○	○
27. Enjoys listening to and discussing stories		27. ○	○	○	○
28. Begins to predict what will happen next		28. ○	○	○	○
29. Chimes in with predictable text		29. ○	○	○	○
30. Asks questions pertaining to the story		30. ○	○	○	○

Comprehension

Objectives	Head Start Outcomes	1	2	3	4
31. Retells stories in own words; acts stories out	Demonstrates progress in abilities to retell and dictate stories from books and experiences, to act out stories in dramatic play, and to predict what will happen next in a story	31. ○	○	○	○
32. Understands the difference between letters and numbers		32. ○	○	○	○
33. Responds accurately to thinking questions following a story		33. ○	○	○	○

Print Awareness/Concepts

Objectives	Head Start Outcomes	1	2	3	4
34. Understands that illustrations carry meaning but can not be read	Demonstrates increasing awareness of concepts of print, such as that reading in English moves from top to bottom and from left to right, that speech can be written down, and that print conveys a message	34. ○	○	○	○
35. Understands that print carries a message, such as label, list, or sign		35. ○	○	○	○
36. Understands that print moves from top to bottom and left to right		36. ○	○	○	○
37. Handles books appropriately, for example, holds a book correctly, turns pages in correct sequence	Progresses in learning how to handle and care for books: knowing to view on page at time in sequence from front to back, and understanding that a book has a title, author, and illustrator	37. ○	○	○	○
38. Understands that books have a title, author and illustrator		38. ○	○	○	○

Objectives	Head Start Outcomes	Recording Periods 1 2 3 4
Print Awareness/Concepts (continued)		
39. Follows print when it is read	Shows progress in recognizing the association between spoken and written words by following print as it is read aloud	39. ○ ○ ○ ○
40. Understands conventions of print, such as groups of letters make up words, words are separated by spaces	Recognizes a word as a unit of print, or awareness that letters are grouped to form words, and that words are separated by spaces.	40. ○ ○ ○ ○
41. Understands the functions of print, such as text, list, labels, and so on	Develops growing understanding of different function of forms of print such as signs, letters, newspapers, lists, messages, and menus Shows increasing awareness of print in classroom, home, and community settings	41. ○ ○ ○ ○
Letter Knowledge		
42. Begins to identify letters	Knows that letters of the alphabet are a special category of visual graphics that can be individually named	42. ○ ○ ○ ○
43. Identifies ten or more letters	Identifies at least ten letters of the alphabet, especially those in his or her own name	43. ○ ○ ○ ○
44. Recognizes letters in words	Increases in ability to notice the beginning letters in familiar words	44. ○ ○ ○ ○
45. Begins to match letters and sounds 46. Recognizes some familiar words, such as mommy, me, daddy	Shows progress in associating the names of letters with their shapes and sounds	45. ○ ○ ○ ○ 46. ○ ○ ○ ○
Early Writing		
47. Attempt to write messages as part of play	Develops understanding that writing is a way of communicating for a variety of purposes	47. ○ ○ ○ ○

Objectives	Head Start Outcomes	Recording Periods
		1 2 3 4
Early Writing (continued) 48. Uses a variety of tools for writing	Experiments with growing variety of writing tools and material, such as pencils, crayons, and computers	48. ○ ○ ○ ○
49. Uses letter approximations to communicate, such as writing name on paper	Progresses from using scribbles, shapes, or pictures to represent ideas, to using letter-like symbols, to copying or writing familiar words such as his or her own name	49. ○ ○ ○ ○
50. Dictates words, phrases and sentences, such as letter writing, labeling, story telling	Begins to represent stories and experiences through pictures, dictation and in play	50. ○ ○ ○ ○

Children's Book Index

Index